Who Gets What from Government

Who Gets What from Government

Benjamin I. Page

UNIVERSITY OF CALIFORNIA PRESS

Berkeley • Los Angeles • London

University of California Press
Berkeley and Los Angeles, California

University of California Press, Ltd.
London, England

1 2 3 4 5 6 7 8 9

Library of Congress Cataloging in Publication Data
Page, Benjamin I.
  Who gets what from government.

  Includes index.
  1. Income distribution—United States.   2. Government spending-policy—
United States.   I. Title.
HC110.I5P27   1983   339.5′22′0973   82-13454
ISBN 0-520-04702-8

To the Institute for Research on Poverty
Madison, Wisconsin

Contents

Tables and Figures

FIGURES

Preface

In this book I have tried to do two things: (1) to discuss how U.S. government policies affect people's incomes and the overall income distribution, and (2) to explore what political factors make government policies take the shape they do. The first task involves reviewing and commenting on a great deal of work by economists; the second belongs in the realm of political science.

The book was written for anyone interested in how and why government policies affect ordinary citizens. It is intended for general readers as well as for students and scholars. Every effort has been made to use clear language and to explain technical terms when they come up.

Still, the subject matter is inherently complicated; government affects people in a wide variety of direct and indirect ways. It is impossible to discuss some of these effects (tax incidence, e.g., or the overall incidence of fiscal policy, or equilibrium effects of regulation, or the common law of property) faithfully, without writing some passages that some readers will find difficult. In such cases I would urge the reader to forge ahead, to get the general drift and perhaps return later to the difficult passage, but not to let it distract him or her from the main arguments.

I have used notes to support some specific points and also as guides to further reading. It is of course impossible to cite all the many relevant works; I have noted those I consider most important or most representative, with (naturally) an emphasis on those I find most nearly correct. I have tried to cite the strongest arguments against my positions, as well.

In some ways this project began in the academic year 1972–1973 when I was a Social Science Research Council post-doctoral fellow in economics at MIT and Harvard. Lester Thurow and Herbert Gintis, in particular, helped kindle my interest in economic inequality, and I was exposed to the teachings of Paul Samuelson, Kenneth Arrow, Jerome Rothenberg, and others on microeconomic theory and welfare economics.

I did much of the work on the book (considerably later) during several summers and one academic year in residence at the Institute for Research on Poverty at the University of Wisconsin, Madison. I am most grateful to the institute and especially to its director at that time, Irwin Garfinkel, for financial and other support. Many economists, political scientists, sociologists, and others in the lively intellectual setting of the Poverty Institute contributed ideas and criticisms, and Scott Milliman provided energetic and able research assistance. Needless to say, the arguments and conclusions are my own and do not necessarily reflect the views of anyone at the Poverty Institute.

In writing the book I also engaged in long dialogues (some real and some imaginary) with economist and political scientist colleagues at the University of Chicago, whose respective concerns with efficiency and equity and with markets and politics helped sharpen my own thinking.

While the book was in press, I spent a very pleasant and fruitful year as a National Fellow at the Hoover Institution, Stanford, working on a project concerning relationships between public opinion and policy making. Although I am very grateful to the Hoover Institution for supporting my other work, it would be quite incorrect to associate the arguments I make in this book with that institution.

I am grateful to many people for making comments, criticisms, and suggestions on part or all of various drafts of the book. I especially want to thank Christopher Jencks, Joseph Minarik, and Sheldon Danziger for commenting on an earlier draft of the entire book. They stimulated many improvements—though not, perhaps, as many as they would like.

Among those who made helpful comments on one or more chapters, I want to thank Robert Lampman, Brian Barry, Charles Anderson, Jane Mansbridge, Richard Merelman, Murray Edelman, Irwin Garfinkel, Robert Haveman, Paul Menchik, Timothy Smeeding, Ted Marmor, John Bishop, Barbara Wolfe, Richard Burkhauser, Peter Eisinger, Russell Hardin, Duncan Snidal, Ira Katznelson, Roger Noll, Douglas Hibbs, and Alex Hicks. Responsibility for the product and its defects, of course, is mine.

Finally, I want to thank Mary, Benjamin, Alexandra, and Timothy, who have been very patient with a long and sometimes painfully intense writing process. I hope the book's account of my egalitarian arguments will be more convincing to them than the dinner-table versions sometimes seemed to be.

Benjamin I. Page

Stanford, California
May 1982

It is evident that any transference of income from a relatively rich man to a relatively poor man of similar temperament, since it enables more intense wants to be satisfied at the expense of less intense wants, must increase the aggregate sum of satisfactions.[1]

1

Why Equality

The question of who gets what from government could mean many different things, depending upon how one chooses to group the population. We might want to know how government actions affect blacks as compared with whites, or the young contrasted to the old, or residents of the Northeast versus the Southwest, for example. This book, while it does touch on such matters, is mostly concerned with what the U.S. government (federal, state, and local) does for high-income people as compared with those of low income—or, to put it loosely, what benefits go to the rich and what to the poor.

The focus is on inequality of income. In this first chapter, I will discuss some reasons why equality is desirable, show that private wealth and income in the United States are very une-qually distributed, and suggest government as the place to look for redistribution. The rest of the book deals with what effects the government actually has on inequality and why, politically, it has the effects it does.

Equality, of course, is not cherished by everyone, especially not by those who are at the top of the heap and want to stay there. The last several centuries of world history have seen a gradual breakdown of rigid inequalities in status based on race, sex, class, ethnicity, and the like. Equality of political and legal rights has advanced, and there has been increasing agitation for more equality in material conditions and incomes as well. Still, the idea of moving toward more equal incomes provokes a lot of resistance, and progress, if any, has been slow and uneven, with many ups and downs.

As this book is written, in fact, the United States is in an exceptionally antiegalitarian mood. Writers and politicians have been telling us that government has gone much too far in promoting equality, that economic productivity and growth have suffered as a result, that it will be necessary to tolerate a high degree of inequality in order to encourage people to work and invest and restore vigor to the economy. Contempt for the poor is expressed in high places. Americans' sympathy for the underdog seems to have dried up.

This may be a good time, therefore, to remind ourselves why a high degree of equality is worth pursuing and to examine the record of government action. Some of the evidence may be surprising even to those who follow public affairs closely. In particular, despite a War on Poverty and large social welfare budgets, the United States has not succeeded much—if at all—in reducing income inequality. And that lack of success does not appear to be dictated by the imperatives of economic growth but follows (at least in substantial part) from biases in the political system.

Arguments for Equality

A substantial degree of equality is required in order to satisfy the aims of liberals, radicals, and conservatives alike. Extreme inequalities of income or wealth undermine the values of order and stability, communal harmony, liberty, self-fulfillment, and equal opportunity. Extreme inequalities reduce the overall happiness of mankind.

In order to realize the conservative values of order, stability, and community, for example, we can no longer rely on traditional mores or deference to authority: a good measure of equality is needed. In the modern world, inequalities breed resentment. Resentment, in turn, damages the sense of fellowship and solidarity essential to social harmony. Ultimately, the discontent of the poor can fuel war or revolution, wholly upsetting the social order. Short of insurrection, the deprived may be driven to crime and violence. Thus, conservatives must grant substantial equality in order to avoid alienation, turmoil, or revolt.

Similarly, liberty, which is a function of choices, requires a degree of material equality. Money expands choices, and those deprived of money are deprived of liberty. Moreover, political and legal equality are impossible in the face of severe material inequality. As Rousseau put it, no citizen should be sufficiently opulent to be able to purchase another and none so poor as to be forced to sell himself. We should allow neither excessive wealth nor beggary.[2]

Self-fulfillment and personal development also require material foundations. Freedom of action is limited without freedom from want. Creative thinking and aesthetic appreciation are not encouraged by an empty stomach or a desperate struggle for existence. As Tawney and Mill have argued, it is only in a society marked by a large measure of economic equality that varieties of individual genius and character are likely to find their full expression. The powers that make for energy and refinement should be liberated and cultivated in all men, not only in a few.[3]

Even the liberal notions of equality of opportunity and fair reward for individual achievement depend upon substantial equality of result. To be sure, equality of opportunity implies a competitive race in which the winners and losers enjoy unequal prizes. But the race is supposed to be a fair one, in which the competitors have an equal start. Those who have considered the problem have increasingly realized that members of a current generation cannot get an equal start unless their parents enjoyed substantially equal incomes, that is, equality of condition.

So long as natural families raise the young, the children of past winners have big advantages in their own contests: inherited wealth, good nutrition, intellectual stimulation, and opportunities to learn skills and motivation from family and friends. To be born rich does not guarantee success, but it certainly helps. Take the matter of motivation. If a child is reared by wealthy, supportive, and ambitious parents, they may instill in him self-confidence and drive and need for achievement. It is hardly fair for society to declare the child a winner and offer him (or her) lavish rewards because of this lucky initial advantage. Thus, any real effort to provide equal opportunity by equalizing starting positions must in the end move toward equality of condition.

In fact, we can go further than that. The very logic of equal opportunity is flawed by the impossibility of arranging equal starts, together with the injustice of rewarding those who have initial advantages. Even if unequal parental influences were minimized (perhaps by kibbutz-style collective child-rearing or by leveling parents' incomes), differences in genetic endowment are still bound to occur. In ethical terms, why should society reward those lucky enough to be born with superior qualities of mind or body? One might argue just the opposite, that those less blessed should be compensated.

In any event, if a genuinely equal beginning were somehow arranged (perhaps through a system of lengthy head starts for disadvantaged children), winning would then become random. What justice is there in unequal rewards for chance victories? And those who happened to take an early lead would be advantaged in any future racing. How long should a race last? How many races, with how many new starting lines and new equalization of contestants, should there be? Why stop short of constantly resetting the starting point, that is, imposing equality of condition?

Nor is it easy, once the start and finish of the race have been defined, to judge winners and determine their rewards. Neoclassical economics offers the observation that in a free labor market, with perfect competition, each person is paid exactly the value of his or her marginal product. We might be tempted to call that a fair reward for labor. But even setting aside market imperfections that distort wages—no small matter—we cannot consistently assign the same marginal product to each comparable worker when workers as a body produce more than a simple sum of marginal products. Production is genuinely collective. Nor, if we could do so, would it be just to assign rewards in this way since a worker's marginal product depends

upon uncontrollable features of consumer demand, labor supply, and the prices of other factors, as well as on the worker's
own skills (themselves not all under his control) and efforts.
Rare is the economist who claims that free market wages provide just rewards.[4] Rarer still are alternative suggestions for
working out the liberal ideal. The very concept of "to each according to his work" is not a clear one.

In fact, to most modern free market advocates, the argument
for unequal incomes is really not ethical but pragmatic: fair or
not, people should be paid more for the more productive work
so that a lot of productive work will get done. But once the matter is acknowledged to be purely pragmatic, everything then
rests upon empirical questions about how great the magnitude
of incentive effects is and whether nonmaterial incentives could
be substituted. As we will see, the empirical evidence does not
provide so much support for inequality as is commonly believed.

The utilitarian aim of maximizing the happiness of mankind,
which many take as their central moral imperative, provides
some particularly important arguments for material equality.
As Pigou concisely pointed out in our opening quotation, if a
poor man would gain more satisfaction from a given sum of
money than a rich man would, happiness in society would be
increased by transferring money from rich to poor.

In fact, if we are willing to accept a few assumptions (as economists are fond of saying), utilitarian reasoning leads to advo-
cacy of complete equality. Suppose we agree with the classical
utilitarian postulate that society ought to be arranged so as to
maximize the total amount (the sum) of happiness of the individuals in it. ("Happiness," of course, may depend not only
upon pleasures of the flesh but also on aesthetic enjoyment,
friendship and sense of community, self-development, and, indeed, anything that people value.) By referring to the sum of
happiness, we admit the possibility—at least in principle—of
adding up and comparing the happiness of individuals. Suppose further that the goods that can be purchased with any
given total amount of money bring the same amount of happiness to each individual. Finally, suppose that money has declining marginal utility for everyone, that is, a dollar brings more

happiness when one is penniless than when one already has $1 million, and the amount of happiness brought by an extra dollar declines steadily with increasing income.

Under these assumptions, if we treat people only as consumers and posit that there is a fixed amount of income to distribute, simple logic shows that the total amount of happiness in society is maximized by a completely equal distribution of income.[5]

To be sure, the assumptions of this argument are not beyond challenge. Such utilitarian thinkers as Bentham, Mill, Edgeworth, and Pigou questioned one or more of them and pulled back from the conclusion of complete equality. Yet the argument must be taken seriously.[6]

True, the cardinal measurement of utility or happiness, so that quantities can be added, is problematic; it is neither necessary nor possible for ordinalist economic theory. But it is important for normative purposes and can be accomplished by subjective methods or by the Von Neumann-Morgenstern technique involving reactions to risk. Declining marginal utility for money, while not easily demonstrated, is quite plausible and deserves acceptance in the absence of evidence to the contrary. A person usually appreciates a dollar more when he is poor than when he is rich.

Interpersonal comparisons of utilities involve real difficulties, but they cannot be ruled out unless we are willing almost completely to forego discussion of distributive justice. To refuse to compare the happiness of different individuals even in principle is virtually to refuse to make evaluations of income distributions and, in effect, to accept whatever the status quo may bring. It is also to shut one's eyes to a form of judgment we make every day. Sympathy and imagination, important human virtues, are both based on putting ourselves in another's place and comparing the other's happiness with our own. Most of us are convinced that the poor are less happy than the rich because we know we would be miserable in their circumstances.

The assumption of identical utility functions for income is not so absurd as it first appears. The point is not that everyone gets the same pleasure from the same things (smoking, symphony going, carpentry) but only that they obtain the same amount of happiness from the same total income, spent in whatever way they choose. If this assumption is not met and individuals differ in their capacities for pleasure, utilitarianism leads to the rather offensive conclusion that the most money ought to go to those who can enjoy it most. If the deaf, mute, or blind get less satisfaction from a dollar than do those in perfect health, a consistent utilitarian would tax the handicapped and subsidize playboys.[7] But we may reasonably be skeptical about claims of widely differing utilities for income. Any refined tastes displayed by the rich (which in any case are easily exaggerated) probably arise more from their riches than from innate capacity for pleasure. Given time and opportunity, very likely anyone can learn to enjoy what money will buy.

Furthermore, considering the difficulty of measuring cardinal utilities and making interpersonal comparisons and the danger that some people will pretend to have keen capacities for pleasure if that will get them a bigger share of the money, prudence suggests refuge in a principle of insufficient reason. Absent strong evidence to the contrary, a theory of distributive justice ought to presume that utility functions for money are identical and carry through with the egalitarian implications of that fact.

By far the weakest assumption in the utilitarian argument for equality, however, is that there exists a fixed amount of resources to be divided up. This assumption obviously fails, and its failure compels the utilitarian to retreat somewhat from complete egalitarianism. Only the extent of the retreat is in question. This, in fact, is the key to many modern objections to equality.

Resources are produced as well as consumed. If material incentives are needed to encourage work, the prospect of redistribution may affect how much is produced. Neither low-income workers who expect to be subsidized nor high-income workers who expect to be taxed may exert their best efforts. Incentives to save and invest may also be reduced and allocations of effort made less efficient. In order to avoid such losses of productivity and consequent declines in happiness, the optimal utilitarian tax might have to stop well short of the steep progressivity that would be needed to equalize incomes. Under these circumstances, even Rawls's "maximin" criterion would dictate some tolerance of inequality in order to maximize the welfare of the least well off.[8]

The extent of disincentive effects from redistribution is an important topic that will come up repeatedly as we proceed. For now, however, we can say that they may not be so serious as they seem at first. Economic theory offers no definite guide, for example, to the impact of progressive taxation: income effects (having to work harder to make up for income that is taxed away) push against substitution effects (choosing more leisure rather than heavily taxed work), and the predicted result depends upon a number of factors. In addition, people may work (even in capitalist countries) for reasons of self-fulfillment, sense of duty, or prestige, as well as for money. Findings from the New Jersey and other income maintenance experiments indicate that work does not decline a great deal when incomes are guaranteed. Similarly, high-income earners apparently keep at it even when tax rates are high. As we will see, the example of a number of European countries suggests that considerable increases in equality above the U.S. level would be possible without retarding productivity.[9]

Moreover, to the extent that disincentive effects are inherent in capitalist or free market economic systems, this need not be taken as an insurmountable obstacle to redistribution. If desirable in order to promote human welfare, it might be possible to reorganize the economy so as to rely more heavily on nonmaterial incentives, like patriotism and sense of community, and incentives inherent in the work itself, like pride in craftsmanship, and self-fulfillment. Granted, because nonmaterial incentives are less finely grained, less rich in information, and less self-executing, they may tend to cause efficiency losses, but this must be balanced against their virtues. By the same token, if saving and investment cannot be managed under capitalism without extreme inequalities, we might want to consider the possibility (it, too, having liabilities as well as advantages) of giving the state a major role in investment.[10]

These matters will come up again when we discuss possible structural determinants of inequality. The facts about disincentive effects of redistribution in actual or possible economies are still so imperfectly known that no precise conclusions about the optimal degree of equality can be drawn. But antiegalitarian implications are easily exaggerated. While human welfare would probably be maximized at some point short of total uniformity of incomes, it would be surprising if the optimum did not require considerably more equality than is found in the contemporary United States.

The Extent of Inequality

The income of Americans is distributed very unequally. According to Current Population Survey (CPS) of the Bureau of the Census, the bottom one-fifth of all U.S. families in 1980 received only 5 percent of the total money income whereas the top one-fifth got 42 percent of the total, about eight times as much. That is, the top group got close to half the income and the bottom group got only one-twentieth of it[11] (see Table 1). Inequality is still greater when unrelated individuals, as well as families, are considered.

These highly unequal income shares have remained about the same for more than three decades since World War II. The census figures indicate that between 1948 and 1977, the share of the bottom fifth of families and unrelated individuals stayed between 3 and 4 percent and that of the top fifth hovered between 43 percent and 45 percent.[12] Apparently, none of the great polit-

TABLE 1   *Distribution of American Families' Money Income, 1980*

Families, Ranked from Lowest to Highest Income	Income Range ($)	% of Total Income
Lowest fifth	0–10,286	5.1
Second fifth	10,287–17,390	11.6
Middle fifth	17,391–24,630	17.5
Fourth fifth	24,631–34,534	24.3
Highest fifth	34,534–	41.6
		100.0
Top 5%	54,060–	15.3

SOURCE: U.S. Bureau of the Census, *Current Population Reports*, Series P-60, #127, Aug. 1981, p. 15.

ical or economic events of the 1950s, 1960s, or 1970s made much difference in the distribution of money income.

One concise way of characterizing the degree of inequality in an income distribution is by means of the Gini coefficient, which can vary from zero (complete equality) to one (total concentration of all income in the hands of one individual). In order to compute a Gini coefficient, people are first arrayed along a line in order of increasing income, and a Lorenz curve is drawn indicating the cumulative percentage of income received by each cumulative percentage of the lowest-income earners. That is, the lowest 10 percent of income earners might earn only 1 percent of the income; the lowest 20 percent might get 3 percent; the lowest 30 percent, 6 percent; and so on, as indicated in the hypothetical Figure 1. (The Lorenz curve for a completely equal distribution would be a straight diagonal line.) The Gini coefficient then measures how far a Lorenz curve deviates from the diagonal; it is calculated as the area between the curve and the diagonal (shaded in Figure 1), divided by the total area under the diagonal.[13] The Gini coefficient for the distribution of American households' money incomes in 1976, based on the CPS data, was 0.406.

So far we have passed over a good many problems of conception and measurement that make it difficult to be sure exactly what the distribution of income looks like. Statistics on income distributions depend upon people's own reports of their incomes, as given to survey interviewers or to the Internal Revenue Service, and such reports are not always accurate. People are sometimes confused or forgetful; in other cases, they deliberately underreport income in order to hide illegal sources or to avoid taxes. Underreporting may conceal the full extent of inequality since self-employed individuals with relatively high incomes, such as doctors and small businessmen, do not have wages automatically reported to the government and fail to report substantial amounts of earnings. On the other hand, some very low-income people with odd jobs also hide income in order to avoid taxes and to stay below the income cutoff points of government welfare programs.

Most figures on income also neglect various kinds of receipts which economists consider income but which others don't think of that way, or which are difficult to measure. It is easy

FIGURE 1 *Lorenz Curve for a Hypothetical Income Distribution*

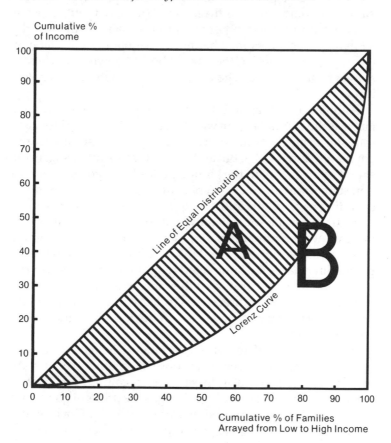

Gini coefficient = area A/area B

enough to add back into income some items which are reported on tax returns but excluded from taxation, such as a portion of the gains from selling stock and other capital assets. It is harder, however, to learn the value of such nonmoney income as the benefits (the "imputed rent") of living in an owner-occupied home; increases in the value of unsold assets; expense account meals and trips; the value of food consumed from one's own farm or garden; or the value of do-it-yourself projects, housework, and other goods and services that are produced and consumed at home. Some of these items (imputed rent, expense accounts, unrealized capital gains) accrue mainly to the wealthy so that total incomes may be more unequal than the money-income figures reveal. Others (e.g., home-grown produce consumed by farm families) go mainly to those with relatively low incomes.

Another complication is that many reported income figures (such as the CPS data upon which Table 1 is based) include cash transfers from government: welfare payments, social security payments, and the like. But at this point we are interested in the extent of inequality in the United States *before* government action so that we can analyze what effects government taxes and spending have on this initial inequality. We want figures on income from private sources only, not from government. Moreover, we want figures on *pre-tax* incomes. This is not so simple as it sounds: we not only need to know how much people earn before direct taxes are subtracted (e.g., by income and payroll tax withholding) but also what their incomes would have been if there had been no indirect taxes (sales, corporation, property taxes), which they may have paid in the form of higher prices and higher rents.

It is hard to calculate "pre-government" incomes, working backwards from the incomes we observe people receiving. As we will see, the effects of indirect taxes are complex and controversial. Government spending changes the prices of goods and services and thereby affects "private" incomes. Government actions affect every aspect of production and distribution by supplying money, enforcing contracts, educating workers, upholding law and order, and the like. It is impossible even to imagine a modern economy without government and impossible to calculate with any precision what people's incomes in the absence of government would be.[14] But we need a starting point, which can be provided by the best available estimates.

One sophisticated effort to estimate the pre-tax distribution of income is that by Pechman and Okner for the year 1966. Pechman and Okner used a broad definition of income (including unrealized capital gains, imputed rent, indirect taxes, and—unfortunately for us—transfer payments, which reduce apparent pre-government inequality). They adjusted for nonreporting and underreporting, and they had unusually good data (a Survey of Economic Opportunity merged with information from income tax returns). As Table 2 indicates, they found even more inequality than the CPS does. The top one-fifth of families got nearly half the total "adjusted family income" in the country whereas the bottom fifth got less than 4 percent. Indeed, the top 5 percent of families received 22 percent of the total income, and the top 1 percent got more than 10 percent. That is, the average family among the top 1 percent of income earners received nearly *sixty times* as much income as the average family in the bottom fifth.[15]

In addition to the problem of defining and measuring income, assessments of inequality are complicated by the fact that income-receiving units differ: there are families of different sizes and unrelated individuals living alone or together. If all "households" or "consumption units" are lumped together (as is sometimes done), measured inequality does not reflect the actual experience of individuals. A family of four is not twice as well off as a family of two (or four times as well off as a single individual) just because it has twice (or four times) the income. One helpful step—which produces less measured inequality— is to omit unrelated individuals. It is better yet to calculate on a household per capita basis so that the whole population can be

TABLE 2   *Distribution of Adjusted Family Income, 1966*

Families, Ranked from Lowest to Highest Income	Income Range ($)	% of Total Income
Lowest fifth	Under 4,038	3.7
Second fifth	4,038–7,679	9.9
Middle fifth	7,679–11,212	16.1
Fourth fifth	11,212–16,000	22.6
Highest fifth	16,000 and over	47.9
		100.0
Top 5%	27,273 and over	22.1
Top 1%	56,667 and over	10.5

SOURCE: Joseph A. Pechman and Benjamin A. Okner, *Who Bears the Tax Burden?* (Washington, D.C.: Brookings Institution, 1974), p. 46.

considered and so that large families don't look too rich compared with small. It is best of all to base the calculations on "equivalent units," which take account of economies of scale and joint consumption: a given amount of per capita income usually goes farther in a large group than a small.[16]

We should note one further problem in interpreting statistics on income distribution: most figures are gathered on an annual basis. In any given year some families may do unusually poorly and others may do unusually well, thus accentuating the apparent inequality in incomes. Moreover, to compare the relatively low earnings of the young and the aged with those of people in their peak earning years can be misleading. For some purposes it would be best to measure the distribution of "permanent income" or income averaged over people's lifetimes. This is difficult to do. Although inequality is always less in lifetime earnings than in annual, research to date has not agreed on how much less.[17]

Wealth, unlike income, is not reported regularly on tax returns. It is hard to find those who hold it or to get them to give honest and complete answers to survey questions. The best survey of Americans' wealth was conducted in 1963 by Projector and Weiss, for the Federal Reserve System. Many respondents, especially those of high income, refused to give financial information, so efforts were made to adjust the data for nonresponses. Projector and Weiss found that the distribution of net wealth was extremely unequal—more unequal than the distribution of income. The top 1 percent of wealth-holding consumer units held about 33 percent of the total wealth and 62 percent of the corporate stock. About one-quarter of the population, on the other hand, had a net worth (including the value of cars and equity in homes) of less than $1,000, and nearly half had less than $5,000.[18]

Another method of learning about the distribution of wealth has been to treat estate tax returns as a "sample" of all property holdings, in which the sample is drawn by death. The total distribution of wealth can be estimated by multiplying each estate by the inverse of the probability of its being drawn from the population (that probability being roughly indicated by the mortality rate of the decedent's age and sex group). Using this estate-multiplier method for the year 1953, Lampman found a high concentration of wealth: the top 1.6 percent of wealth-holders had 32 percent of the total wealth and 82 percent of the corporate stock held in the personal sector.[19] This may actually have been an underestimate because of the tendency of those expecting death to plan for it and avoid estate taxes by giving gifts, setting up trusts, and the like. According to the estate-multiplier method, the concentration of wealth was even higher at the end of the 1920s; it dropped somewhat at the outset of the Depression and again during World War II but then remained fairly constant (reacting, however, to swings in the stock market) from the end of the war through 1969.[20]

Inequality of wealth is itself a source of unequal incomes—from rent, dividends, interest, and the like. In 1978, for example, of all the income reported to the IRS on the 2,041 tax returns listing over $1 million in adjusted gross income, only *16 percent* of the money came from wages or salaries; most was derived from ownership of capital.[21] In addition, unequal wealth yields unequal well-being of sorts not easily captured in income statistics: political and economic power, status, and the ability to give (and often to control after giving) large gifts and bequests.

Unequal wealth is partly generated in the first place by capitalizing an idea or a process: for example, by incorporating, selling some stock, and retaining a substantial part of the ownership of a growing business. To a large extent wealth is then passed on to the accumulators' children, and inequality is perpetuated across generations.[22]

It is still true, as Harrington wrote more than twenty years ago, that the poor are largely invisible to white suburban Americans. In 1980, for example, according to the official definition of poverty (the cutoff was an income below $8,414 for an urban family of four), 29.3 million Americans—13 percent of the whole population—were poor in terms of money incomes. About half of these people were members of female-headed families; more than one-third (11.4 million) were children under the age of fifteen, and another 3.8 million were age sixty-five or over so that, for many, to work was difficult or impossible. But most of these millions of people were out of sight, in rural areas or central city ghettos. More than one-third of them were black (8.6 million) or Hispanic (3.5 million); in fact, the black and Hispanic populations of the United States had poverty rates of 32.5 percent and 25.7 percent, respectively.[23]

The human meaning of inequality goes beyond dry statistics about income or wealth: it touches every aspect of life. Judging by people's own reports, those with low incomes tend to be significantly less happy than are those with high incomes. The poor die younger. They eat unappealing food and suffer from malnutrition. They live in small, poorly constructed, uncomfortable living quarters, often with inadequate heat, plumbing, or electricity. In central city ghettos, especially, multiple families are often squeezed into a small, cold apartment in a dirty and dangerous neighborhood.[24]

Many cannot work. For those at the bottom of society who can, jobs are not easy to get or to hold. Much time is spent in searching, in the degrading position of unemployment. The jobs that exist not only bring low wages but are themselves repetitive, boring, and unpleasant. Working conditions actually accentuate the unequal satisfactions brought by unequal incomes: the doctor, lawyer, and businessman are paid far more for their efforts than the waitress or the assembly-line worker; they also get more variety, more control over their activities, and more chance for creativity and self-fulfillment.[25]

The point is not just that many Americans receive less than a minimum standard of the necessities of life. If one accepts an absolute definition of poverty, based on some minimum standard, there is always reason for optimism: economic growth (barring setbacks like those caused by the food and energy crunches of the 1970s) may eventually lift most Americans above the minimum. Indeed, the poor of the United States are already rich by the standards of much of the world. But the problem is that poverty is not only absolute; it is also relative. Regardless of the average level of income, or the minimum level, a high degree of inequality causes unhappiness.

People judge their well-being not only by standards of biological survival but also by how well they are doing compared with what they think possible. In the United States, what is possible is judged by the opulence of the surrounding society. As polls have long shown, what the average American figures that a family "needs to get along" is relative to average neighborhood incomes—in fact, more than one-half the median. Those with lesser jobs and incomes suffer. They see themselves as deprived: they feel inadequate and lose self-respect, quite aside from questions of material comfort.[26] The phenomenon of relative deprivation adds to the arguments mentioned earlier and indicates that we should be concerned about the degree of inequality in incomes—not merely absolute poverty or minimum standards but inequality itself.

The Role of Government

As we have seen, the private economy of the United States generates very unequal incomes. If we view inequality as harmful to society and destructive of human welfare, it is natural to conclude that the state ought to redistribute income so as to achieve more equality.

In the twentieth century, a redistributive role for the state has been widely taken for granted. Students of public finance, for example, generally consider redistribution to be one of the major functions of government, along with allocation (remedying market failures for efficiency purposes) and stabilization (moderating business cycles and aiming for a desired rate of economic growth).[27] Since conservatives, liberals, and radicals all have reasons to oppose extreme inequalities, they all tend to favor at least some state action to counteract the income inequalities that would result from the unhindered operation of the private economy.

In addition to the idea that government *ought* to reduce inequality, there is reason to expect that democratic governments *will* do so. After all, most citizens have low incomes compared with the wealthiest. One might expect that the low-income majority would vote to tax those with high incomes and share the proceeds.[28]

Certainly, during the last two centuries of broadening popular participation in Western countries, many political theorists and ordinary people have either hoped or feared that democracy would entail a redistribution of income and wealth. If we take account of altruistic preferences, that is, that the rich may acquiesce in some spreading of the wealth, this prediction seems all the more compelling. Indeed, most people assume that the Western democracies do engage in large-scale redistribution. Whether they are pleased or outraged, most people take redistribution as an established fact.

It is the purpose of this book to look more closely at the conventional wisdom and to explore what effects—intended or unintended—U.S. government policies in fact have upon inequality. To what extent, and how, is the redistributive function actually performed? And why, politically, do policies have these effects or noneffects?

We will examine a broad range of government programs and policies, first separately and then in their total impact. Chapter 2 deals with taxes: which income groups bear the burden of taxes on personal and corporate income, payrolls, property, sales, and the like; what net effect these taxes have upon the distribution of income; and what determines the shape of tax politics.

Chapter 3 is concerned with social welfare programs, broadly construed: cash transfers under Social Security and Unemployment Insurance and Aid to Families with Dependent Children; in-kind benefits, including Food Stamps, Medicare, Medicaid, and housing assistance; and programs of aid for education and employment.

Chapter 4 turns to programs less directly aimed at individuals, with more of a "public goods" quality: military spending; international affairs; science and space exploration; energy development; the environment and natural resources; agriculture; and transportation.

Chapter 5 considers the distributive effects and the politics of various kinds of law and regulation: regulation of price and quality; macroeconomic policy, fiscal and monetary; and the constitutional and legal framework within which the economy operates.

Finally, Chapter 6 summarizes the findings and offers some general observations about the politics of redistribution. It discusses political possibilities and political limits.

As the reader will soon see, many problems beset any effort to discern exactly what effects government has upon inequality.

What can be established fairly clearly, however, is that after all government actions are taken into account, with their tremendous range and magnitude, after New Deals and Fair Deals and Wars on Poverty, the incomes of Americans remain very unequal. The welfare state may help establish a minimum level of existence for its citizens, but (in the United States, at least) it does not produce a substantial degree of equality. This fact must be explained in terms of the political process.

2

Who Bears the Tax Burden

Taxes affect people's real incomes—the amounts of goods and services they can consume—by taking away money before they can spend it and by changing the prices they have to pay. Thus taxes can, either deliberately or accidentally, change the distribution of income. They may fall more heavily on the rich, or on the poor, or on people in the middle. They may leave the rich and the poor closer together—or farther apart—after taxes than they were before.

Taxes could be used deliberately to increase equality. When the private economy generates highly unequal incomes, government could tax income away from the rich and give it to the poor. A strongly progressive tax system, that is, one in which a much higher proportion of income is taken from the rich than from the poor, would advance equality even if the proceeds were paid right back to the citizens in equal amounts or in shares proportional to income—all the more so if most of the money went to the poor.

The personal income tax, especially, could be used in that way. Utilitarian arguments for equality were developed largely in the course of advocating a progressive income tax. Public finance economists, even rather conservative ones, argue that government should perform a "distributive" function by means of progressive taxation of personal income together with cash transfer payments to the poor.[1]

We tend to assume that that is exactly what the U.S. government does. Historically, much agitation over the income tax has concerned issues of redistribution. The original impetus for a federal income tax, which culminated in the Sixteenth Amendment to the Constitution, came from populists and progressives, who aimed to curtail great fortunes and to tax on the basis of "ability to pay." It was opposed on the Senate floor as "socialism, communism, devilism."[2]

To be sure, the Taft and Wilson administrations and their legislative supporters who helped enact the income tax in 1913 did so largely in order to make up revenue lost by lowering tariffs rather than from any intention of soaking the rich. The rates were initially set far too low (7 percent on the top bracket) to have any substantial redistributive effect. Still, statutory tax rates became quite progressive during World War I, reaching a high of 77 percent on income over $1 million.

There was a sharp decline in the progressivity of the tax schedule in the 1920s, a rise in the 1930s and during World War II (with a top rate of 90 percent in 1944), and a moderate decline in the 1960s and later. But since 1932 the *nominal* rates of the federal income tax, that is, the rates published in the official schedules, have generally looked quite progressive. In the 1970s, for example, the rates for single persons were 14 percent on taxable income below $500, 28 percent on $8,000–10,000, 50 percent on $22,000–26,000, and 70 percent on income over $100,000.[3]

The reality of U.S. tax policy, however, and the *effective* rates that people actually pay, are quite different from this appearance, especially when we go beyond the personal income tax to consider the whole tax structure. Although certain taxes have complex economic effects that make it hard to be sure who actually bears the burden, it is clear that the net effect of all U.S. taxes, federal, state, and local, is not very progressive, if progressive at all.

Who Pays Federal Taxes

The Personal Income Tax

The federal income tax is more egalitarian than other taxes. But the progressivity of actual effective rates—as contrasted with the nominal scheduled rates—is rather mild and has been eroded over time. Taxes on the rich are not very high. In 1976, for example, income taxes as a proportion of total money income (IRS "adjusted gross income" plus excludable dividends, moving expenses, sick pay, and such "tax preference" items as excluded capital gains) were about 1 percent for incomes around $4,000, 10 percent around $14,000, and 24 percent in the $50,00–75,000 range. They reached a high of only 33 percent for incomes between $200,000 and $500,000 and actually declined to 28 percent for incomes of $1 million and over.[4]

The actual tax rates, in other words, were substantially progressive up to incomes of about $75,000, and then they leveled off and even declined for the highest incomes. The peak effective rate of 33 percent was a far cry from the nominal 70 percent found in the rate schedules. Income equality could not be achieved by taxing away only about one-quarter of incomes over $1 million.

Income tax rates look even less progressive when taxes are calculated as a percentage of the more broadly defined "adjusted family income," including imputed rent and unrealized capital gains and the like. Goode, using Pechman and Okner's 1966 data (but subtracting imputed taxes from incomes) found that the top 1 percent of income earners, with average earnings of nearly $100,000, paid only 18 percent in income taxes.

As Goode points out, the tax is both less heavy and less progressive than is commonly believed. Since only about 9 percent of all the adjusted family income in the country is taken by the income tax, it could not possibly accomplish much redistribution of income unless practically all of the tax were concentrated in the high brackets. But that is not the case. In fact, the impact of the tax on income distribution is not impressive. The percentage share of the top 1 percent of units in after-tax income was only about one-tenth smaller than their share in before-tax income (8.3 percent compared with 9.2 percent), and the differences are smaller for other groups[5] (see Table 3).

At present the income tax is probably even *less* progressive than these past data indicate. Progressivity was increased slightly in 1974, 1975, and 1976, but these changes were reversed when taxes on capital gains were reduced in 1978 and 1981, and the top marginal income tax rate was cut from 70 percent to 50 percent in 1981.[6]

Why isn't the income tax as redistributive as it looks? In mechanical terms, the answer is that various exclusions and exemptions and deductions from taxable income greatly benefit the rich.

Figure 2 illustrates how these provisions reduce tax progressivity. The nominal rates are represented by the steeply sloped solid line at the top of the figure, running from about 23 percent on the lowest incomes to more than 65 percent on the highest. Actual effective rates are tracked by the broken line at the bottom of the figure, which rises more gradually from about 10 percent to less than 40 percent and then declines slightly. The other lines (and the size of the gaps between lines) indicate how

TABLE 3   *The Income Tax and Net Adjusted Family Income, 1966*

Before-Tax Income Groups	% of All U.S. Income Received by Group		Mean Income ($) Before Tax	Effective Tax Rate (%)
	Before Tax	*After Tax*		
Top 1%	9.2	8.3	92,425	18.0
Next 4%	11.7	11.5	29,340	10.6
Rest of top quintile	25.8	25.6	17,257	9.8
Fourth quintile	23.2	23.4	11,638	8.3
Third quintile	16.1	16.4	8,076	7.2
Second quintile	10.0	10.5	5,016	5.1
Lowest quintile	4.0	4.3	2,006	2.5
	100.0	100.0		

SOURCE: Richard Goode, *The Individual Income Tax*, rev. ed. (Washington, D.C.: Brookings Institution, 1976), p. 250.

much particular provisions cause the effective rates to drop at each income level.

Certain kinds of economic benefits are not even defined as income or required to be reported for tax purposes: unrealized capital gains (i.e., the increased value of property which has not yet been realized or sold), imputed rent from owner-occupied dwellings (i.e., the value of the housing received by the owner, which is a kind of income from capital), and many fringe benefits including the consumption value of business meals and travel and entertainment. Since these kinds of income go mostly to the wealthy, their exclusion from taxation lowers the effective tax rates of the rich.

In addition, the tax code takes note of certain kinds of income but explicitly excludes them from tax liability or treats them spe-

FIGURE 2   *Influence of Various Provisions on Effective Rates of the Federal Individual Income Tax, 1976*

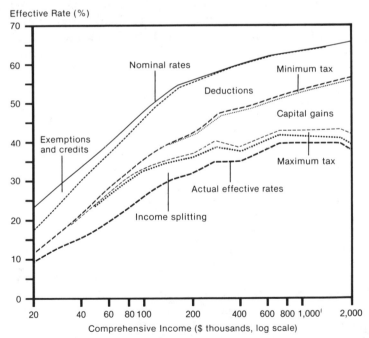

SOURCE: Joseph J. Minarik, "Who Doesn't Bear the Tax Burden," in *The Economics of Taxation*, ed. Henry J. Aaron and Michael J. Boskin (Washington, D.C.: Brookings Institution, 1980), p. 59.

cially. One-half (since 1978, 60 percent) of realized capital gains—the profits from selling stock or other property—are excluded from taxation altogether, and the top tax rate on the rest is now 50 percent, for a maximum net tax of *20 percent*. All income from tax-exempt state and local bonds and the first $100 or $200 of stock dividends are subtracted from taxable income. Tax-free bonds are a favorite investment of the rich and save them a great deal in taxes.

The special treatment of capital gains is particularly important to the well-to-do; by itself, as of 1976, it reduced the highest income tax rate from the nominal 69 percent to an effective rate of 49 percent.[7] (Also see Figure 2.) It may seem odd that income from stock market speculation is taxed much more lightly than income from people's labor. After a number of efforts to tighten the treatment of capital gains in the 1960s and early 1970s, however, they were treated even more leniently in 1978 and 1981.

Income splitting between husband and wife—the use of joint returns to treat the income of one spouse as if it were earned one-half by each—also benefits high-income families with one main earner since lower tax rates applied to the two halves add up to less than a higher rate applied to the total. This effect is most beneficial for those in the $25,000–100,000 range, where tax progressivity is steepest; it cuts some 6 to 7 percent off the nominal tax rates for those people.[8]

In addition, deductions reduce the taxes of the wealthy. A deduction of a given number of dollars is worth more to a rich man in a high nominal tax bracket than to a poor man in a low bracket. For example, one dollar given to charity by a millionaire may save him 50 cents (before 1981, 70 cents) in taxes whereas it would save someone with $100 of taxable income only 14 cents. (Flat dollar *credits* against taxes do not have this feature; they proportionately favor those of low income, especially if they are refundable when no tax is due.) Thus deductions for charity, casualty losses, interest, and state taxes cut the income taxes of upper-middle- and upper-income earners.

This point is true even of fixed dollar personal exemptions and standard deductions, which save the rich more dollars (though a lower percentage of their income) than they do the poor. But in addition, more is spent on most deductible items by high-income than by low-income people so that many deductions actually lower the *percentage* of income paid by the rich more than they do the poor. Deductions of interest payments and property taxes are especially valuable to those who have mortgages on expensive homes or borrow money to invest it. Charitable contributions overwhelmingly are given by those of high income. Pechman estimates that deductions cut 18 percent, more than one-quarter of the total scheduled rates, from the nominal tax rates of those in the higher brackets.[9]

To be sure, some exemptions and deductions have social purposes; they are designed to affect behavior, not just to lighten the tax load. The tax exemption for state and local bonds, for example, increases demand for such bonds and thereby enables states and localities to borrow money more easily (and at lower interest rates) than they otherwise would. It is partly a federal subsidy for state and local governments. Similarly, deductions for charitable contributions encourage private giving.

Furthermore, when we take account of these behavioral effects, the impact of deductions upon progressivity becomes harder to assess. It can even be argued that in a perfectly free market, many such tax benefits would be "competed away" and would not help the rich at all. An investor who put $10,000 into municipal bonds, for example, might find that the marketplace had driven tax-free interest rates down to 3 percent so that the yield of $300 a year would be no greater than the $300 another investor would get, after taxes, from $10,000 put in 10 percent industrial bonds with that interest taxed at a 70 percent rate. He would not really "save" anything from the tax exemption.[10]

There is confusion and controversy, however, about how strong these effects are, how well they accomplish social purposes, and to what extent the rich end up benefiting. The deduction of charitable contributions undeniably does encourage giving, perhaps even stimulating more than one dollar's worth of gifts for every one dollar in tax revenue given up. (The total effect was greater before 1981, of course, when the top marginal tax rates were higher.) But there is no guarantee that the recipients spend the money as well as the government would for genuinely public purposes; in particular, it is not clear that the poor benefit. As to municipal bonds, at least part of the benefit probably "trickles up" to the rich since municipal bond yields are higher than they would have to be to equalize after-tax returns for top-bracket taxpayers. And to the extent the subsidy to local government works, it may be a bad one, encouraging borrowing for inefficient construction that yields less than a fair market return on the capital.[11]

Tax relief for the rich reaches its highest point with "tax shelters," in which earned income is protected from taxation by means of large artificial losses conjured up through clever use of the tax code. In many tax shelters the trick is to borrow heavily, taking tax deductions for interest payments, and to deduct for depreciation in the investment on an accelerated basis—faster than the actual decline, if any, in the value of the assets. These deductions produce "losses" which offset ordinary income and prevent its taxation at high rates. Ultimately the assets are sold, and the profits are usually taxed at the lower capital gains rates.

Many a Manhattan doctor has become an oil or cattle baron for tax purposes. In response to periodic outcries about these loopholes, Congress has enacted restrictions and recapture provisions, but the ingenuity of tax lawyers and investment brokers easily keeps pace. With changes in the law, fashions in tax shelters simply shifted from the old standbys of oil, ranching, and real estate to the newer equipment leasing, sports franchises, and motion pictures—many of which, for sound business reasons, are pornographic.[12]

Payroll Taxes

Since World War II the moderately progressive income tax has constituted the largest single source of federal government revenue. In recent years it has provided just under half of the total. But a fast-growing rival has been payroll taxes, which were begun under the Social Security Act of 1935. Payroll taxes accounted for only 10 percent of federal revenues in 1954, nearly 20 percent in 1964, and over 30 percent by 1975 (see Table 4).[13]

Payroll taxes are very regressive in the upper income ranges, that is, the richer a person gets, the lower the percentage of his income he or she has to pay in payroll taxes. The reason is that the taxes are levied at a flat percentage rate on all wages up to a ceiling of about $30,000–40,000; above the ceiling, wages are entirely free of the tax. Thus the tax constitutes a larger propor-

TABLE 4   *Sources of Federal Government Revenue, 1940-1980*
            (percentages)

	Year				
Source	1940	1950	1960	1970	1980
Individual income taxes	17.5	39.9	44.0	46.7	46.9
Corporation income taxes	15.4	26.5	23.2	16.9	12.4
Social insurance (payroll) taxes	27.0	11.1	15.9	23.4	30.9
Excise taxes	29.0	19.1	12.6	8.1	4.7
All other receipts	11.2	3.4	4.2	4.9	5.1
Total receipts	100.0	100.0	100.0	100.0	100.0

SOURCES: U.S. Office of Management and Budget, "Federal Government Finances," Jan. 1979, p. 7; U.S. Office of Management and Budget, The *Budget of the United States Government*, fiscal year 1982 (Washington, D.C.: U.S. Government Printing Office, 1981), pp. 560-62.

tion of total income for those below or near the ceiling than for those way above it. A corporate president making $900,000 per year is not much burdened by a small tax on his first $40,000 of salary. Moreover, nonwage income (dividends, interest, rent, capital gains), which accrues mostly to the wealthy, is not subject to the tax at all.

Since the very poor earn little in taxable wages, payroll taxes as of 1977 were somewhat progressive for income up to $12,000; roughly proportional from $12,000 to $22,000, where the flat rate applied; and substantially regressive thereafter. Based on comprehensively defined family income, the rates ranged from a peak of about 11 percent on incomes of $15,000, down to 6 percent on $45,000 and approaching zero on the highest incomes.[14]

One complication in figuring the incidence of payroll taxes is that about half the Social Security (and all the unemployment) payroll tax is officially paid by employers rather than by workers. But economists are virtually unanimous in maintaining that this distinction is a fiction. The part employers pay is almost certainly subtracted from wages that workers would otherwise get. Employers are not inclined to pay more for the same work just because part of their wage cost takes the form of a tax; and since coverage of the taxes is nearly universal, workers have nowhere else to go and can't drive wages up to compensate for taxes and pay cuts. (If unions have power to exact wages above competitive levels, however, and choose to exercise that power on the occasions when payroll taxes are imposed, all or part of the taxes might be shifted to consumers in the form of higher prices.)

If payroll taxes are partly shifted to consumers, they are even more regressive. The taxes remain regressive in the upper ranges since the rich consume a smaller proportion of income than the poor. And shifted payroll taxes would be regressive even over the very lowest parts of the income scale since the poor must spend a high proportion of income on consumption items whose prices may be increased by payroll tax shifting (see Figure 3).

There is a different way of looking at payroll taxes that somewhat modifies the point about their regressivity. These taxes are linked to Social Security, medical care, unemployment insurance, and other programs, which (as we will see in the next chapter) are somewhat pro-poor in their distribution of benefits. Since payroll taxes are channeled into special trust funds for use in benefit payments, one may wish to consider them as elements of unified programs rather than analyzing the taxes separately. You can take your choice. In the end, whether one considers Social Security as involving separate programs of regressive taxes and pro-poor benefits or as an integrated program which (as we will see) gives back to each income class roughly the same amount it takes away, the result is the same: there is not much net redistribution of lifetime incomes, not much increase in equality.

Payroll tax rates have been rising. In 1977 the OASDI (Social Security) rate was 5.85 percent of wages from employees and the same from employers, for a total of 11.7 percent; in 1978 it went up to a total of 12.10 percent; and in 1981, to a total of 13.3 percent. In addition, the unemployment tax is 3.4 percent (lower in some states) on the first few thousand dollars of income. So these regressive taxes are becoming a larger and larger burden on low-income wage earners. By 1977, in fact, the Social Security payroll tax became the highest tax paid by about two-thirds of the nation's income recipients.[15]

FIGURE 3   *Effective Rates of the Payroll Tax, 1977*

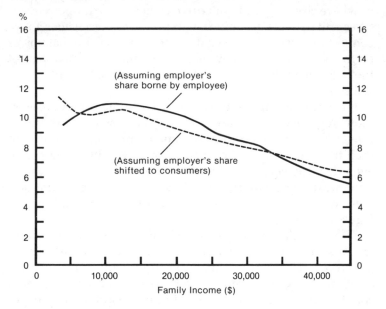

SOURCE: Joseph A. Pechman, *Federal Tax Policy,* 3rd ed. (Washington, D.C.: Brookings Institution, 1977), p. 207.

a. Tax is 11.7 percent for wage earners and 7.9 percent for the self-employed. Maximum earnings subject to tax are $16,500.

b. Both the employer and the employee portions of the tax are assumed to be borne by the employee; the self-employment tax by the self-employed.

c. The employer tax is distributed in proportion to consumption by income class; the employee tax and self-employment tax by the employee and the self-employed, respectively.

d. The tax is applied to *taxable income* as defined in the income tax law for 1977.

e. *Family income* is a *comprehensive definition* of income, which includes estimated accrued capital gains.

The regressivity of the tax over the middle-income range has been reduced somewhat by increases in the maximum amount of wages subject to the tax: from $16,500 in 1977 to $25,900 in 1980, $32,100 in 1982, and a projected $42,600 in 1990. But to a large extent this only compensates for inflation rather than taxing higher real incomes.

The Corporation Income Tax

The tax on corporations' "income" (i.e., net profits) in the years before World War II often produced more revenue than the individual income tax or any other tax. After the war it fell into second place, and in the late 1960s it was overtaken by the payroll taxes as well. By 1980 it yielded only 12.4 percent of federal revenue, less than half of what came from payroll taxes (see Table 4). In recent years the rates have been cut, and generous provisions for accelerated depreciation allowances, investment tax credits, and credits for foreign "taxes" (often disguised royalties—on oil, for example) paid by multinational corporations have further eroded effective rates. The 1981 investment tax credit and accelerated depreciation provisions virtually eliminated the tax for many corporations.[16]

The corporation income tax raises some of the knottiest questions for the understanding of tax incidence. It is very hard to tell which income classes actually bear how much of the burden of the tax.

At first glance the matter seems simple enough. Since the tax is levied as a percentage of corporations' profits, it presumably cuts after-tax corporate earnings and thereby lowers returns to each share of stock—most of which are owned by the wealthiest Americans. Thus the tax would seem to be paid heavily by the upper-income classes, as popular rhetoric favoring corporate taxation suggests. But this conclusion is thrown into doubt by the possibility that the tax is *shifted*, through the actions of corporations and reactions in the marketplace, onto workers in the form of lower wages or onto consumers in the form of higher prices.

To complicate matters further, even if corporate stockholders pay all of the tax in the short run, it is possible that investment patterns are affected—decreasing corporate, and increasing noncorporate, investment. Then less efficient noncorporate investments may be made, and the marginal rate of return (and, therefore, the rate of return that the market pays capital, generally) may go down until it equals the after-tax corporate return. If so, the tax is ultimately borne by owners of all capital, corporate and noncorporate alike.

It makes a great deal of difference what sorts of shifting, if any, occur. If consumers pay the tax, it is regressive because low-income families generally spend a much larger share of their income on consumption. If stockholders pay, it is a very progressive tax since the ownership of corporate stock is highly concentrated among wealthy people. If some intermediate amount of shifting occurs, there are intermediate distributive effects.

Economists disagree about whether and how much the tax burden is shifted. Under the perfect-market competitive assumptions embraced by conservative economists like Harberger—and with the additional, rather odd, assumption of a fixed supply of capital—the tax would be borne entirely by capital. In the short run, a profit-maximizing firm would not change its production decisions—there would be no use to manufacture an extra unprofitable unit or to forego manufacturing a profitable one merely because the tax would take away part of the new profit or save part of the loss—and prices would remain the same. Even a profit-maximizing monopolist would have no reason to alter quantity or price. In the long run, with equity financing, funds would move to the noncorporate sector until rates of return were equalized and the tax was borne equally by owners of capital in general.[17] (Debt financing complicates this picture since interest is a deductible expense; with full debt financing the tax may be borne entirely by stockholders. Financing by debt rather than equity has increased greatly in recent years.)

On the other hand, if markets are imperfect and oligopolistic, with firms engaging in cost-plus or after-tax-target-rate-of-return or other behavior that does not strictly maximize profits, the tax may be shifted forward to consumers or backward to workers. It seems doubtful that such "irrational" behavior would persist since a profit-maximizing competitor could seize most of the market by offering lower prices and/or higher wages. But some empirical evidence suggests that shifting does occur: Krzyzaniak and Musgrave arrived at econometric estimates of 100 percent or more shifting.[18] And after-tax rates of return reported by corporations were no lower (in fact, slightly higher) in the 1950s and 1960s than in the late 1920s when the tax had been much lower.

Given the confusion and disagreement, the best that can be done is to report who pays the corporate income tax under alternative incidence assumptions. Pechman, using 1970 data, found that if half the tax is shifted to consumers, it is mildly regressive for low incomes, proportional (at around 3 percent of broadly defined income) from about $10,000 to $50,000, and somewhat progressive—reaching a peak of nearly 9 percent— for the highest incomes. If it is fully shifted to consumers, of course, it is quite regressive. If the tax is borne by owners of capital in general, it is at first slightly regressive and then substantially progressive. If it is borne entirely by stockholders it is very low (under 1 percent) for incomes below $20,000 and then sharply progressive up to a peak of 32 percent on incomes over $1 million (see Table 5).[19]

Total Federal Taxes

Other federal taxes are small and could not possibly have much redistributive effect regardless of their incidence. Estate and gift taxes, for example (such as they are) fall mainly on the rich. But the exemption levels are set so high and the rates are so

TABLE 5   *Effective Rates of the Corporation Income Tax, 1970*

	Effective Rate (%)		
Income ($ Thousands)	If Half Borne by Capital and Half by Consumers	If All Borne by Capital in General	If All Borne by Stockholders
0–3	4.6	3.1	0.8
3–5	3.5	2.9	0.6
5–10	3.1	2.2	0.7
10–15	2.7	1.8	0.6
15–20	2.6	1.9	0.8
20–25	2.5	2.0	1.3
25–30	2.6	2.3	1.7
30–50	2.9	3.3	2.9
50–100	3.8	5.5	7.0
100–500	5.0	8.2	14.1
500–1,000	7.7	12.1	27.6
1,000 and over	8.6	13.4	32.0

SOURCE: Joseph A. Pechman, *Federal Tax Policy*, 3rd ed. (Washington, D.C.: Brookings Institution, 1977), p. 136.

low and so easy to avoid through skillful tax planning that few pay them. Only 1.2 percent of total federal revenue in 1980 came from estate and gift taxes.[20]

Indeed, the 1981 tax bill essentially abolished estate and gift taxes for nearly all Americans, in a series of steps scheduled to result in a cumulative exemption of $600,000 (up from $175,625) in 1987, and a maximum rate of 50 percent (down from 70 percent) in 1985.[21] Inequality is perpetuated by preserving large fortunes intact. In addition, equal opportunity is abridged when people can inherit great wealth without any demonstration of merit.

The bulk of federal excise taxes are levied on alcohol, gasoline, tobacco, and telephone calls, goods and services upon which low-income citizens spent a much larger proportion of their money than the rich do. Moreover, since demand for these goods is relatively inelastic, the burden of the taxes is not significantly shifted to producers through declines in demand. Thus those with incomes below $3,000 paid about 2.5 percent of their incomes in excise taxes in 1970; those above $100,000 paid only 0.4 percent. But excise taxes, which (together with customs duties) provided the bulk of federal revenue through the nineteenth century, now produce only a small and declining fraction—4.7 percent in 1980.[22] Their regressivity, like the progressivity of estate and gift taxes, is largely irrelevant to the total redistributive effect of taxes.

The net effect of federal taxes taken all together depends somewhat upon disputed matter of incidence, especially of the corporate income tax. But the controversial taxes provide only a small part of the revenue. Even under a variety of incidence assumptions, therefore, the general shape of the federal tax burden stays much the same. It is somewhat progressive, with the regressive payroll tax diluting the moderate progressivity of the individual income tax.

According to Pechman and Okner's data (updated by Okner to 1970), if corporation taxes fall half on property income in general and half on consumption, and the employers' part of payroll taxes is paid half by employees and half by consumers, total federal taxes in 1970 were nearly proportional over much of the income scale (14.6 percent on incomes between $5,000 and $10,000, 17 or 18 percent from $10,000 to $50,000) and then rose to about 27 percent on incomes over $1 million. That is according to incidence variant "3b," the most regressive considered in the study. On the other hand, if corporation taxes fall half on dividends and half on property income generally, and employer payroll taxes are paid entirely by employees (variant "1c," the most progressive assumptions considered), then federal taxes are a little more progressive. They rose from 7 percent on the lowest incomes to more than 33 percent on the highest. But again they were flat (17–18 percent) over most of the income range.[23] And a top rate of 33 percent on incomes over $1 million a year would not be nearly sufficient to equalize incomes.

In short, despite uncertainties about tax incidence, we can be fairly sure that federal taxes have some moderately redistributive effects. The rich pay somewhat higher rates than the poor. But even if all the revenue were given to those with low incomes, it would not go far toward income equality. And federal taxes are not the only taxes Americans pay.

State and Local Taxes

The progressive effect of federal taxes may be wholly nullified by regressive state and local taxes. The states and localities draw most of their revenue from sales taxes, which are distinctly regressive, and from property taxes, the incidence of which is in doubt.

Sales Taxes

General sales taxes, with flat rates ranging from 2 to 7.5 percent, are used by virtually all states. Together with excises, they provide a large share of state tax revenues. General sales taxes are very regressive because consumption of the taxed goods takes up a much larger proportion of income from the poor than the rich. They are not shifted to producers since, if all goods are taxed, demand has nowhere to go, and neither the prices nor the quantities produced change.[24]

For partial relief from the regressivity of sales taxes, more than half the states exempt food purchases, and most exempt medicine. But all states impose regressive excise taxes on alcohol, cigarettes, and gasoline. According to the Pechman and Okner 1966 findings, sales and excise taxes (including some federal taxes) were regressive throughout the income scale, taking 9 percent of the incomes of those in the $0–3,000 range, 4 percent from $25,000–30,000, and only 1 percent of incomes over $1 million.[25] Regressive sales taxes, like payroll taxes, are growing rapidly.

Property Taxes

Property taxes, the main source of revenue for local governments and school districts, are subject to great controversy about who bears the burden. As with corporate income taxes, the matter seems simple enough at first glance: property tax bills are paid by those who own real property, that is, land and buildings. (Personal property and inventories of goods are less often taxed because they are harder to locate and evaluate.) Thus the tax seems to fall upon the owners of homes, apartment houses, and businesses—mostly high-income people.

As with the corporate income tax, however, it is possible that those who initially pay property tax bills are able to shift the burden to others. Apartment owners may raise rents so that the tax is borne by renters; businesses may raise prices so that taxes on their buildings and inventories are borne by consumers. If property taxes are heavily shifted in this way, they fall mostly on lower-income people and are regressive.

There is much disagreement about whether, or to what degree, the property tax is shifted. Most economists have taken the supply of land as fixed and agree that landowners bear the entire burden of a tax on land in the form of declines in market value when the tax is imposed or anticipated. (Even this point ignores certain complexities, such as the interdependence of value of land and improvements, which renders the quality of land supplied variable; and the possibility of movement of investment from land to reproducible capital, which would reduce the return on capital, in general, and shift the tax to owners of capital generally.)

Some have maintained that a property tax on structures is shifted forward to users (renters and the consumers of goods produced in factories) on the grounds that the supply of structures is completely elastic. Rates of return are equalized every-where: unlimited capital is available to build new structures if the returns they yield go up, but none is available if (e.g., be-cause of a tax) the return should drop below that for other uses of capital. Upon this assumption Netzer, Musgrave, Pechman, and Okner (variant "3b") and others have estimated that prop-erty taxes are substantially regressive, ranging from 6 percent or 7 percent on incomes under $3,000 down to about 3 percent on incomes around $100,000 and less than 1 percent on incomes over $1 million.[26]

Recently Henry Aaron has argued that even under these in-cidence assumptions the past estimates of tax burdens by in-come class have been incorrect because of the use of annual rather than permanent income figures, because the proportion of income consumed in housing does not vary much in different income classes, and because value-to-rent ratios rise with hous-ing values so that taxes on value are more progressive. Using 1967–1971 panel data, Aaron estimated that property taxes are slightly regressive for renters and slightly progressive for homeowners, with a net result of being roughly proportional to income. But this must be qualified if (as appears to be the case) property taxes are unfairly administered so that lower effective tax rates are imposed on the most valuable property.[27]

Most important, Mieszkowski and Aaron and others have introduced a new view of property tax incidence, which makes it appear to be a quite progressive tax, falling upon owners of capital. The essence of the argument (and a questionable as-sumption) is that the total supply of capital is fixed—it does not respond to the rate of return. Consequently, a uniform tax on capital in general would be borne entirely by capital; there would be no way to shift assets or (without losing money) to raise prices. The variations in tax rates by location and type of capital goods produce some "excise" effects, in which invest-ments move from one place to another and prices change. But it is plausible that these effects mostly cancel out, leaving the own-ers of capital to pay the tax.[28]

Based on these assumptions, embodied in Pechman and Okner's incidence variant "1c," the property tax in 1966 was very slightly regressive in the low income range but stayed mostly proportional, around 2 to 3 percent, for incomes up to about $25,000 a year; it then became progressive and rose to 6 percent on incomes of $50,000–100,000 and 10 percent on incomes over $1 million.[29] Thus it makes a great deal of difference what we believe about incidence; the property tax may be either substantially regressive or substantially progressive (see Table 6).

The effects of property taxes are complicated by the fact that they, more than any other commonly used tax, are subject to great variations and inequities in administration. Before the tax is imposed, someone has to put a value on the property to be taxed, and in the assessment process there is room for delay and inefficiency, random error, systematic biases of various sorts, and outright corruption. Tax rates themselves vary greatly from one locality to another not only in proportion to services ren-

TABLE 6   *Effective Rates of the Property Tax, 1966*

	Effective Rate (%)		
Adjusted Family Income ($ Thousands)	*If Borne in Proportion to Property Income Generally*	*If Borne by Landowners*	*If Tax on Improvements Shifted to Consumers*
0–3	2.5	2.4	6.5
3–5	2.7	2.8	4.8
5–10	2.0	2.2	3.6
10–15	1.7	1.9	3.2
15–20	2.0	2.2	3.2
20–25	2.6	2.8	3.1
25–30	3.7	3.7	3.1
30–50	4.5	4.4	3.0
50–100	6.2	6.1	2.8
100–500	8.2	7.8	2.4
500–1,000	9.6	8.8	1.7
1,000 and over	10.1	8.7	0.8

SOURCES: Henry J. Aaron, *Who Pays the Property Tax?* (Washington, D.C.: Brookings Institution, 1975), p. 47; Joseph A. Pechman and Benjamin A. Okner, *Who Bears the Tax Burden?* (Washington, D.C.: Brookings Institution, 1974), p. 59.

dered by government but also in relation to the happenstance of how much taxable property is available.

Some of the variations in level of assessments and in tax rates are virtually random, producing "horizontal" inequities of a sort which should not be taken lightly but which do not differentiate among income classes. Other variations do affect the progressivity or regressivity of the system. Business property is usually assessed (and therefore taxed) more heavily than rental property, which in turn is assessed and taxed more than owner-occupied homes. If the tax is partly shifted to consumers and renters, then those relatively low-income individuals may pay higher rates than upper-middle- and upper-income homeowners.

More importantly, the most valuable homes are often assessed at a lower proportion of their value than are the less expensive ones. In Boston, a fairly typical city, some wealthy people's houses were assessed at only half the ratio of lower-income people's. Similarly, some corporations and big property owners receive conspicuously low assessments on large holdings, like Anaconda's timberland in Montana that was assessed at $9.7 million but sold for $117 million, or U.S. Steel's South Works plant that was underassessed by $150 million. And property tax rates tend to be higher in central cities, where average incomes are low, than in affluent suburbs. Even if the property tax is borne largely by property owners, therefore, those of low income may bear a heavier share than those of high income when the vagaries of administration are taken into account.[30]

Total State and Local Taxes

State income taxes have been growing but still produce about the same amount of revenue as sales taxes. They generally follow the federal model and have progressive nominal rates. But they are much less progressive (even regressive) in effect because the nominal progressivity often ends at a point low in the income scale. Usually a flat rate is imposed on all income over $25,000 or so. And state tax payments are deductible from federal taxes; this deduction is worth far more to those in high federal brackets than in low.

States vary a great deal, from the rather progressive income tax in New York and Minnesota, to nearly flat rates in Indiana, to no tax at all in Texas. But in most states the marginal burden of the state income tax for those in the highest federal tax bracket is less than 2 percent, and in many states it is less than 1 percent. State income taxes fall more heavily on those of lower and middle income.[31]

Most states impose corporation income taxes, but the rates are low and the distributive effects, regardless of incidence, are minor.

The total effect of state and local taxes depends heavily upon who actually pays property taxes. Under Pechman and Okner's most progressive assumptions (variant "1c"), in which the property tax is taken to fall on property income in general, as of 1970 the effective state and local tax rates followed a "U" curve, starting at about 15 percent on the lowest incomes, dropping to 7 or 8 percent in the $10,000–50,000 range, and rising again to a peak of just under 20 percent on incomes of $1 million and over. On the other hand, if property taxes on improvements are shifted to shelter and consumption (variant "3b"), state and local taxes were more sharply regressive at low levels, somewhat regressive at high, and flat in the middle. They fell from 20 percent on the lowest incomes to about 8 percent in the $20,000–100,000 range, to about 6 percent on incomes of $1 million and more.[32]

Even at best, then, state and local taxes are regressive or proportional over the range of most Americans' incomes and do not reach a very high rate on the highest incomes. At worst—and there is reason to suspect the worst—they are quite regressive. Generally speaking, proposals to "turn over" policy responsibilities to the states imply less progressive financing.

When all federal, state, and local taxes are taken together, the net effects again depend somewhat upon incidence assumptions. Under the regressive ("3b") assumptions, the total effect of all taxes in 1970 was almost exactly proportional, taking around 26 percent of incomes at most levels, with slightly higher rates of 30–35 percent on the very lowest and the very highest. Under the most progressive ("1c") assumptions the rates rose markedly over the upper end of the income scale (above $50,000 or $100,000), reaching a peak of nearly 53 percent. But for the vast majority of Americans, with all but the top 1 or 2 percent of incomes, the rates were very nearly proportional, varying only from 22 percent to 27 percent (see Table 7).[33]

In short, regardless of incidence assumptions, the U.S. tax system is virtually proportional for the vast majority of American families. It is not an important means of redistribution. At best, Pechman and Okner say, taxes reduce the Gini coefficient of income inequality by less than 5 percent.[34]

Tax Politics

Why is this so? Why aren't U.S. taxes very progressive, despite expectations that the poor would take from the rich in a democracy, and despite the special emphasis upon taxes as appropriate instruments for income redistribution? As

TABLE 7   *Total Effective Rate of All Federal, State, and Local Taxes, 1970*

	Effective Rate (%)	
Adjusted Family Income ($ Thousands)	*Under Progressive (1c) Incidence Assumptions*	*Under Regressive (3b) Incidence Assumptions*
0–3	22.2	31.4
3–5	19.4	24.4
5–10	22.4	25.2
10–15	24.1	26.3
15–20	24.5	26.3
20–25	25.0	26.1
25–30	25.7	26.2
30–50	27.3	26.5
50–100	32.7	29.3
100–500	39.1	30.6
500–1,000	51.9	36.7
1,000 and over	52.7	32.9

SOURCE: Benjamin A. Okner, "Total U.S. Taxes and Their Effect on the Distribution of Family Income in 1966 and 1970," in *The Economics of Taxation*, ed. Henry J. Aaron and Michael J. Boskin (Washington, D.C.: Brookings Institution, 1980), p. 74.

we will see, similar puzzles arise in other policy areas. If we can find the answers about tax policy, some of them may illuminate fundamental aspects of the political process generally. Others may reflect peculiarities of taxation.

A general possibility that must be considered is that democratic forms may conceal undemocratic realities. Perhaps the will of the people is thwarted. This could happen in a variety of ways.

Chairmen and Committees

Journalists and students of American government make much of the role of legislative committees, especially in the House of Representatives. Many assert that the "powerful" chairmen of the House Ways and Means and the Senate Finance committees play important parts in shaping tax legislation and in preventing it from taking a very progressive form.

It is true that such men as Wilbur Mills and Russell Long have, over the years, championed a series of regressive measures and resisted progressive reforms.[35] Long, for example (from the oil-producing state of Louisiana) was an ardent defender of the oil depletion allowance even after it became a symbol of regressive loopholes. Committee chairmen have regularly opposed moves to tighten the taxation of capital gains, and Al Ullman and Long were leading figures in the 1978 loosening of capital gains taxation. The chairmen have also resisted financing Social Security from general (e.g., income tax) revenues rather than regressive payroll taxes.

It is hard, however, to see how committee chairmen could be fundamental causes of regressive tax policy. One would want to know why conservative chairmen were repeatedly chosen over a period of decades. And why would state legislative committee chairmen fit the same mold? Moreover, if chairmen were seriously out of step with their committees, we would expect them to be overruled in policy making or, if necessary, to be replaced. As it happens, successful chairmen are usually quite in tune with their committees and tend to anticipate or respond to committee wishes rather than oppose them. Democratic tax committee chairmen have sometimes had voting records more conservative than their fellow Democratic committee members, but they have been rather close to the average of their committees as a whole. In the late 1970s, Chairman Ullman was actually somewhat more liberal than his committee.[36]

If the chairmen are not tyrannical conservatives, perhaps the tax committees themselves are unrepresentative, more conservative than their parent bodies. Such unrepresentativeness might result from self-selection to committees or from influence by corporations and large campaign contributors upon elections and the legislative assignment process. It is true that tax committees get abundant campaign money from interested groups and individuals. Perhaps the committees, marking up bills in secret and relying upon "closed rules" to push their legislation through without amendments on the floor, impose their antiprogressive wills on Congress.[37]

Again, however, it is difficult to see how the composition of committees could be a fundamental cause of tax policy. If they are atypical of Congress as a whole, why don't other congressmen insist on a better balance, or why don't they at least overrule minority legislation on the floor? Closed rules could be rejected by the membership. (And why would Congress allow an unrepresentative composition of the Rules Committee, which would be necessary to grant such rules in the first place?)

In fact, voting records indicate that Senate Finance Committee members are more conservative than the Senate as a whole and often load their tax bills with "Christmas tree" loopholes, but these bills are open to amendment—and are frequently amended—on the Senate floor. The House Ways and Means Committee, on the other hand, is very successful at getting its bills through the House, but its members are quite representative of that body; Ways and Means is virtually a microcosm of the House as a whole. Thus one committee may have the inclination to go against its parent chamber but lacks the power; the other committee, whether or not it has the power, lacks the inclination.[38]

What about the general membership of Congress, then? Legislators may be more conservative than the public. Certainly the many millionaires in the Senate have self-interested reasons to oppose progressive taxation. In the low-information context of congressional elections, citizens must rely upon cues of party and incumbency; they cannot be sure they are electing congressmen who reflect their policy preferences.[39] Money counts. The rich and well organized have great advantages in electing friendly representatives, especially since low-income citizens are the least likely to participate.[40]

Some evidence about representation is available from surveys of constituency opinions and their relations to congressmen's attitudes and roll call votes. Because of small and nonrandom samples of district opinion, it is hard to be sure exactly how much correspondence there has been between congressmen and their constituents. But clearly the correspondence is less than perfect. Even on rather salient questions of social welfare (federal help with jobs, medical care, and the like) citizens and their representatives often disagree.[41] It is quite possible that in the complex, less visible area of taxation the representational linkage is even weaker. On the other hand, some aggregate public opinion data (discussed below) suggest that tax policy may not depart very far from Americans' wishes.

Political Parties

Party differences play a part in tax policy. When tax questions come to a vote, Republican and Democratic congressmen tend to take opposite sides, with the Democrats (especially Northern Democrats) favoring more progressive policies. The Democrats have mostly sought tax credits for those with low incomes, extension of payroll taxes to high incomes, and the like whereas Republicans have voted for cuts in corporate and capital gains taxes. The 1974–1976 period witnessed a particularly lively struggle between the Democratic Congress and Republican President Ford, and the 1981 tax bill provoked conflict between congressional Democrats and President Reagan.

Yet party differences, when all is said and done, have been rather modest. A Republican administration presided over the regressive changes of 1954, but Republican presidents also signed the progressive measures of 1969, 1974, 1975, and 1976 (pushed, to be sure, by Democrats in Congress). Democratic administrations enacted the progressive tax cuts of 1964, but also the regressive changes of 1962 and 1978. In 1981 the Democrats, led by Ways and Means Chairman Dan Rostenkowski, engaged in a bidding war with Reagan to see who could offer more lucrative tax breaks to business.

Over the years there have been some zigzags in the degree of progressivity of tax policy, but those zigzags have been limited in effect and have not followed any consistent relation to party control. What is most important is that *neither* party has embraced highly progressive tax policies of the sort advocated by the social democratic parties of Europe. Neither Lyndon Johnson, with his huge Democratic majority of 1964, nor Jimmy Carter, with his solid congressional majority and his talk of tax favoritism for the rich as a "disgrace," transformed the tax system into an instrument of redistribution. Instead, Carter signed some of the most regressive changes of the post-war decades.[42]

Implementation

Implementation certainly has something to do with the effects of tax policy. Even when the law appears to tighten a loophole or to move in a progressive direction, new legal maneuvers or favorable rulings or court decisions often open a new loophole or preserve the old one. In some cases, as McConnell argues, the implementation process may be completely captured by private interests.[43]

This is not very plausible in the case of the Internal Revenue Service (IRS), which has a reputation for integrity—although some odd IRS rulings, after onslaughts of private lobbying, can be found. (And periodic proposals to tax fringe benefits are usually dropped quickly.) It is more plausible with respect to state and local taxes, especially the property tax, where assessment practices may often be tainted by corruption. Local assessors may be tempted to supplement their incomes by undervaluing and undertaxing the property of the wealthy.

An important feature of implementation is the role of high-priced tax lawyers, who are hired by the rich to find legal ways to outwit the law. Top legal talent is capable of great ingenuity. Just as the bar in England for centuries preserved the aristocracy's power to tie up land, despite repeated court decisions to the contrary, so American tax lawyers seem able to invent new tax shelters, find new ways to take depreciation allowances and capital gains, no matter what Congress does.

If cattle herds lose their appeal, equipment leasing or pornographic movies may do the trick. If estate taxes threaten to take a real bite, estate planners can devise trusts or foundations that avoid taxes but preserve a good measure of control. If Uncle Sam tries to capture some of the profits made by U.S. multinational firms abroad, judicious shifting of gains from one subsidiary to another, or persuasion of foreign governments to assess "taxes" rather than royalties, may keep the tax collector at bay. None of this is illegal or violates lawyers' ethics. The point is simply that with a system of free enterprise law, the brains and the ideas go into the service of the rich and undermine progressive taxation.

At the same time, implementation can hardly account for the broad shape of tax policy. Those who write the laws are also experts, with skillful staff support. If they wanted a steeply progressive tax system, they could create one. They could treat capital gains as ordinary income, repeal various deductions, convert the payroll tax to a graduated schedule with no exemption for high incomes. Such progressive changes would survive attacks by the best lawyers in the country. But the will is not there. Loophole closing is often pursued in a half-hearted or ritualistic manner. The way the law will be circumvented is sometimes apparent to everyone even before it is enacted.

Interest Groups

Lobbying and interest group influence play a part in several of the arguments we have already considered. It is a fact that organized groups tend to overrepresent the wealthy, especially commercial, industrial, and professional interests, because of the "free rider" barrier against organizing more diffuse interests. (It is hard to get low-income taxpayers to contribute to a union of small taxpayers since any individual would benefit from its efforts even without contributing; but business organizations already exist for purposes other than lobbying.)[44]

The rich have more money and more organizational clout for getting friendly congressmen and tax committee members elected; for lobbying, persuading, or even purchasing executive action or legislative votes; and for influencing implementation.

Despite the rise of public interest lobbies like Common Cause, Taxation with Representation, and Tax Analysts and Advocates, the overwhelming thrust of tax lobbying activity still favors high-income individuals and corporations.

At the beginning of the 1980s, for example, an examination of organizations focusing on federal tax policy revealed that conservative groups had *twenty-two times* as large budgets as did liberal and labor groups. Business-oriented groups like the U.S. Chamber of Commerce's Tax Policy Committee, the National Association of Manufacturers, American Business Conference, and the Tax Foundation spent more than $4 million on tax policy issues. "Balance the budget" groups like the National Taxpayers Union and the National Tax Limitation Committee spend another $2.7 million. By contrast, liberal organizations like Citizens for Tax Justice and the Public Citizens Tax Reform Group spent only $365,000.[45]

It is important to recognize that lobbying can take perfectly legal and apparently benign forms. As Stanley Surrey points out, tax legislators need specialized information about the effects of proposed provisions; often they must rely upon the multitude of special interest groups for that information, with the main counterbalance coming from the Treasury Department— which cannot effectively resist every plea for special favors.[46] Especially if the congressmen are favorably predisposed to regressive tax measures by their own wealth and by the fact that the wealthy elected them, no pressure or bribery is necessary. Their predispositions are reinforced by the testimony they hear, private conversations, and interaction with like-minded legislators.

It is easy enough to recount anecdotes about lobbying by groups or individuals. In one colorful example, the Ways and Means Committee late at night at the end of the 1975 session passed a special loss carryback provision which would have given H. Ross Perot some $15 million in benefits. The *Wall Street Journal* revealed that the provision had been drafted by Perot's lawyer, former IRS commissioner Sheldon Cohen. Moreover, Perot had recently contributed $27,400 to twelve Ways and Means Committee members, some unopposed for reelection, ten of whom backed the provision in a 14–12 vote. Amidst general embarrassment the provision was rescinded.[47] It is reasonable to suppose that less publicized efforts to get special favors have been more fruitful.

In the late 1970s, Representatives James Jones (D) and Barber Conable (R) urged business lobbyists to unify behind a single proposal to cut corporate taxes. The U.S. Chamber of Commerce, National Association of Manufacturers, Business Roundtable, American Council for Capital Formation, and others held a series of informal meetings at the Carlton Hotel in Washington, and their attorneys drafted legislation for "10-5-3" accelerated depreciation allowances.[48] (The numbers refer to the "tax life" of various assets: the total cost of an automobile, e.g., could be deducted from taxable income over the course of three years, even if it kept running for ten years. The effect of such short tax lives is to cut taxes sharply, by several billion dollars, for capital-intensive firms.) After an intense lobbying effort, and after the 1980 elections produced a more conservative Congress, "10-5-3" depreciation was enacted into law in 1981.

Systematic evidence of group influence is difficult to obtain, however. Often it is possible to show that favorable provisions follow lobbying activity and campaign contributions; sometimes congressmen or executives even reverse their positions after being lobbied. But many such incidents are open to alternative interpretations, such as extortion by politicians (threatening unfavorable action merely to drum up campaign money); or provision by groups of important information that a conscientious legislator should heed. And the more cosy kind of group influence, in which the wealthy and well-organized simply elect like-minded representatives, never shows up in specific incidents of lobbying activity at all.

It is even possible for intelligent people to deny altogether that groups and lobbyists have any significant influence upon policy. Some prominent political scientists have done exactly that.[49] On the other hand, most observers of the tax policy-making process are convinced that lobbying is crucial. Whatever the extent of effects, the direction of influence is clear. There is not much of a lobby for serious tax progressivity. The AFL-CIO talks against Republican "trickle-down" economics but doesn't fight very hard for steep progressivity. A few public interest groups try harder, but they have limited resources, and some hold only rather mild upper-middle-class ideas about what the optimal tax system would be. Much of the field is left to business and conservative groups.

Public Opinion

Any account of tax policy that asserts that the public's will is thwarted must explain why an aroused citizenry does not rise up and throw out unresponsive officials. A possible answer is that citizens do not have the necessary information; they do not know that taxes are not, in fact, progressive. This might be particularly true of tax policy since the issues are so technical and complicated. In Schattschneider's phrase, the "scope of the conflict" is narrow, and the public can be virtually ignored. Moreover, as Edelman maintains, symbols may be used to deceive the public about what is happening.[50]

The particularly regressive nature of state and local taxation may reflect its even lower visibility. State and local governments, despite their geographical closeness to the people, actually get less publicity and less attention and less participation than their federal counterparts. The stakes of local government appear to be relatively low and not worth much investment of citizens' time or money. They may, as McConnell argues, be less subject to popular control.[51] If so, special interests may more easily prevail and regressive taxes result.

Survey research indicates that people know little about the tax system. "Don't know" responses are frequent, and pollsters don't even bother to ask about really complex issues. Few Americans understand the differing effects of credits and deductions, let alone accelerated depreciation or intangible drilling expenses.[52]

Some symbols are available to convince people that taxes are more progressive than they are. The nominal rate schedules themselves have that effect: a casual reader of the tax forms could easily conclude that the rich pay 50 percent or 70 percent of their earnings in income taxes rather than the 20 percent or so they actually pay. (It is easy to confuse nominal with effective rates, and marginal rates with average rates.) Similarly, periodic outcries against "confiscatory" taxation may help convince some that the rates are high.

The "minimum tax," devised in response to public outrage over the fact that 257 persons with incomes over $200,000 had paid no federal income taxes at all in 1968, also helps sustain the myth of progressivity. The minimum tax for a time shortened the list of those paying zero taxes, and quieted the protests, but did not make anyone pay very much and did not significantly increase the progressivity of the rate system.[53]

It is conceivable, therefore, that legislators could get away without enacting progressive taxes precisely because the people think they already have progressive taxes. This and all the previous suggestions about different ways in which the political process could contradict the will of the people, however, presume that the popular will is, in fact, contradicted. But there is some evidence that Americans actually favor tax provisions and effective rates closely resembling those that exist.

Polls indicate, for example, that most people oppose "tax loopholes" in the abstract but favor such specific provisions as income splitting, deductions for all medical and dental expenses, and deductions for college tuition and room and board—all of which favor high-income taxpayers. They judge sales (as opposed to income or property) taxes to be the "fairest" state and local taxes. And, in the 1970s, many more Americans considered capital gains taxes "too high" than "too low."[54]

For a fairly precise measurement of preferences about the redistributive effects of taxation, we must turn to a series of Gallup questions often asked in the 1940s and 1950s but last used in December 1962. Gallup asked each respondent to suppose that he or she was a member of Congress setting the amount of taxes for people to pay in the coming year. Taking a typical family of four, with a total income of $3,000 a year, how much should they pay in personal income taxes? What about people earning $5,000? $10,000? $50,000? $100,000? Gallup then calculated the median response concerning each hypothetical family.

The Gallup findings, displayed in Table 8, are quite interesting. The average American favored a progressive income tax all right, but a very mild one, rising from nothing on $3,000 to 3 percent on $5,000, 7 percent on $10,000, and 10 percent on $50,000, to a peak of only 20 percent on $100,000. The degree of progressivity desired was substantially less than that on the rate schedule.[55] What is most remarkable is that the rates which the median American preferred were quite close to the actual 1966 effective rates as computed by Pechman and Okner, taking account of adjustments, deductions, and exclusions (compare Table 3).

The 1962 evidence, then, indicates that Americans were getting about as much income tax progressivity as they wanted. We should not assume that preferences have remained exactly the same since that year, but the Gallup findings did have a great deal of stability over the years they were asked, from 1937 through 1962. And more recent surveys show rather little sentiment for "increas[ing] the tax rate for high incomes," or for "the federal government trying to make a fairer distribution of wealth of the country," or for "do[ing] something to reduce income differences between rich and poor."[56]

A poll done for H & R Block in the summer of 1977 helped blunt the post-1976 movement for tax reform by indicating little public enthusiasm for more progressivity. Large majorities (80 percent or more) considered twelve special provisions that favor the rich to be "reasonable," and smaller majorities even approved the exclusion of municipal bond interest and one-half of capital gains.[57]

This sheds a different light upon the hypotheses of interest group influence or unrepresentative congressmen. It suggests

TABLE 8   *Income Tax Rate Preferences of the Public, 1962*

Annual Income of Family of Four ($)	Median Rate Preferred by Public ($)	(%)	Actual Effective Rate, 1966 (%)
3,000	0	0	1–2
5,000	150	3	3–5
10,000	720	7	6–7
50,000	5,000	10	10–14
100,000	20,000	20	14–18

SOURCES: George H. Gallup, *The Gallup Poll: Public Opinion, 1935-1971*, 3 vols. (New York: Random House, 1972), III, 1,800; Joseph A. Pechman and Benjamin A. Okner, *Who Bears the Tax Burden?* (Washington, D.C.: Brookings Institution, 1974), p. 59.

a much simpler and happier explanation for the lack of progressivity in tax policy: perhaps democracy works, and the people get exactly what they want.

Manipulation of Opinion

A simple correspondence between policy and the preferences of the public, however, does not in itself demonstrate governmental responsiveness to the public. It is possible that citizens' preferences are consequences rather than causes of policy; or that the relationship between the two is spurious, that some outside factor (perhaps interest groups) affects both; or that preferences are only proximate causes, themselves influenced by some more basic determinant. The democratic implications of the correspondence are thrown into doubt if preferences do not actually cause policy or if preferences are caused to depart from the true interests of the citizens, that is, from the preferences they would express if fully informed.[58]

Tax law complexity and lack of information may permit public preferences to be *manipulated* so as to diverge from true interests. The rational citizen must form his policy preferences on the basis of available information about the effects of alternative policies. The available information may be biased because of the influence of monied sectors of society upon schools, the media, and government itself.[59] Even presuming that the provision of information responds perfectly to market forces (though the difficulties in selling information may cause it to be underprovided), the market will respond to money rather than to democratic votes. The rich know what's going on, but the average taxpayer does not necessarily get the information he needs to judge what tax policies would be in his best interest.

The most casual observer can see that the public is offered abundant misinformation about taxes. We have noted how nominal tax rates and misleading rhetoric could fool the unwary into thinking they have a very progressive tax system. Similarly, acceptance of particular provisions may depend upon mistaken impressions of what effects they have. Deductibility of mortgage interest sounds good to the middle-income homeowner if no one mentions how much more it benefits the rich. The sales tax seems fair (it is paid by everyone in small easy doses) if there is no discussion of the higher proportion of income taken from poor than rich. Loose talk of "capital shortages" may frighten the average man into approving easy treatment of capital gains.

More fundamentally, manipulation of preferences may affect people's opinions about progressive taxation itself. If academics and politicians and the media overstate the extent of work and savings disincentives from progressive taxation, the average person may conclude that progressivity would retard the economy and harm him. If schools exaggerate the possibilities of social mobility, an ordinary citizen may decide that inequality should be preserved so he or his children will have a chance to get to the top. If civics books and television say the free market rewards each according to his work, the average American may conclude that the rich deserve what they have and that it should not be taxed away. Without question, ordinary working people tend to oppose equalizing incomes even if they would benefit from it.[60]

Evidence about the extent of manipulation is elusive. We need to know what information is transmitted to the public, whether it is true or false, what the public believes, and what impact the information has on beliefs. There is only limited evidence on any of these points. But we can be sure that the public has some mistaken beliefs about taxes and that there is much misinformation in the air.

Economic Structure

The other side of the coin is the argument that people may approve of the present tax system because it is in fact optimal, given the constraints of our economic system. That is, perhaps there are *structural* reasons for the shape of tax policy and for the similar configuration of public preferences. Perhaps it is true that material incentives are essential within a capitalist system in order to promote work and investment and economic growth. Perhaps highly progressive taxation would destroy these incentives, inhibit growth, and leave the average man worse off than if he had accepted inequality and let the economy flourish. Maybe citizens are aware of these truths and have no desire for zero-sum redistributive politics but prefer a positive-sum, dynamic game in which they put up with inequality and are better off in the long run.[61]

Structural theories of politics take two quite different forms. On the political right, some neoclassical economists (including contributors to the "optimal taxation" literature) argue that a free market system is the ideal form of economy, that private enterprise requires unequal rewards to operate effectively, and that people must accept inequality as an inevitable feature of a smoothly running economy. Highly progressive taxation would be counterproductive.[62] Such arguments became very popular in the 1970s.

On the left, Marxist structuralists agree that under capitalism the workers must bribe entrepreneurs with high salaries and must let corporations accumulate fat profits in order to achieve economic growth and produce largesse for later distribution to workers. They agree that the capitalist economic structure itself prevents substantial redistribution by making redistribution counter to the immediate self-interest of any class in society. Where they differ from conservatives is in assuming that an alternative economic system would be superior. Under socialism the state would direct investment and use nonmaterial incentives to encourage work so that prosperity could be attained along with equality.[63]

Marxist structuralists must account for why the workers in capitalist economies do not perceive the postulated advantages of socialism. This could be explained by resorting to arguments of group power and manipulation of consent: the capitalists have control and prevent the workers from learning the virtues of socialism. Or, more in the structuralist spirit, it can be argued that rationally self-interested workers accept the local optimum of inequality under capitalism because it is too costly to obtain information about the possible global optimum of socialism. Better to stick with the satisfactory known, they think, than to gamble on the ideal unknown, especially if the benefits would accrue only to their grandchildren.

Both Marxist and neoclassical structuralist theories are consistent with the lack of progressivity in U.S. taxes and with the apparent acquiescence of the public. But how true are they?

Certainly, much of the rhetoric of tax policy making has been consistent with structuralist reasoning. In the 1920s, for example, Secretary of the Treasury Andrew Mellon asserted that the high progressive income tax rates of World War I had driven the rich to invest in tax-exempt bonds. Sounding like "supply-side" economists of the 1970s, Mellon declared that

> the sources of taxation are drying up; wealth is failing to carry its share of the tax burden; and capital is being diverted into channels which yield neither revenue to the government nor profit to the people. . . . [A] decrease of taxes causes an inspiration to trade and commerce which increases the prosperity of the country so that the revenues of the government, even on a lower basis of tax, are increased.[64]

Under Mellon's leadership the tax rates on high incomes were cut drastically, and the present special treatment of capital gains was begun.

Even the representatives of organized labor gradually came to the view that taxing the rich too much would hurt everyone. In 1962, to take one instance, the AFL-CIO went along with the Investment Tax Credit (ITC), which granted a huge windfall to the largest and most profitable corporations. The Democratic Kennedy administration, following the Republican Mellon's example, advocated the ITC on the grounds that it would stimulate economic growth and improve the lot of the poor and working people, as well as increasing national strength for the struggle with communism.[65]

In the early 1970s there was a strong movement for tax reform, manifested in George McGovern's presidential campaign and in the rise of "public interest" lobbies. It seemed possible that various regressive tax provisions (e.g., the special treatment of capital gains) might be rolled back, and some progress was made in 1974, 1975, and 1976. But an intensive campaign claiming an urgent need for capital formation stopped the movement toward progressivism. Amidst concern about incentives and economic growth, there was a very substantial *cut* in corporate and capital gains taxes in 1978, and even more in 1981.

Yet such examples are not conclusive. The rhetoric of economic imperatives may sometimes be a smoke-screen for businessmen and others with a selfish interest in regressive tax policies.[66] And acquiescence by labor may represent compromising for some quid pro quo, or resignation to the inevitable, rather than conviction on the merits. The economic "facts" which convince people may be incorrect either because of biased research and publicity or from simple unmotivated error, in which case tax policy depends not upon the actual economic structure but upon misunderstandings of that structure, which could presumably be corrected. (It is notable, e.g., that taxes on property and on corporate income began to be cut sharply just when economists had started to argue that they were not shifted but fell on capital.)

As this book is written, practically all Americans—and certainly President Reagan and his economic advisers—appear to believe that highly progressive taxes are incompatible with productivity and growth. But the foundations of that belief are flimsy. It is unclear what boundaries, if any, a capitalist economy places upon the degree of progressive taxation that is feasible or desirable.

Despite intuition and economic theory, researchers have not actually found compelling evidence that people work much less when they are taxed at high rates. When asked open-ended questions about their finances and their work, the affluent seldom spontaneously mention taxes as entering into their decisions. Nor do they attribute much effect to taxes when specifically asked, or behave much differently in high brackets than low.[67] Motivations are partly noneconomic. And the income effect of needing to work harder for the same standard of living may cancel out the substitution effect of choosing more leisure.

On the other hand, such studies are based on taxes in the current (not very high or progressive) range. If taxes approached total confiscation in high brackets, there would presumably be some slacking of work effort. We don't know at what point this would occur. Comparative examples suggest that executives and professionals continue to work hard in a capitalist system even when taxes take a high proportion of their incomes.

Over the broader range of ordinary workers' incomes, econometric studies indicate that taxes probably do discourage work somewhat, especially among women and second-wage earners. One recent estimate finds a significant effect on men as well: as of 1975, income and payroll taxes apparently reduced the hours typical men worked by about 8 percent. But as discussants pointed out, that would be a relatively modest effect that need not perturb policy makers. It would be a fairly small price in inefficiency to pay for some equality. Moreover, all such estimates are subject to methodological difficulties and uncertainties; they do not foreclose the possibility that highly progressive taxes could be imposed with little economic loss.[68]

Even strong disincentive effects in the present economy would not necessarily rule out increases in equality. We know little about whether nonmaterial incentives could replace material incentives in getting people to work. Perhaps, if the economic system were transformed, managers and technicians might be persuaded to put forth their best efforts for the sake of excellence itself, or the common good, for social approval rather than for individual material gain. To the extent that this is true, equality may be obstructed only by material incentives, not by the nature of well-functioning economies generally.

Savings and investment present even greater uncertainties. There is some doubt, first of all, about the role of high rates of investment in promoting economic growth. Technological change may be far more important. And trying to increase investment (by taxing the wealthy less) in times of unused capacity and slack demand can actually slow growth—by reducing funds available for consumption by ordinary people. Factories won't produce more if people can't buy more. Furthermore, the role of private savings is unclear when so much capital is derived from retained corporate earnings. And even if there were a definite connection between private savings and investment and growth, it is not certain to what extent progressive taxation reduces savings.[69]

Nor do we know how well investment by the state might substitute for any private saving that was discouraged by redistribution of income. Some socialist economies have grown rapidly. Investment may be easier to handle without material incentives for individuals than work is. Within the present system, econometric evidence indicates that taxes probably have some effect on savings and investment, but the extent of effect is very much in doubt.[70] Again, highly progressive taxes might entail only moderate (if any) reductions in economic growth.

Moreover, the particular pattern of regressive tax provisions in the United States is so odd, so economically erratic, as to cast great doubt on the argument that it is required by the structure of the economy. The lenient treatment of capital gains is very extreme and encourages land speculation and collections of antiques, as well as investment in productive assets. Accelerated depreciation overcompensates for inflation so thoroughly as to produce *negative* tax rates (i.e., subsidies greater than the money invested) under some circumstances and distorts investment incentives across industries and types of assets.[71] "All-savers" tax-free certificates were plainly a wasteful sop to savings and loan associations. Very likely such provisions have had more to do with interest group activity than with economic structure.

Definite conclusions about political causes and effects are hard to come by, for taxation and for other policy areas as well. But I can offer some observations about the most likely reasons tax policies take the shape they do.

We should be skeptical of the simplest versions of interest group theory, in which campaign contributions and lobbying by the wealthy and machinations by members of the tax committees bring about regressive tax policies and thwart the will of the people. Processes of group influence undoubtedly occur, and they certainly have a pro-rich bias. But the resulting policies do not appear to clash with the expressed preferences of the public. If interest group arguments are to be sustained, therefore, they must encompass the facts of popular preferences about taxes, perhaps by showing that public opinion is manipulated.

Tax policy is an area in which preferences are particularly susceptible to manipulation because of the technical complexity of the issues and the paucity of accurate information. Much misinformation is spread about, in some cases probably deliberately. Very likely the public is deceived about particular tax provisions, and perhaps it is also deceived about the pros and cons of tax progressivity itself. If so, public education should be a top priority of the tax reformer. Increases in the visibility of the tax process and correct information provided by scholars and publicists and public interest lobbies could profoundly affect the tax system of the future.

What to make of structural constraints is difficult to say. No doubt the workings of a capitalist economy make it impossible to completely equalize incomes without disastrous consequences for all concerned. Just when structural constraints would begin to pinch, however, we cannot be sure. If the dynamics of capitalism prove to put severe limits on the extent of possible equality, an egalitarian should be willing to consider socialist alternatives. (We will return to this point in later chapters.) But surely there would be considerable leeway to increase the progressivity of U.S. taxes without running up against any such limits.

3

Who Gets the Social Welfare Dollar

Even though taxes do little or nothing to redistribute income in the United States, substantial redistribution could still be achieved if most of the tax money were spent for the benefit of the poor.

Again, many would have us believe that that is exactly what happens. We are told that massive, fast-growing income transfers go to the poor; that we cannot afford so much equality because the resulting tax burden crushes the middle class and income transfers permit the lazy to avoid work; that the "welfare mess" is full of fraud and waste.[1]

The U.S. government does in fact spend an enormous amount of money, more than half its budget, on social welfare programs, that is, programs dealing with income assistance, jobs, food, medical care, housing, and education. It is here, if anywhere, that we would expect to find redistributive spending. And a substantial part of that money does go to low-income Americans. Yet, as we will see, the equalizing effects are much less than one might imagine.

To put social welfare programs into context, it is helpful to consider the trends in government spending generally. In terms of absolute dollar figures, the federal government has grown rapidly in the last hundred years or so. In the nation's first sixty years, from 1789 to 1849, it spent a minuscule total of $1 billion for all purposes. In the second half of the nineteenth century, with the Civil War and industrialization, spending totaled $15 billion. During the World War I years of 1916-1920, it came to $40 billion. At the peak of World War II, in the single year of 1945, about $90 billion was spent, and this stood as a record until the end of the 1950s. But by 1970 the annual figure neared $200 billion, and in 1980 it easily passed $500 billion: about $2,500 for each man, woman, and child in the country.[2]

Part of the increased spending, however, is an illusion caused by general price rises, especially during the recent period of inflation. In terms of constant prices (i.e., looking at what could actually be bought with the money), between 1970 and 1980 the federal budget only increased by 30 percent, not 170 percent (see Figure 4). And part of the increase simply reflects a growing economy. In fact, as a proportion of the Gross National

FIGURE 4   *Trends in Budget Outlays, 1950–1982*
            (Constant 1982 Dollars)

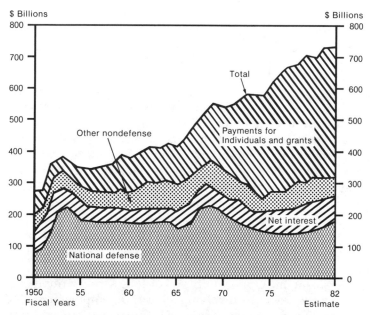

SOURCE: U.S. Office of Management and Budget, *The Budget of the United States Government, Fiscal Year 1982* (Washington, D.C.: U.S. Government Printing Office, 1981), p. 6.

Product (GNP), spending stayed nearly constant during the 1970s, in the 20-22 percent range. This was a high figure for the United States historically but relatively low when compared with the spending habits of most other industrialized nations.

In 1980, for example, the total of all U.S. federal, state, and local government taxes was only 30.7 percent of the Gross Domestic Product (GDP)—GNP excluding net income from abroad. Eighteen Organization of Economic Cooperation and Development (OECD) countries averaged 36.6 percent, and their tax burden had risen much faster, on the average, than that of the United States: by 11.9 percent of GDP, as versus the United States 7.1 percent, between 1955 and 1980. Only four countries (Italy, Portugal, Ireland, and Japan) imposed lower tax burdens than the United States in 1980; Japan's was only 26 percent. But the prospering West Germans paid 37 percent of GDP in taxes; Britain paid 36 percent; and Sweden 49.9 percent.[3]

Still, the U.S. federal government has—by any measure—grown substantially during the twentieth century, and much of that growth is related to social welfare. During most of our history social welfare policy was left to state and local governments; even today nonfederal spending (mostly on education) remains large: $164 billion or 62 percent of the federal contribution in 1979. But a great story of the last fifty years has been the growth of national social welfare programs, first in reaction to the Great Depression and then following the civil rights and antipoverty movements of the 1960s.

The Social Security Act of 1935 established social insurance programs for the retired and unemployed and welfare programs for the blind, the impoverished elderly, and dependent children. To this was added Aid to the Permanently and Totally Disabled, Aid to Families with Dependent Children (AFDC), and Disability Insurance. Low-income housing was also subsidized to a modest extent. In the late 1950s and early 1960s, after the science scare associated with the Russian Sputnik, the U.S. government began to offer some aid to education.

The Economic Opportunity Act of 1964 set up a number of antipoverty programs involving education, employment, and training. In that same year the Food Stamp program was begun, and in 1965 Medicare health insurance for the aged and Medi-

caid for the indigent were passed. During the 1960s and 1970s
these programs expanded rapidly, as did the benefit levels and
coverage of social insurance and AFDC. The share of the federal
budget devoted to social welfare (according to the Social Security Administration definition) jumped from 28 percent in 1960
to 40 percent in 1970 and a peak of 57 percent in 1976, dropping
to 55 percent in 1979. As a proportion of GNP, total federal,
state, and local social welfare spending also declined after the
1976 peak of 20.4 percent, to 18.5 percent in 1979.[4]

According to the slightly different definition used in our Table 9, social welfare spending rose from about 28 percent of the
federal budget in 1960 to 37 percent in 1970 and 52 percent in
1980—declining slightly in the late 1970s and early 1980s (see
Table 9).

Social Security

As Table 9 indicates, by far the largest federal social welfare program is Social Security. In 1980, well over $100
billion was spent on Social Security's Old Age, Survivors, and
Disability Insurance (OASDI). Together with the money devoted to railroad retirement and to federal employee retirement
and disability, this amounted to about one-quarter of the entire
federal budget, up from 17 percent in 1970.

In one sense Social Security represents an enormous transfer
of income to the poor. In 1974, according to Danziger and Plotnick, about 60 percent of Social Security payments went to those
whose incomes (before government transfers) fell below the official poverty line. That is, most of the money went to those who
would apparently have been poor without it. Social Security is
largely responsible for the fact that most of the aged poor have
been raised out of poverty—a great achievement.[5] (See Table 10,
which gives a detailed breakdown of the size and pro-poor impact of a number of social welfare programs, as of the mid-
1970s.)

Social Security has been renowned as a simple, efficient program, involving little more than the mailing of checks. Direct

TABLE 9   *Federal Social Welfare Outlays, 1960–1980*

Function	% of Total Budget		
	1960	1970	1980
Retirement and disability (Social Security and federal employees)	16.9	17.3	23.9
Unemployment insurance		1.7	3.1
Public assistance and other income supplements	2.5	2.9	6.3
(food and nutrition)			(2.4)
(housing)			(0.9)
(other)			(3.0)
Health	0.8	6.7	10.0
Education	1.0	2.5	2.4
Training, employment	0.4	0.9	1.9
Social services	0.1	1.0	1.1
Veterans' benefits	5.9	4.4	3.7
Total social welfare (% of entire budget)	27.6	37.4	52.4
Total budget outlays ($ billions)	92.2	196.6	579.6

SOURCE: Calculated from U.S. Office of Management and Budget, *The Budget of the United States Government*, fiscal years 1971, 1980, and 1982 (Washington, D. C.: U. S. Government Printing Office, 1970, 1979, and 1981); 1960 budget categories are adjusted for comparability.

administrative expenses of the old age portion, as of 1979, were estimated at a remarkably low 1.3 percent of benefits paid; the disability part of the program, involving more complex questions of eligibility, cost only 2.7 percent to administer.[6]

Still, the redistributive impact of Social Security is limited. For one thing, no one gets rich from the program; benefits are too low to equalize incomes or to raise recipients close to the average. In late 1981, for example, the average benefit for a retiree was $384.46 per month ($4,614 per year), no princely sum, in fact a very sparse living indeed, unless supplemented somehow. Or, to put it another way, Social Security on the average replaced only about 40 percent of a worker's pre-retirement earnings. A replacement rate of about 70 percent (taking account of its nontaxability and lower living expenses) would be

TABLE 10 *Major Income Transfer Programs and Benefits to the
Pre-Transfer Poor, 1965 and 1974 ($ millions)*

	1965 Expenditures ($)	1974 Expenditures ($)	% Spent on Pre-Transfer Poor in 1974
Federal Programs			
Social Security	16,488	53,564	58.8
Railroad retirement	1,118	2,671	58.8
Railroad disability	44	28	58.8
Public employee retirement	3,216	10,776	40.5
Unemployment Insurance	2,506	5,316	20.8
Workers' Compensation	73	1,237	45.2
1. Regular	73	271	–
2. Black lung	–	966	45.2
Public assistance	2,614	6,925	85.9
1. AFDC	956	4,009	91.8
2. OAA, AB, APTD, and Emergency Assistance	1,658	1,047	77.8
3. SSI	–	1,869	77.8
Veterans' income support	4,108	6,763	43.0
1. Compensation and pensions	4,042	6,616	–
2. Other	57	103	–
Food Stamps	36	2,718	83.0
Housing assistance	227	1,968	65.0
1. Public housing	219	1,233	73.0
2. Rent supplements	–	137	77.0
3. Homeownership and rental housing assistance, sec. 236	–	523	46.0
4. Other	2	59	89.0
Health	1,990	15,120	58.0
1. Medicare	–	9,557	59.0
2. Medicaid	271	5,563	73.0
State and Local Programs			
Public employee retirement	1,861	5,682	40.5
Temporary disability insurance	253	481	27.0
Workers' Compensation	1,690	4,152	45.2
Public assistance	2,148	5,658	86.1
1. AFDC	768	3,362	91.8
2. OAA, AB, APTD, and General Assistance	1,379	1,652	77.8
3. SSI	–	643	77.8

TABLE 10   *(continued from page 65)*
*Major Income Transfer Programs and Benefits to the
Pre-Transfer Poor, 1965 and 1974 ($ millions)*

	1965 Expenditures ($)	1974 Expenditures ($)	% Spent on Pre-Transfer Poor in 1974
Veterans' bonuses and compensation	20	156	43.0
Housing assistance	80	545	73.0
Medicaid, vendor medical payments	252	4,174	73.0

SOURCE: Sheldon Danziger and Robert Plotnick, *Has the War on Income Poverty Been Won?* (in preparation); Sheldon Danziger, Robert Haveman, and Robert Plotnick, "Income Transfer Programs in the United States: An Analysis of Their Structure and Impacts," prepared for the Joint Economic Committee of the United States, Special Study on Economic Change, University of Wisconsin, Madison, May 1979, p. 20.

required to maintain the same standard of living as before retirement.[7]

Moreover, most of the aged who are poor in the particular years they receive Social Security payments have not been destitute over their whole lifetimes; most have previously been middle-class workers with substantial lifetime incomes. The Social Security system performs the important function of smoothing out lifetime income streams, forcing people to save, through payroll deductions, when they are working—presumably substituting in part for private savings.[8] It then pays money back when people retire. Social Security also has an important insurance element: in effect, workers buy insurance against being disabled, or leaving a widowed spouse, or living so long that private savings run out. Thus, it insures against the risk of certain kinds of poverty. Without government help the private market would probably not provide such insurance even if people would like to buy it.[9]

What Social Security does *not* do to any great extent, however, is increase equality among the lifetime incomes of different income classes.

It is important to remember that Social Security benefits are financed by regressive payroll taxes. There is a linkage between taxes paid in by an individual and the benefits received, so that workers with relatively *higher* incomes tend to benefit more when they retire. To the extent that average benefits for the retired match the contributions they made as workers, the program is simply one of compulsory retirement insurance and does not redistribute income among income classes at all.

To be sure, certain features of the Social Security program do not, in fact, fit the pure insurance model and do provide for some transfers to those with low lifetime earnings. The benefit schedule has been somewhat progressive, with replacement rates ranging from as low as 33 percent (for high-income workers) to as high as 66 percent for those with very low previous earnings.[10] The minimum benefit regardless of contribution and the uniform dependent's benefit and earnings test have also tended to redistribute income. And for many years of the program, when population was growing rapidly so that there were many more workers than retirees in any given year, the payroll taxes on current workers provided enough money to give retirees much more than they themselves had contributed. Thus there was a transfer across generations, from today's workers to yesterday's. As of 1972, Burkhauser and Warlick estimate that the average beneficiary got over $1,000 per year more out of the system than he or she had put into it.[11] (Virtually everybody got the same dollar amount, which constituted a bigger percentage gain for low-income earners than high.)

In the long run, however, this system (scathingly referred to by conservatives as a Ponzi game) could not continue unless the population or productivity continued to grow fast enough so that each generation of retirees would be supported by a much larger or more productive group of workers. Now, with declining population growth and no offsetting productivity surge, benefits have had to be brought more nearly into line with contributions and early retirement discouraged. Benefit levels are rising at a slower rate than payroll taxes. The redistributive element of the program is shrinking. In 1982, for example, the minimum benefit began to be phased out.

These comments about Social Security apply with even more force to the federal employee retirement program. Most government workers are not poor. Any retirement money paid to them over and above a compulsory insurance scheme benefits people of middle and upper incomes. Federal pensions have been generous and have grown quickly. Many federal workers in the 1970s even managed to collect double retirement benefits, under a loophole in the law, by working briefly for private employers and collecting Social Security as well as their government pensions.

Unemployment Insurance

Unemployment Insurance (UI) is another large social insurance program with less redistributive impact than one might expect. On the surface it seems obvious that unemployment benefits must help the poor, that is, people without jobs. But in fact a person must first have a job in order to be "unemployed" and receive UI. Often, therefore, unemployment insurance covers temporary painful episodes in the lives of people who are usually working at good wages. Only to a lesser extent does it help those at the bottom of the economic heap who have a hard time getting jobs in the first place, or stay jobless after the benefit period runs out, or get so discouraged that they stop looking for work. Only a meager one-fifth of unemployment insurance payments goes to the pre-transfer poor (see Table 10).

Nor are the benefit levels very large. In early 1981, UI provided an average of $106 per week for a totally unemployed worker to support his family. The amount under this state-administered program varied from less than $80 per week in Mississippi, Alabama, Georgia, and Florida to over $120 in the District of Columbia, Minnesota, Ohio, Pennsylvania, and Wisconsin.[12]

As a matter of fact, unemployment insurance may actually increase unemployment. It subsidizes wages in cyclical work like construction where layoffs are a matter of course. Since the government helps take care of the workers during off periods, employers are encouraged to employ lots of people (paying them less than they would have to without UI) and then lay them off, and workers are encouraged to stay out of work. More workers and investments flow into cyclical industries than otherwise would.[13] The administration of unemployment insurance also involves some inefficiency—many officials and requirements to come and stand in line. In addition, for some who are unable to find work, to appear at the unemployment office represents a public humiliation. And the system does not use the productive abilities of the jobless.

UI is an important and necessary program for alleviating the damage of short-term, "frictional" unemployment for ordinary workers. But it does not and cannot accomplish much redistribution of income. For dealing with high levels of long-term unemployment, a far superior remedy would be to provide jobs.

Cash Assistance

The cash assistance programs aimed at the very poor tend to be relatively small. Aid to Families with Dependent Children (AFDC) is the prototypical public aid or "welfare" program, providing assistance to female-headed families with children. More than 90 percent of AFDC money has gone to people whose incomes, without government help, would have fallen below the official poverty line. A cynic might conclude that it is precisely the pro-poor nature of this program that has made it the target of misleading attacks about "welfare Cadillacs" and lazy no-goods. The fact is that fraud is uncommon, and AFDC has made life bearable for millions of people in desperate circumstances. This is not to say, of course, that AFDC is an ideal program or that it should form the basis of egalitarian policy. By refusing help to male-headed families (except, in about half the states, those headed by unemployed males), it encourages family breakup, or a certain kind of "cheating"—denial of male presence. It does little to impose responsibility on fathers or to discourage profligate childbearing and multiple generations of dependence; it offers no clear path out of the system.[14]

Guaranteed jobs and a universal guaranteed income for those unable to work (or whose time should be devoted to child rearing) would be much better. Still, lacking superior programs, AFDC is an essential last resort for destitute mothers and children. And it would be better yet if more money were spent in order to lower the implicit tax rates on work (by tapering off benefits more slowly with increased outside income) and thus encourage work by those who can.

During the 1960s and 1970s AFDC grew from small beginnings ($1 billion total in 1965) to become a substantial program, involving $4 billion of federal funds in 1974 and over $6 billion (plus large state contributions) in 1978. But by the late 1970s the growth of AFDC had slowed down. Most of the eligible people who had once failed to participate finally joined up; benefit levels (in real terms) were held down during inflation. AFDC remained only a small fraction of the size of Social Security. At the end of 1980, AFDC average payments per recipient ranged from a tight $147 per month in California to a paltry $29.83 in Mississippi.[15]

The Supplemental Security Income (SSI) program of 1974 resembles AFDC in that it makes cash payments that go mostly to the poor. SSI now provides a nationwide minimum income for the aged, the blind, and the disabled. But these payments are small, and largely substitute for—rather than add to—OASDI pensions.[16] Even when AFDC and SSI are added together, they amount to little more than one-tenth of the expenditures on social insurance (retirement and disability) programs or about 3 percent of the total federal budget.

Certain other cash payments by the federal government are not particularly pro-poor. A substantial part of veterans' benefits, but less than half, goes to the pre-transfer poor. Many veterans are healthy, productive, even well-to-do members of society, and many never saw wartime service. It makes most sense to look at veterans' benefits as part of the compensation paid to members of the armed forces rather than as a redistributive program. More strikingly, the billions of dollars paid to farmers in the form of price supports—which might be considered cash assistance—are distributed roughly in proportion to farm production and, therefore, to total income, so they go overwhelmingly to the wealthiest farmers.[17]

When we bear in mind that many of the "poor" who receive social insurance payments are in poverty only temporarily, it is clear that the total cash transfers by the federal government do not accomplish a fundamental redistribution of income. This does not mean they are bad programs: they lift many people out of absolute poverty and insure against financial disaster. But they do not equalize incomes.

Much the same thing can be said of state and local programs. The states and localities devote a substantial proportion of their income assistance budget to the poor, via contributions to AFDC, supplemental SSI, and general assistance (see Table 10).

But the total amount spent for these purposes does not quite match the modest federal total. The states also spend substantial amounts on public employee retirement and workers' compensation, which mostly help middle-income people.

In-Kind Programs

In the 1960s and 1970s there was dramatic growth in "in-kind" programs, which deliver goods and services rather than cash. A prime example is medical care, which became one of the largest social welfare programs. Food Stamps were begun, and housing assistance increased.

In-kind programs have been criticized as inferior to cash transfers in several respects. They require more administrators and red tape than is needed for putting a check in the mail. They may be more open to fraud. Sometimes they tend to enrich the providers of services, such as doctors and nursing home proprietors, instead of wholly benefiting the recipients. They may limit the freedom of choice of the recipients, who might prefer to use their assistance in other ways. In-kind programs are often inefficient because they give people things which are less valuable to them than they are costly to the taxpayers.

Presidents Nixon and Carter both attempted to change the social welfare system by unifying the welter of cash transfers and emphasizing cash rather than in-kind benefits.[18] Both failed. Part of the political appeal of in-kind programs may reflect the power of bureaucrats and social workers and others who administer the programs or provide services. They also appeal to Americans' paternalistic instincts: they seem to provide such basic necessities as food, shelter, and health care while trying to keep people from "wasting" the assistance on alcohol, cigarettes, or entertainment.

Still, in-kind benefits can have some important advantages. For one thing, paternalism is not necessarily bad: if people cannot or do not look after their own or their children's health and nutrition, perhaps government should do so. Indeed, many people may favor certain kinds of paternalism toward themselves. Just as workers may be glad that Social Security forces them to save for retirement when otherwise, under the pressure of daily living, the money might slip away, so also poor people may be glad to get food and medical care and education and school lunches for their kids rather than cash that might go elsewhere.

Furthermore, in-kind programs have a potential advantage (not always realized in the United States) of improving the symbolism and spirit of redistribution. If food, shelter, health, education, and jobs are considered basic *rights* and are given to everyone through "universal" programs, then it should be possible to minimize the political resentment by those who are taxed most to pay for them and to avoid grudging or degrading treatment of those who receive benefits. It should be possible, in a rich country, to provide such goods and services and opportunities efficiently—and with a warm and generous (or, perhaps better, a matter-of-fact) spirit.

Food Stamps

Among U.S. in-kind programs, Food Stamps are unusually efficient and unusually pro-poor. More than 80 percent of the benefits go to the pre-transfer poor (see Table 10). In fact they are the only benefits that can be obtained by *all* poor people, even by able-bodied males of working age. In effect they provide a small guaranteed income for all Americans in the form of coupons which can be redeemed at grocery stores. At first recipients had to pay part of the face value of the coupons, the proportion depending on their income; then different amounts of coupons were simply given to those with different incomes.

The Food Stamps program was enacted in 1964. Beginning with 600,000 recipients getting only $32 million in bonus value (i.e., the value of the coupons in excess of recipients' payments) in 1965, it grew to 3.2 million participants getting $228 million in 1969. During the Nixon years the program was extended to all counties in the United States (some had previously opted out). Purchase requirements were lowered and eventually eliminated. By 1975, nearly 20 million participants received a total of more than $4 billion.[19] During the late 1970s and especially in the Reagan administration, however, eligibility was tightened and benefits were allowed to lag behind inflation.

From an egalitarian standpoint, the chief shortcoming of the Food Stamps program is that it is very small, hardly taking up more than 1 percent of the federal budget. It provides rather meager benefits.

The Food Stamps program avoids some of the usual defects (and virtues) of in-kind programs because the stamps are virtually equivalent to cash; most recipients (90 percent) would buy at least as much food anyway if they were given money instead of stamps. Thus, the question arises whether it would not be better simply to give people the money and avoid the bother of printing and distributing special coupons. (Administrative costs are not in fact very high but are not insignificant, and counterfeiting attempts are occasionally successful.)

In principle, the answer ought to be that, by its in-kind form, the program establishes that all Americans have the *right* to enough food for minimum subsistence. Indeed, that rationale contributed to its political feasibility at a time when the idea of a guaranteed cash income was unpopular. In practice, however, the voters have not fully accepted such a right. President Reagan apparently echoed a widespread sentiment when he remarked, in his first State of the Union address, that Food Stamp "abuses" are obvious to anyone who has stood in line at a grocery counter. Many feel that poor people should not use Food Stamps to get potato chips or ice cream for their children. In fact, many feel that Food Stamp recipients are freeloaders and no-goods. In some communities, therefore, coupon users are stigmatized: they must endure hostile stares or demeaning comments at the check-out counter and would be better off with inconspicuous cash.

If the poor (who, like the rest of us, are bombarded by slick advertising for junk food) don't in fact budget their food purchases well, it might be wise for the government to invest in educational efforts and to help them with economical and nutritious food preparation, or even to require certain restrictive kinds of purchases. But specific purchase requirements could become a bureaucratic nightmare. And it is worth remembering that there are often good reasons why the poor can't act like the middle class: they seldom have freezers to store bulk purchases, or the time and transportation to patronize bulk outlets, or the unharried afternoons to prepare meals from basic ingredients. Fast food can be a blessing after a long day of scrubbing floors and a tedious bus ride home. An occasional Coke may add a bright spot to a child's drab day.

Medical Care

By far the largest in-kind transfer programs involve medical care. By 1980 some 10 percent of the federal budget went to health care services (mainly Medicare and Medicaid), an amount dwarfing all other social welfare programs except Social Security.

National health insurance was discussed as early as the Franklin Roosevelt administration but was omitted from the 1935 Social Security legislation. Various medical care proposals by the Truman administration in the 1940s and by Democratic legislators in the 1950s were rejected. The government has, of course, long provided some medical help to the military and to others through the Veterans Administration and (much less) through the Public Health Service. In the 1950s and 1960s there was some regulatory activity and some aid for medical training and buildings, as well as assistance to states for medical care for those on public assistance. But only with the enactment of Medicare for the aged and Medicaid for the poor in 1965 did the federal government enter the health care area in a big way. Outlays for health care services mushroomed from virtually nil in 1960, to $11 billion in 1970, and about $50 billion in 1980 (see Table 9).

Under Medicare, all recipients of Social Security and certain other retirement plans are insured against hospitalization for periods up to several months. If hospitalized, they have to pay only an initial deductible amount and then a co-insurance portion of the bill for the later part of their stay. Nearly all beneficiaries, about 97 percent, also enroll in a voluntary Supplementary Medical Insurance (SMI) plan which covers physicians and other nonhospital care. Medicare now pays a substantial share—though well less than half—of the medical bills of elderly Americans.

Medicare, like Social Security pensions, is not fundamentally a redistributive program and was not so intended. It is primarily a system of compulsory insurance, established for the good reason that most people can't or won't buy comparable private insurance.[20]

Of course, most of those who get the benefits have low incomes at the time they receive them: it is hard to work from a hospital bed. And many would be in desperate shape without help. In this sense, the program alleviates poverty. But recipients do not necessarily have low lifetime incomes. Medicare, like Social Security, covers virtually the entire elderly population and is oriented primarily toward the middle class. Like Social Security, it is financed by a regressive payroll tax, and there is a rough equivalence between the value of insurance that the average person gets from the program and what he has to pay during his working years.

In the beginning, at least, low-income people actually benefited less from Medicare, on the average, than higher-income people because they were discouraged by having to pay the deductible and co-insurance amounts. Some even failed to sign up for the physician coverage. An early survey found that Medicare benefits were about 70 percent higher for elderly persons with family incomes above $11,000 than for those below $6,000, even though the poor tend to be sicker than the well-off. (There is some evidence that the difference in benefits later decreased.)[21]

Moreover, the huge cost of the medical programs gives an exaggerated impression of what patients actually receive. In 1980, only about 38 percent of the medical expenses of the elderly were covered.[22] Furthermore, in health care it is particularly hazardous to assume that every dollar spent by the government gives a dollar's worth of benefit to the recipient.

True, medical services have definitely expanded and improved. But inflation in medical costs during the 1960s and 1970s proceeded much more rapidly than inflation generally, and much of the new money went for the same quality of care at higher prices. Doctors and hospitals, rarely cost-conscious anyhow, found that when the government pays the bill, people will purchase medical care with little regard to price. They naturally supplied more services, some unnecessary, and raised their rates. (The boards which decided whether fees were reasonable and should be reimbursed were strongly influenced by doctors.) Hospitals expanded, even when beds were empty, and bought lots of fancy equipment.[23]

In addition, some medical assistance money (not a high percentage) has been stolen, not usually by the greedy welfare mothers caricatured in the popular press, but by unscrupulous nursing home operators and doctors and "Medicaid mills." Bills have been submitted for services that were superfluous or were never rendered at all or even for patients who didn't exist. This and the cost of inflation may be inevitable results of subsidizing free enterprise, fee-for-service medicine, as opposed to publicly providing health care by salaried physicians.

Medicaid, unlike Medicare, is explicitly designed to help the poor. It is a joint federal-state program which pays for medical care received by those on AFDC or other welfare programs and—in about half the states—by the "medically indigent," who would be made poor by their medical expenses if they didn't get help. It is not merely an insurance program for the middle class; it represents a large redistributive transfer from high-income to low-income people. It has brought health care to millions of people who rarely saw a doctor in the past and has dramatically improved many lives. Infant mortality rates among the poor, for example, declined 32 percent between 1965 and 1974.[24]

At the same time, we should not exaggerate these benefits either. Many of the poor have not received Medicaid at all because they are ineligible. Coverage varies from state to state, and the South is particularly stingy. Those facing nonfinancial barriers such as lack of nearby physicians, poor transportation, or discrimination get less help. (In particular the rural poor and blacks have not done as well.) The poor now use more medical services than they did, but they tend to get lower quality care than others do. The poor do not participate in mainstream medicine; they mostly attend crowded, dreary clinics with long waits and few amenities. Care is episodic, fragmented, and impersonal, often involving a different physician on each visit. There is a real difference between health care in Scarsdale or Palo Alto and that on the south side of Chicago.

In any event, Medicaid benefits are often not worth as much to the poor as they cost to provide. Some of the money never gets to recipients at all; it is lost to administrative overhead or fraud. What gets to recipients is worth to them, according to one estimate, only about 68 cents on the dollar.[25] Some of this results from the perverse incentive to use hospitals, which has turned hospital emergency rooms into costly clinics. Part of the enormously inflated hospital bills and doctors' fees represents redistribution to high-income rather than low-income individuals. The doctors, who at first bitterly resisted government involvement in medical care, have profited greatly from it.

Medicaid's effort to insure the poor against the costs of injury or sickness is a worthy one. But if the aim is generally to improve the health of the poor, there are better ways to accomplish it. Instead of just paying to patch people up when they are sick or hurt, more money could be spent on nutrition, housing, job safety, public health, and preventive medicine. Medical care might be provided by salaried physicians with group practices in community health centers, perhaps under a national health service. Care at home also deserves thought.[26] Health insurance programs like Medicare and Medicaid, in the context of private enterprise, fee-for-service medicine, enrich doctors and other health care providers.

Some federal medical programs have reached the poor more effectively, but they are small. Maternal and child health expenditures support some clinic projects which have probably helped reduce infant mortality in certain areas. The few Neighborhood Health Centers (only 125 for the whole country in 1976) have greatly improved access and convenience and emphasized preventive medicine.[27] In addition to their contributions to Medicaid, the states (often through county governments) operate some public hospitals and mental institutions, which—though far from ideal—are the last resort of the destitute. But all such programs have been far outweighed by the money spent on, for example, veterans' medical services ($6 billion by 1980), of which less than one-quarter goes to the poor.

Housing

Decent housing for everyone might be considered another "right" in a civilized country, but many Americans don't have it: they endure crowded, deteriorating, and sometimes rat-infested dwellings. Federal efforts at housing assistance for low-income people have not been very extensive or successful. Public housing, the largest such effort (until rent supplements came to equal it in the 1980s) provides subsidized apartments for low-income families, usually in large apartment buildings constructed for that purpose. In many cases usable old housing units have been bulldozed in order to make way for new public buildings. But the newness doesn't last long. Poor people, crowded together in apartments in which they have no financial stake and little supervision or social structure, tend to create run-down, demoralized, dangerous high-rise slums. Successful tenants tend to leave as soon as they can and become ineligible even if they would like to stay; only the most miserable and least capable are left. Efforts to scatter smaller public housing units around middle-class neighborhoods understandably encounter angry resistance from those who do not want the poor among them. The full cycle of public housing became apparent when the Pruitt-Igoe development in St. Louis was itself bulldozed.[28]

This does not, of course, mean that publicly owned housing is inherently hopeless: with careful design, sufficient investment, proper supervision and maintenance, and sensible administrative arrangements, the United States could probably provide good living quarters, just as many other countries do.[29] But the effort has not been made.

U.S. public housing exemplifies the flaws of in-kind programs at their worst. The subsidy is worth much less to tenants than it costs the government; by Smeeding's estimate it amounts to only 56 cents on the dollar.[30] Perhaps the chief beneficiaries are those who build the buildings: contractors, concrete and material manufacturers, and construction workers, few of whom suffer from low incomes.

After the failures of U.S. public housing had become obvious, the rent supplement program was enacted. The idea is to help the poor afford housing in ordinary neighborhoods, preserving much of their freedom to choose where to live and integrating them into normal communities, while making sure that no one has to pay more than a quarter of his income for housing. By increasing the purchasing power of the poor, it also encourages private developers to build more houses and apartments.

Rent supplements have most of the virtues of general cash transfers, except for the red tape involved in determining who is eligible for how much assistance. Like AFDC and Food Stamps, they mostly help those with the lowest incomes. The chief limitation of the program is that it is very small: in 1980, less than one-third the size of Food Stamps. Most who want rent supplements and are eligible cannot get them. Less restricted housing allowances have proved very successful on an experimental basis, but we have not been willing to pay for a full program.[31]

The federal government has a long history of guaranteeing and subsidizing mortgages for the purchase of homes, mostly for the middle class. The Federal Housing Administration (FHA), established in 1934, revolutionized mortgage markets by providing lower down payments, longer repayment periods, and lower interest rates. Together with the Veterans Administration (VA) and Farmers Home Administration (FmHA), FHA covers a good many mortgages—as many as one-third of the total—and influences the terms of other lending as well. But the redistributive impact of these programs is small because they help mainly people of middle or lower-middle income. Most low-income people cannot afford to buy houses. Only a little of the benefit trickles down to the poor by increasing housing supply and lowering rents. Indeed, for many years these programs bled cities of the relatively affluent and promoted segregated suburban neighborhoods.[32]

With the Housing and Urban Development Act of 1968 the government tried to extend some FHA-type help to low-income Americans by guaranteeing and subsidizing private mortgages for those not ordinarily qualified to buy. The effort was a spectacular and expensive failure. When the program worked, it worked like FHA and gave some marginal aid to lower-middle income home buyers rather than the poor. But many unscrupulous mortgage lenders and realtors signed up high-risk customers to buy defective houses at inflated prices. When these buyers defaulted on the payments, the lenders invoked the federal guarantee, took a quick profit, and left the government holding the bag. The purchasers fled or were evicted; thousands of homes stood idle and were vandalized and burned. The result was a traumatic experience for would-be home buyers, guaranteed profits for mortgage lenders and realtors, and the destruction of several thousand houses.[33]

As it happens, I lived a block away from a once elegant old Victorian house that was sold under the mortgage guarantee program. The buyers defaulted and abandoned it, and the house was vandalized and ultimately burned down. This was just one case of hundreds in Chicago alone.

The low-income homeowner program was suspended in 1973 amidst scandal, legal indictments, and officials' resignations. In later years it limped along, supporting mortgages that had already been authorized. The experience, like that with medical care, seems to stand as a monument to the peculiar American way of contending with problems through private enterprise and public money.

After the sharp rises in heating costs of the 1970s, a small Low-Income Home Energy Assistance program was begun to provide free fuel for the poor. But during the icy winter of 1982 only $1.75 billion was made available (cut about 3 percent from the previous year), and only about 50 to 75 percent of the estimated 15 million eligible families received aid. The *Wall Street Journal* told of a seventy-two-year-old Philadelphia widow, hospitalized when the metal screws implanted in her hip began to freeze, who was assured she would get fuel but was found eight days later alone in her room, at a below-freezing temperature, with five blankets around her.[34]

Over the years the largest program of housing assistance has not appeared in the budget of federal outlays at all. It is the system of subsidies, or "tax expenditures" built into the Internal Revenue Code, which allows homeowners to deduct mortgage interest and property taxes on their federal income tax. These deductions are worth billions of dollars each year ($29 billion in 1981) and mainly benefit high-income people who own expensive homes.[35]

Social Services

"Social services"—for example, counseling by social workers—are provided jointly by the state and federal governments as an adjunct to AFDC and other cash assistance programs for the poor. Ideally, such counseling could help poor families organize their budgets, locate needed goods and services, and establish harmonious personal relationships. In practice, however, it is not always very effective. Social workers are sometimes seen as intruders, to be hustled or avoided, especially when they have power to check on eligibility and cut off benefits. At best, brief intermittent visits are unlikely to transform family life. Some of the enthusiasm for welfare services, like other in-kind programs, comes from the providers rather than the recipients.

A number of small in-kind programs flourished under the Office of Equal Opportunity (OEO) during the 1960s; most of them declined in the disillusionment of the 1970s. The largest of these, Community Action (later rebaptized under new names), mobilized the poor and badgered concessions out of local government, while enraging established politicians and putting some blacks into new leadership positions.[36] OEO programs for health and nutrition, legal services (a notable success), migrant farmworkers, and community economic development focused their expenditures very heavily on the poor. Some were incorporated into other agencies when OEO was dismantled. But even with the addition of programs for Indians, Cuban refugees, and the aging, the amount of money spent has been very small.

Jobs

Job training and employment programs are perhaps most important of all because they are supposed to help people help themselves through productive work. Working contributes more to society than living on the dole; it leads to more self-fulfillment and independence; and it avoids the social conflict that can arise between those receiving cash transfers and those paying for them. If we talk in terms of "rights," surely the right to hold a job must rank high.

Much political rhetoric and action has emphasized the importance of jobs, from the hopeful training programs of the Kennedy years, to the work "requirements" and work incentives of the late 1960s, to the public service employment programs that grew in the 1970s. But the rhetoric has run up against the troubling reality that many of the poor cannot or should not work; that for those who can, it makes no sense to require work when no jobs are available; and that to train people or to create jobs is very expensive. Americans do not seem willing to pay the price. No great commitment of resources has been made: only about 1 percent of the federal budget in 1970 and 2 percent in 1980.

In the 1960s, manpower training was seen as a major answer to unemployment and depressed incomes. If Appalachian coal miners were out of work, they would be retrained for other jobs. Ghetto youths would be taken out of their discouraging environment and taught skills in the Job Corps. But the cost of processing each individual proved to be great, and it was difficult to find permanent work for them after training. Earnings of trainees tended to rise only moderately and often, after a time, to fall back to what they would have been without the program.[37] Voters and politicians were reluctant to pay the costs, and the program shrank.

Later, a very small program, Supported Work, managed to turn some hard-core members of the underclass—ex-convicts, drug users, and street hustlers—into productive citizens through a combination of intensive training (focused on self-presentation, personal organization, and work habits), subsidized work experience, and job placement efforts. Despite the frustration of a tight labor market and high unemployment that faced the graduates (and faced Americans generally), this program seemed to demonstrate that even some of the most intractable problems can be dealt with if society is willing to invest the necessary money and effort. Again, however, no such investment has been made.[38]

In the 1960s and 1970s, various work "requirements" were attached to welfare programs. But the requirements often amounted only to registering willingness to take jobs that didn't exist. And there was reluctance to bear the expense of making welfare benefit schedules less punitive toward those who work (i.e., by not removing all benefits at once when earned income reached some arbitrary threshold or by not imposing a high implicit tax rate on work). Elaborate tax incentive schemes were devised to get private employers to hire the unemployed, but always the question was whether they simply displaced other workers. And the unemployed could be hired for a while, fired, and then new unemployed hired for a new government subsidy.[39]

In any event, so long as unemployment rates remain high, training programs and employment incentives merely tend to speed up the game of musical chairs. When the music stops, lots of people are still left without jobs.

In the 1970s the United States turned to an idea that had been used in social democratic Europe for decades: to create government jobs. Under the Comprehensive Employment and Training Act (CETA), spending for public service employment went from almost nothing in 1970 to $5 billion (about half of all the money devoted to job assistance) in 1980. The successful WPA and CCC programs in the 1930s had left a legacy of useful buildings, improved parks, and even fine art. CETA, however, instead of starting new public works or conservation projects, delegated job creation to state and local governments, essentially without central control. Under the guise of new jobs the states often spent federal money for work they would have done anyway so that the effect was one of revenue sharing rather than new employment. When genuinely new jobs were created, they were sometimes of a make-work sort, producing little. Nor was there any real guarantee that the job would be permanent.

The creation of a few hundred thousand new jobs definitely did help, though it could not greatly alter the unemployment rate or the distribution of income. But in any case, virtually the entire CETA program was eliminated in 1981, leaving no public jobs program.

Education

Education occupies a special place in the liberal vision. The aim is to equalize opportunity. It is hoped that poor children, given good schooling, can get ahead on their own, make productive contributions, and earn good incomes in the private labor market. Education programs are supposed, therefore, to have substantial effects on the distribution of income.

State and local governments spend more on education (about $96 billion in 1979)[40] than on any other program. The bulk of it goes for elementary and secondary schools. Aside from early land grants and later vocational aid, the federal government was slow to get involved, but beginning in the late 1950s it supported some higher education fellowships and loans (many of them science-related) and then—after the Elementary and Secondary Education Act of 1965—offered assistance to elementary and secondary schools. During the 1970s federal attention was mainly devoted to helping disadvantaged students at all levels. About 2.5 percent of the federal budget was devoted to education, and more than half of that went to elementary, secondary, and vocational programs, assisting school districts that had children from low-income families, the handicapped, Indians, and students with limited English-language skills.

The vast amount of state and federal spending on elementary and secondary schools clearly involves a great redistributive transfer of income. In fact this is one respect in which the United States does better than much of the industrialized world. All children are offered a free public education, and the poor have a much larger share of the nation's children than they do of its money. Any benefits that are distributed among children help low-income families more than high. Nonetheless, the redistributive impact of school spending is limited in several ways.

First, neither school expenditures nor their benefits are actually spread evenly over all school children. Less money is spent on schools where income levels are lower. Because schools are mostly financed by local property taxes, wealthy suburbs can often afford better schools than impoverished central cities. The poor tend to get old buildings, crowded classrooms, less experienced teachers, and inferior books and equipment.[41] Even more important, the private housing market leads to residential segregation by race and income. Unless there is busing, poor children, therefore, tend to be surrounded in school by other poor children with relatively low academic skills, weak motivation, and little effective parental encouragement. Unequal schooling is reinforced by unequal peer influence.

Second, the benefits are not always what was hoped. There appear to be real limits to the capacity of education to produce higher incomes in later life. For any one individual the effects of family background, native intelligence, peer group influence, and just plain luck are so great that schooling cannot have an overwhelming impact. For society as a whole, as average educational levels rise, the credentials required for any given job rise as well, and the people who start on the bottom tend to stay near the bottom. The slots that people are sorted into remain very unequal. Income inequality does not change.[42]

Only part of school expenditures is, in fact, designed to upgrade the "human capital" of students. Some of the money goes to the custodial function, benefiting parents: schools act as enormous babysitting services. (This, of course, can be a great boon to low-income families.) Some money goes to entertainment and social life for the children. And some goes to increase the incomes of middle-class teachers and administrators.

The net effect of education programs may be initially less equalizing than would be achieved if the money spent on schools were simply divided up equally among children (or their parents) instead. Still, in the long run, spending on schools is probably better since neither children nor parents, left to their own devices, might invest adequately in education. "Vouchers," to be used in any school desired (public or private), would presumably increase efficiency, forcing schools to try to attract customers, but would probably increase segregation by race, income, and academic skill, thus increasing inequality.

Some argue that contemporary public schooling in America actually tends to *reinforce* rather than overcome economic inequalities. The public school movement of the nineteenth century arose partly in response to the needs of an industrializing society for a disciplined, willing labor force with orderly work habits. Even today public schools devote a great deal of effort to inculcating the habits of neatness, punctuality, and obedience. Of course, some of these traits are admirable and important— one sees few messy, late business executives—and ghetto schools should perhaps work even harder to promote them. But insofar as schools in poor and working-class neighborhoods emphasize discipline and little else, they merely train people for subordinate positions in society. Moreover, school books encourage approval of capitalism and propagate the belief that unequal incomes result from unequal merit. The existence of some social mobility through schooling, so that a few poor children escape their destiny and make it to the very top, lends a color of justice to the overall pattern of inherited inequality.[43]

Special efforts to improve the education of deprived children through Head Start and other pre-school programs have been perceived as somewhat disappointing. Test scores may not have improved much (this is a subject of controversy), and what short-run effects there are, may not last. (On the other hand, there have been gains in health and emotional well-being.) Still, Head Start is probably one of the many Great Society programs that "failed" only in relation to excessive expectations. A few hours a day of pre-schooling can hardly overcome the total effects of broken families, impoverishment and malnutrition, and ghetto demoralization. Again, no major public investment has been made.[44]

Higher education absorbs relatively little government spending, but the amount has increased markedly in recent years, especially state spending for community colleges and university systems. These expenditures are considerably less egalitarian than those for primary and secondary education. No universal right to higher education has been established. Even though some financial aid is available, college students come disproportionately from upper-income families, who can afford to pay the expenses and can defer going to work. The system may look less pro-rich if one considers taxes at the same time, especially if they are borne by high-income homeowners or owners of capital; and long-run effects of education on earnings are hard to estimate. But the fact remains that the children of the poor are less likely to go to college, less likely to stay if they go, and therefore less likely to benefit from the money spent on higher education.[45] Federal programs do tend to help the disadvantaged more than state and local spending, but a good many subsidized student loans went to high-income families before the sharp cuts in student aid of all kinds at the beginning of the 1980s.

All in all, education programs are essential to accomplish egalitarian purposes but could be made much more effective and more equalizing than at present.

The Impact of Welfare Spending

Taken all together, the billions of dollars spent on social welfare programs have a definite redistributive impact. They have raised the living standards of millions of poor Americans and have greatly reduced poverty as officially defined. But the effect upon income inequality has been far less impressive.

The casual newspaper reader could easily believe that the United States has lifted its poorest citizens right into the ranks of the middle class, greatly equalizing incomes. A few economists have encouraged such an impression. Edgar Browning, for example, claims that in 1972 the bottom fifth of the population, which got only about 2 percent of private money income, actually received some 12 percent of all the net income in the country when all government social welfare programs (including in-kind benefits) are taken into account. Therefore, he concluded, the average income of the top fifth was only 2.7 times that of the bottom, not 7.7 times as great.[46]

Browning's figures, however, are based on a mixture of fanciful assumptions and curious calculations. He assumed that in-kind transfers were worth to the poor what it cost the government to provide them instead of the much lower cash equivalent values. He treated education expenditures as worth their cost as well and allocated the bulk of them equally among parents of children under age eighteen. Most remarkably, he counted as income the "potential earnings" of those not employed even if their unemployment was involuntary due to disability or lack of jobs. He attempted to subtract taxes paid but left out the regressive sales taxes and the employer's half of payroll taxes. Each of these steps made incomes look more equal than they actually are. Smeeding's revised calculations—correcting most of these errors—indicate that taking taxes and social welfare programs into account, the lowest fifth of the population got only 6.5 percent of the income, half of Browning's 12.5 percent.[47]

Without indulging in Browning's excesses, several other economists have overstated the amount of money transferred from high-income people to low because they have relied upon simple assumptions about how benefits are distributed. Even for the year 1960, before the great expansion of programs, Gillespie calculated that social welfare expenditures overwhelmingly benefited people of low income because he conveniently but mistakenly assumed that expenditures for Social Security, health, and education went primarily to the poor. For 1968, Musgrave, Case, and Leonard estimated that social welfare expenditures (especially by the federal government) doubled the total income of the lowest income class. They too valued all transfers at cost and allocated Social Security almost exclusively to the poor and education expenditures equally to students. Reynolds and Smolensky offered similar estimates of the effects of social welfare spending in 1970, though they hedged their results by noting the weaknesses of the methodology employed in such studies. (Their work is discussed further in the next chapter.)[48]

As we have seen, when social welfare programs are examined in more detail, it becomes clear that those which go mostly to the poor—Food Stamps, AFDC, housing allowances, Supported Work—tend to be small. The largest programs, like Social Security and Medicare, help mostly those in the middle-income ranges.

For the years 1965, 1968, and 1972, Plotnick and Skidmore gathered estimates on the proportion and the actual amount of money in each program that went to the pre-transfer poor. They then calculated the total benefits received by the poor and the reduction in the poverty population due to these programs. They found that in 1972 $185 billion, or 46 percent of all federal, state, and local government budgets, was spent on social welfare programs; of that amount 42 percent, or $79 billion, went to people whose earned income fell below the official poverty line. This was enough to cut the number of poor people from 40 million (20 percent of the population) before cash transfers to 24 million or 12 percent after. Taking into account in-kind transfers and underreporting of income, the proportion of poor may have fallen as low as 6 percent, far below the figure at the beginning of the War on Poverty.[49]

At the same time, Plotnick and Skidmore also looked at "relative poverty," that is, inequality, as measured by the proportion of families whose "welfare ratios" (the ratio of their current income to the poverty line as defined for their type of family) fell below about half the median value for the whole population. I have argued that a relative definition of poverty, which reflects the degree of income inequality, is more relevant than the official poverty definition based on absolute levels of consumption.

According to the relative measure, post-transfer poverty decreased not one bit between 1965 and 1972, before and after the growth of the Great Society. In both years, government transfer payments appeared to remove about one-third of the pre-transfer destitute from poverty, but more than 15 percent of the U.S. population—some 30 million people in 1972—remained poor.

Danziger and Plotnick did similar analyses with more recent data and found much the same thing. At the end of the 1970s, government income transfers apparently reduced the number of absolutely poor persons from about 20 percent to 11 percent of the population, or to as low as 4.1 percent, taking account of underreporting, taxes, and the cash equivalent value of in-kind benefits. (Weaker than assumed economic conditions in 1980 may have put the actual figure closer to 6 percent.) Of course, even the great achievement of getting absolute poverty down to 4.1 percent would mean that some 9 million people—mostly children—still fell below the government's rather stingy minimum standard for decent living.

But most distressing, in relative terms more than 15 percent of all Americans remained poor in 1978, virtually the same proportion as in 1965. By this measure, inequality was as great after the War on Poverty as before (see Table 11). On the other hand, the income share of the lowest quintile may have been increased by 5 or 6 percent, and the Gini coefficient of inequality may have been reduced by some 19 percent below that for pre-transfer inequality.[50]

In one sense, these less than outstanding figures may actually overstate the extent to which social welfare expenditures redistribute income. Since they are based on annual incomes, they reflect the fact that Social Security, unemployment, and medical payments tend to go to those whose incomes are low for the year benefits are paid but ignore the fact that the lifetime income of the recipients may be quite high. (This is not to say that short-term poverty is unimportant but rather that long-term equality matters as well.) The figures may also attribute excessive value to some transfers.

Furthermore, calculations of the amount of redistribution in any one year presume that the difference between pre- and post-transfer incomes represents the full effect of government transfers. But the transfers themselves very likely have depressed the "pre-transfer" incomes of the poor and thereby counteracted part of their own impact. Unemployment insurance, for example, may encourage unemployment and thereby

TABLE 11 *The Trend in the Incidence of Poverty Among Americans, 1965-1980*

	Income Concept		
Type of Poverty Measure (Year)	Pre-Transfer Income (%)	Post-Transfer Income (%)	Adjusted Post-Transfer Income (%)
Absolute measure			
1965	21.3	15.6	12.1
1968	18.2	12.8	10.1
1970	18.8	12.6	9.4
1972	19.2	11.9	6.2
1974	20.3	11.6	7.8
1976	21.0	11.8	5.9
1978	20.2	11.4	n.a.
1980	n.a.	n.a.	4.1
Percent change, 1965-1978	-5.2	-26.9	-66.1
Relative measure			
1965	21.3	15.6	n.a.
1968	19.7	14.6	n.a.
1970	20.8	15.1	n.a.
1972	22.2	15.7	n.a.
1974	22.9	14.9	n.a.
1976	24.1	15.4	n.a.
1978	23.9	15.5	n.a.
Percent change, 1965-1978	+ 12.2	-0.6	n.a.

SOURCE: Sheldon Danziger and Robert Plotnick, "The War on Income Poverty: Achievements and Failures," in *Welfare Reform in America: Perspectives and Prospects*, ed. Paul Sommers (The Hague: Martinus Nijhoff, 1981).

take away from earned income part of what it restores in transfer payments; Social Security may somewhat discourage savings for retirement and work by the elderly and hence reduce the pre-transfer income that old people get; AFDC and Food Stamps may do the same for the welfare population. Pre-transfer inequality has increased over the years, and social welfare programs may have contributed to this trend. In actual fact, the effect is small: transfers have apparently added only about 1 percent of the population to the "pre-transfer" poor.[51] Still, the findings that substantial amounts of income have been redistributed each year are less reliable than the findings that, over time, income inequality (where income includes social welfare benefits) has not decreased despite the big rise in social welfare spending.

Government has had to act vigorously just to compensate for increased inequality in private earnings. Moreover, to at least a small extent, government action has negated itself, creating some of the pre-transfer inequality it purports to remedy.

In short, social welfare spending in the United States has done much less than most people imagine to increase the equality of incomes. As it set out to do, the Great Society raised many people out of misery and guaranteed a minimum level of food, money, and medical care for most of the population. But it has not brought about substantial increases in income equality. In that sense the War on Poverty has certainly not been won.

Welfare Politics

Political Parties

Political parties play a major part in the making of social welfare policy. Since the New Deal era of the 1930s there have been real differences between the Republican and Democratic parties, with the Democrats considerably more enthusiastic about expanding government programs in this area.

Many of the foundations for a U.S. welfare state were laid by the Democratic administration of Franklin Roosevelt: Social Security retirement and disability programs; unemployment insurance; public works jobs.[52] Harry Truman in the late 1940s proposed a number of extensions, including national health insurance, but was mostly thwarted by Republicans in Congress. The Eisenhower years of the 1950s brought a Republican interlude of inaction.

John Kennedy and particularly Lyndon Johnson, with the Democratic congresses of the 1960s, signed into law a flood of New Frontier and Great Society programs, including aid to depressed areas, manpower training, community action, aid for elementary and secondary education, Medicare and Medicaid, Food Stamps, and housing assistance. In contrast, the subsequent Nixon and Ford administrations produced few innovative social welfare policies, except when prodded by the Democratic Congress.[53] Carter picked up social welfare activity a bit; Reagan slashed it back.

As this sketch indicates, American political history in recent years has tended to follow a cyclical pattern, in which Democratic social welfare activism has been followed by Republican quiescence and then a new outpouring of Democratic activism. One complete turn of the cycle, chronicled by James Sundquist, occurred during the 1950s and 1960s. Eisenhower and his appointees from 1953 through 1960 took few social welfare initiatives. Democratic senators, bureaucrats, academics, and others worked out many proposals, but their legislation was either defeated by Republican and Southern Democratic opposition in Congress or was vetoed by President Eisenhower. From 1961 to 1963 Kennedy's bare majority of liberal Democrats was able to pass only a few new laws. Then the shock of Kennedy's assassination, together with Lyndon Johnson's legislative skill and the overwhelming Democratic majority accompanying Goldwater's defeat in 1964, facilitated a surge of Great Society programs in 1964 and 1965. Soon, however, the Vietnam War, urban unrest, and general disillusionment with government activism led to a slowing of activity. The cycle had returned to its starting point.

Party differences can be traced to the stable coalitions of activists, money givers, and loyalists with distinctive policy preferences, which gather under a given party label in times of crisis and electoral realignment. During the Great Depression working people, immigrants, Catholics, Jews, blacks, and organized labor rallied to the Democrats; white, native-born, Protestant, middle- and upper-class people, along with most of the business world, continued to support the Republicans.[54] Since then the parties have not just sought votes by competing for the middle of the political spectrum; they have retained their distinctive policy orientations, drawing upon the money and work of traditional loyalists to win elections.

There are predictable, systematic differences between the platforms of the Republican and Democratic parties, between the stands of Republican and Democratic candidates, and between the roll call votes of Republican and Democratic congressmen.[55] Party differences are usually sharpest early in an alignment period when the policy disagreements underlying the alignment are fresh and relevant. As time passes, the differences tend to fade and the parties "dealign," as Burnham puts it. Eventually new parties may emerge, or new issues may divide the old parties, or the system may muddle along in confusion and disaffection as it did in the late 1960s and the 1970s.[56]

So long as any life is left in a particular alignment, party alternations in power are likely to lead to zigzags in the direction of public policy. A party may come to power for reasons somewhat independent of its policy stands: the charisma of its candidates or the opposition fumbling into war or depression. But once in office the party leaders push for the policies they favor until they are displaced and the opposition does the same. The ship of state veers right and left and right once again.

Clearly, however, party alternations in power do not account for the overall shape of policy. What matters in the long run is not the back and forth but the net impact of Democratic zigs and Republican zags. Over a period of years the result may be the same as if a single grand coalition had been in power all the time or there had been no parties at all. (To be sure, if by chance a party with unrepresentative views somehow held power for a long time or one party managed to persuade the citizenry to share its policy preferences, that party might actually shape long-run policy.) The chief effect of party competition may be to increase information levels and popular control, not to enact the program of a party elite.

Furthermore, party differences on social welfare policy are not as great as the noise of partisan warfare sometimes makes them seem. Party line votes often involve small marginal differences, not fundamental disagreements over policy. Republicans in office have not generally tried to repeal Democratic programs. Eisenhower didn't innovate, but neither did he dismantle the New Deal; instead, he consolidated it and gave it new legitimacy among Republicans. Nixon, despite his 1968 rhetoric about getting millions "off the welfare rolls," actually proposed a guaranteed income (his Family Assistance Plan) and substantially expanded benefits under Food Stamps, Medicaid, and Social Security. Reagan's extreme cutting of domestic programs soon gave way to compromise.

Similarly, it would be a mistake to think of the Democratic party as a whole-hearted advocate of equality. Even with their huge majority after 1964 the Democrats did not attempt any massive redistribution of income or wealth. Some of the benefits from New Deal and Great Society programs go to people of medium and high incomes—teachers, social workers, and other professionals—who make up an important part of the Democratic coalition. And, as we have seen, the biggest programs provide social insurance for working people of the middle class, not the poor. Organized labor, with its money and its army of doorbell ringers and vote registrars and other party workers, stands at the heart of the Democratic coalition.[57] But it is American organized labor, seeking a piece of the capitalist pie, not the more egalitarian and socialistic labor movement of Europe. The modest extent of party differences is apparent in any time series (e.g., Figure 4) on social welfare spending.

Interest Groups

Interest groups may play a smaller role in the making of social welfare policy than in other areas because of the relatively high visibility of welfare politics and the relatively active involvement of parties and the general public. Yet interest groups must be taken into account both as members of party coalitions and as independent actors.

The American Medical Association (AMA) and the American Hospital Association (AHA), for example, exerted considerable influence upon Medicare and Medicaid. The AMA's intensive lobbying and propaganda campaigns of the 1950s eventually (after a long holding action) lost the battle to keep the government out of medical care. But the AMA and AHA won the war in the sense that the legislation took a form which greatly benefited the doctors and hospitals, and they might well have prevented congressional enactment if it hadn't. An enormous amount of public money was poured into medical care while the structure of free enterprise medicine—private practice, fee-for-service, doctors' control over fees and standards—remained essentially intact.[58]

For many years food politics were ruled by farm interests working through the friendly congressional Agriculture Committees. Food Stamps were enacted only after a protracted struggle when farmers became convinced they would increase the demand for farm produce, and the civil rights movement overcame the resistance of Southern whites who feared that their social order would be upset. Similarly, proposals for shifts from in-kind to cash benefits and for a guaranteed income have been resisted by the providers of social services.[59]

Again, home mortgage lenders lobbied hard for the disastrous low-income home purchase subsidies of 1968. The National Education Association of teachers keeps a keen eye on aid to education. The construction industry, with close ties to the Democrats and Republicans as well, has obtained large bricks-and-mortar expenditures for schools and hospitals. Above all, organized labor has made sure that most social welfare programs benefit workers by focusing on unemployment and retirement and disability insurance, which mainly help working people. When unions' interests conflict with those of the poor, as in the case of the minimum wage (which eliminates jobs for those on the bottom but cuts low-wage competition and makes unionization easier) labor generally wins and the poor lose.

To be sure, it is hard to prove interest group influence, but it is not unreasonable to infer something when groups are organized and active, when they participate directly in the legislative process, and when the final outcome closely reflects their desires.

Public Opinion

The general public probably has more direct influence over social welfare than over any other type of policy. Jobs, food, housing, education, and medical care are central to people's lives. People care about what government does, inform themselves relatively well, and vote for sympathetic politicians. In

Schattschneider's phrase, the scope of the conflict is wide.[60] The broad thrust of policy, if not all the details, must respond to citizens' preferences.

The political parties provide links between citizens' preferences and policy. One type of linkage we have already noted: parties offer distinctive policy programs and win the votes of those who agree. In the full "responsible party" version of this process the two parties not only zigzag around the center of citizens' preferences; they also influence citizens' thinking by enlightening people as to their true interests.[61] A second type of linkage that also occurs (after the fashion of the "economic theory of democracy"), dampens the zigzags and drives both parties, in their competition for votes, to take similar stands near the middle of public opinion.[62] Either way, that is, in both ways, parties tend to achieve a long-run correspondence between what government does and what the citizens want.

The American public favors maximum individual liberty and has long been wary of big government. Most Americans believe in meritocracy: equality of opportunity but unequal rewards for individual skill and effort. There is little discernible interest in large-scale redistribution of income, and the polls have regularly shown heavy opposition to the idea of a guaranteed income. Lockean liberalism is deeply ingrained.[63]

Since the second half of the nineteenth century, there has been increasing acceptance of the idea that government ought to smooth off some of the rough edges of capitalism: that workers should not be left penniless because of economic depression, old age, or disability and that women and children should not be excessively exploited. Survey data show that after the Great Depression, Americans generally came to favor relief for the unemployed, pensions for the retired, and aid for the disabled. Gradually support increased for government help with medical care, education, housing, and especially jobs.[64]

At the same time, however, Americans loathe waste or inefficiency, which they tend to associate with bureaucracy and government programs, especially in the social welfare area. And they do not want to be taken advantage of; they hate loafers or freeloaders or welfare "cheaters," whom they believe to be frequent recipients of welfare payments. Thus they more strongly support aid for the disabled and the elderly, and other gories of people whose condition is clearly beyond their own control, than they do for the poor generally. They do, however, favor programs of education and job training and work so people can help themselves.[65]

The overall shape of social welfare policy, then, is broadly consistent with the expressed preferences of the public for social insurance and some assistance to the needy but not much redistribution of income. In social welfare policy there are few cases of sharp divergence between what the public says it wants and what government does. Policy changes tend to be congruent with opinion changes, and congressmen's votes on legislation correspond fairly closely with the preferences of their constituents.[66] Perhaps the greatest divergence is in the lack of any government guarantee of jobs.

Work Incentives and Economic Structure

Once again, however, we should not leap to the conclusion that democracy works perfectly and that's that. The *sources* of the public's preferences must be considered. One issue involves possible work disincentive effects of social welfare programs. Americans want every able-bodied person to work and tend to suspect that the poor are lazy and that welfare or other transfer programs encourage loafing. If they are right, there may be structural constraints on the possibility of redistribution. Really egalitarian programs might reduce work effort so much that societal productivity would decline and everyone would be worse off. If so, a minimal welfare system focusing upon involuntary categories of people (e.g., the aged and disabled) would make sense and would in fact be imposed by the structure of the economy. But if the public is deceived about work disincentives, it may be less a case of democratic responsiveness and more one of manipulation.

The facts are not very supportive of public images. To begin with, when asked survey questions about whether they want to work, how important work is to their self-esteem, whether they would want to work even if they didn't need the money, and so forth, the poor generally express just as much enthusiasm for the work ethic as other people do. Even the sons of long-term welfare mothers agree. By this measure, the poor *do* want to work. They accept welfare only because they are discouraged by lack of ability or lack of jobs. (In fact the "WIN" work training program found only 10 percent of welfare mothers eligible for training and was able to land jobs for only 20 percent of those.)[67]

These attitudes seem to be real, not just facile answers to survey interviewers. A variety of econometric studies of labor supply, including some based on the income maintenance experiments, indicate that government payments only moderately depress work. Most notably, wives tend to work 20 percent to 25 percent fewer hours when their families are guaranteed an income at the poverty level. But whether this represents any loss at all to society is a real question. (The housework and child care done when wives are not forced to work outside the home does not show up as "earnings" but are just as valuable as paid employment.) When income is guaranteed, husbands and female family heads also reduce work, but by much less.[68]

In fact even current welfare programs, with their perversely high tax rates on work (sometimes withdrawing benefits entirely for earnings above some arbitrary figure) have reduced the supply of labor only to a moderate extent. Danziger, Haveman, and Plotnick, after an exhaustive review of the literature on labor supply effects, offered a cautious "guesstimate" that the total number of manhours worked in the United States would have been only about 4.8 percent higher in the absence of all cash and in-kind transfers. And since most transfer recipients would be low wage earners anyhow, the total earnings (i.e., value of work) lost would have been only about 3.5 percent. This would seem a small price to pay for the reduction of poverty. Moreover, they note that these may be overestimates since private charity might be substituted for some of the public transfers and itself discourage work and since unemployment might prevent full replacement of transfers by earned income.[69] Separate estimates of the work disincentive effects of major transfer programs are given in Table 12.

Furthermore, various proposed reforms could further decrease poverty and increase income equality, with little or no additional loss of work—or indeed with a gain. Simulation studies by Betson and others, for example, indicate that a Negative Income Tax program with a guaranteed income floor at 75

TABLE 12 *Reduction in the Labor Supply of Recipients of Major Income Transfer Programs as a Percentage of Total Labor Supply of All Workers*

Program	Reduction of Work Hours by Transfer Recipients as a % of Total Work Hours of All Workers
Social insurance:	
Old age and survivors insurance	1.2
Disability insurance	1.2
Unemployment insurance	0.3
Workers' compensation and Black Lung	0.7
Railroad retirement	*
Veterans' disability compensation	0.4
Medicare	*
Public assistance:	
AFDC	0.6
SSI and veterans' pensions	0.1
Food Stamps and housing assistance	0.3
Medicaid	*
Total	4.8

*Denotes under 0.05%.

SOURCE: Sheldon Danziger, Robert Haveman, and Robert Plotnick, "How Income Transfer Programs Affect Work, Savings, and the Income Distribution: A Critical Review," *Journal of Economic Literature* 19 (Sept. 1981): 996.

percent of the official poverty level, and an implicit tax (i.e., benefit reduction) rate of 50 cents for each dollar earned in the marketplace, would lead to a substantial decrease in the Gini coefficient (of 10-18 percent) and the poverty rate (of 16 percent), with only a tiny (0.1 to 0.6 percent) decrease in hours worked, and actually a small (0.4 percent to 1.8 percent) rise in total U.S. earnings.[70] The main barrier to such a program is not disincentive effects but unwillingness to pay for it.

On the other hand, this does not mean that incomes could be totally equalized by cash transfers without cutting productivity. If offered a completely free ride, some Americans would no doubt be content to take the cash and go on extended vacations. Yet the existing studies tell us little about what would happen to productivity if all able-bodied people were required (and allowed) to work but their pay were equalized. Some people would presumably resist taking hard jobs or fail to strive for promotion and responsibility, but the losses might be considerably less than the production decreases caused by equivalent cash transfers. Nor do the studies indicate how well the economy could work if nonmaterial incentives were substituted for material ones. Examples as diverse as present-day Germany and China suggest that motives of patriotism and regard for the common good, together with desire for social approval, can encourage solid work efforts.[71]

The exact terms of what Okun calls the "big tradeoff" between equality and efficiency, then, are still uncertain.[72] The structural limits to redistribution are not yet fully known. Hardly any other subject seems more deserving of study.

It does appear, however, that much more redistribution could occur in the United States without great loss of productivity. If so, the antiegalitarian character of policy and public opinion in the United States requires a nonstructural explanation, which may perhaps be found in the peculiarities of American history. The United States was settled at the outset as a middle-class country, practically without feudalism—except for Southern slavery. The Protestant ethic was unencumbered by communal ties of the traditional feudal sort. Material abundance and the open frontier encouraged belief in free enterprise and individual mobility. Furthermore, the ethnic diversity of American immigrants, coupled with this capitalist ideology, discouraged the development of a strong labor movement of the sort that emerged in most European countries. Thus the United States has no real socialist movement, no true labor party, and a public resistant to redistribution from rich to poor.[73] This is an unusual situation in the contemporary world.

The causal connections among these and other factors are not easy to sort out. Whatever the roots of the matter, it is clear that the configuration of parties, interest groups, and public opinion pushes the United States toward social welfare policies that are not very egalitarian.

4

Spending on Public Goods

About half the U.S. federal budget involves more or less "public goods" like the military, science, energy, the environment, transportation, and law and order (see Table 13). Such spending is not usually designed to redistribute income but has quite different purposes. And it is often hard to calculate how much of the benefits go to people of different income classes. Yet public goods, like cash or in-kind transfers, clearly do provide real benefits to people and do therefore affect the net distribution of income in society. We must take them into account in our overall assessment of who gets what from government.

A pure public good or social good is one which is consumed in equal amounts by everyone. If the good is produced, it is not possible to exclude anyone from using it. Moreover, it does not cost the producer any more when many rather than few use it. Consumption is "nonrival." A classic example is navigational help from a lighthouse. When the light is on, it is difficult to prevent any nearby ship from seeing it and taking advantage of it, and it costs no more for many ships to use it than for one.

The private market economy does not do well at providing public goods. If no one can be excluded from consumption, there is no way to charge a price for use of the good and therefore no incentive for private entrepreneurs to produce and sell it. It's

TABLE 13 *Federal Outlays on Public Goods, 1960–1980*

	% of Total Budget		
Function	1960	1970	1980
Military	49.8	39.9	23.4
International affairs	3.3	2.2	1.8
Science, space, technology	0.4	2.3	1.0
Administration of justice	0.3	0.5	0.8
General government	1.2	1.0	0.8
Energy	*	0.5	1.1
Natural resources, environment	1.5	1.6	2.4
Transportation	4.4	3.6	3.6
Agriculture	2.9	2.6	0.8
Commerce, housing credit	1.8	1.1	1.3
Community and regional development	0.1	1.2	1.7
General fiscal assistance	*	0.3	1.5
Interest on debt	9.0	9.3	11.1
Total Public Goods (% of budget)	74.7	66.1	51.3
Total Budget Outlay ($ billions)	(92.2)	(196.6)	(579.6)

*Substantially less than 1%.

Note: These budget categories only roughly approximate the theoretical definition of public goods. Because some offsetting revenues are not included, the proportions of total net spending given here and in Ch. 3, Table 9, sum to more than 100 percent.

SOURCE: Calculated from U.S. Office of Management and Budget, *The Budget of the United States Government,* fiscal years 1971, 1980, and 1982 (Washington, D.C.: U.S. Government Printing Office, 1970, 1979, and 1981); 1960 budget categories are adjusted for comparability.

hard to make money by building a private lighthouse. So if private enterprise is left to itself, public goods tend to be underproduced relative to what consumers want, or not produced at all.[1]

By the same token, public "bads" which people can't avoid consuming, like pollution, tend to be overproduced. People can't easily avoid breathing dirty air. If industries don't have to pay anything to discharge filth, they pollute at will.

To make matters worse, even if people could be selectively excluded from consuming a public good so that a price could be charged, the nonrivalness of consumption means that for purposes of economic efficiency the optimal price would be zero. Since it costs nothing to provide the good to each additional consumer after the first, there is no point in discouraging additional consumers by charging them money. Society would be best off if consumption were maximized by giving the good away. But plainly no private entrepreneur is going to produce something for free. In actual practice, where there is nonrival consumption but exclusion is possible, private monopolists tend to take over and charge too high a price and underproduce the good.

The failure of the private market to deal efficiently with public goods leads most people—even most economists—to recommend that government step in. To be sure, some devotees of free enterprise argue that the costs of government bureaucracy and interference with liberty are so great that they outweigh the deficiencies of the market and private enterprise ought to be left alone to do what it can. But most think the state should cope with the problem of public goods in one way or another through regulation or contracting or producing the goods itself.[2] For some, this allocative role of the state, remedying imperfections of the private market, is the chief justification for government activity of any kind.

In reality, of course, there are no pure public goods. It is almost always technically possible to exclude from consuming a good those who don't pay. Even a lighthouse might send out coded electronic transmissions that could only be unscrambled by rented equipment and mix in decoy signals from scattered locations to confuse any direction-finding efforts by pirates. But, as this fanciful example illustrates, exclusion is often *costly* and inefficient.

Similarly, consumption is never perfectly nonrival. Something is used up by each consumer, some bit of physical substance or at least some space for consuming. Even the use of a lighthouse might become rival if a dense concentration of ships blotted out its sight from their short-masted brethren. But again, consumption can be *relatively* nonrival. Over a significant range of production there are often increasing returns to scale, that is, it is cheap (and increasingly cheaper) to provide the good for each new consumer, and the market mechanism fails to set an efficient price.

Thus the pure public good is only an extreme hypothetical case of two real problems, nonexcludability and nonrivalness of consumption. Often exclusion is physically difficult or costly, or property rights are hard to define or enforce so that there are "externalities"—what Pigou called "neighbourhood effects."[3] People produce or consume goods or bads without being paid or having to pay for them. Often, too, consumption is relatively nonrival in the sense of increasing returns to scale. In either case, without government action the private economy would perform poorly. Without government involvement, private industry would pollute the air and water; protection of life and property (left to private Pinkerton-type agencies) would be spotty and go only to those who could afford it; scientific research would be relatively neglected; defense would be provided only locally, by private armies.

When government provides public goods, those goods add to the net incomes of the citizens who receive them and therefore affect the total distribution of income. Different people would benefit to different degrees even in the case of a pure public good with equal consumption since some people always need or want a good more than others do. To calculate just how much each person benefited would be far from easy. In principle one might want to measure how much better or worse off a citizen was than he would be in "Lindahl equilibrium" where his taxes exactly matched his benefits. In practice, however, the detailed information about citizens' preferences needed for such measurement is unobtainable.[4] Moreover, since there are no pure public goods, actual levels of consumption vary. And the provision of public goods, just like the in-kind benefits discussed in the last chapter, can also affect the incomes of the producers of the goods as well as the consumers. For all these reasons it is quite difficult to sort out the precise effects of public goods expenditures upon the distribution of income.

Military and International Affairs

National defense has some of the features of nonexcludable consumption and increasing returns to scale that are characteristic of a public good. Once Washington, D.C., is defended from attack, it is difficult to exclude any particular resident of that city from enjoying protection. To defend the whole city is little more expensive than defending only the Capitol building and White House. Hence, the armies purchased by individuals in a private market would be ineffective, too small. Virtually everyone agrees that if armed forces are needed, government should provide them.

U.S. military spending consumes an enormous amount of resources. In 1980 some $136 billion, about one-quarter of the total federal budget, went to the military. In addition to about 2 million men in uniform, the Department of Defense had nearly 950,000 civilian employees, far more than any other agency, and close to half the government total. The $136 billion in spending represented over 5 percent of the GNP and more than $500 for every man, woman, and child in the country.[5]

Historical trends in military spending, of course, reflect alternations between war and peace. Little was spent throughout the nineteenth century, except for the Civil War, but the amounts jumped up sharply for World War I and World War II. From about $1.5 billion (only 16 percent of the federal budget) in 1940, military outlays soared to $82 billion (88 percent of a greatly swollen budget) in the peak war year of 1945.[6]

Military spending never seems to decline as fast after wars as it rises during them. There is a ratchet effect. New weapons systems are retained; the troops are not completely demobilized. (In addition, there is some spillover to civilian activities since veterans' benefits and interest payments on the national debt increase, and wartime taxes do not all get repealed.) In the three years immediately after World War II, military outlays dropped from the $82 billion peak to just under $8 billion in 1948—a drastic decline but not down to pre-war levels. Then, with the onset of the cold war, they crept upward once again to nearly $12 billion in 1949. For the Korean War they jumped to $22 billion in 1951 and $43 billion in 1952, which is about where they stayed through the next decade (see Table 14).

The trend in military spending since the Korean War, in constant dollars, was given in Figure 4 in Chapter 3. The Vietnam War brought a new surge of spending, from $47.5 billion in 1965 to nearly $79 billion in 1968. Vietnam involved a massive U.S. effort, including some 500,000 fighting men, thousands of so-

TABLE 14 *Trends in Military Spending, 1940–1980*

Year	Current $ (billions)	Constant 1972 $ (billions)	% of Federal Budget	% of GNP
1940	1.490	6.0	15.8	1.6
1945	81.858	252.0	88.3	37.7
1948	7.845	20.3	26.3	3.2
1950	12.407	29.4	29.1	4.7
1953	49.912	96.3	65.6	13.8
1955	39.834	75.8	58.1	10.5
1960	45.168	73.8	49.0	9.1
1965	47.456	69.3	40.1	7.2
1968	78.755	101.4	44.0	9.5
1970	78.553	90.3	40.0	8.2
1975	85.552	67.1	26.2	5.9
1980 (est.)	125.830	70.4	23.7	5.0

SOURCE: U.S. Office of Management and Budget, "Federal Government Finances," unpublished, Jan. 1979, pp. 36–37, 45–49, 51–55.

phisticated aircraft, and millions of tons of high explosives poured into that small Asian country. Military spending declined markedly as the war ended. Yet what is strikingly clear from Figure 4 is that Vietnam spending represented only a medium-sized hump on top of an essentially flat twenty-five-year level of military outlays. In constant dollars, that is, correcting for inflation, about the same amount was spent on the armed forces in 1980 as in 1955. Since the whole economy and the rest of government spending grew substantially during this period, military spending fell from 58 percent of the federal budget in 1955 to 23 percent in 1980, and from 10.5 percent to 5 percent of the GNP.

By 1980, however, there was a strong trend toward a rising military budget. The Carter administration planned for spending increases of 4 to 5 percent a year in real (constant dollar) terms, with most of the new money going to modernization of equipment, deployment in Europe of Pershing II and ground-launched cruise nuclear missiles, an expanded navy, increased air and sea mobility (airlift capacity, pre-positioned supplies, and Persian Gulf bases), and research and development. There was talk of substantially expanding forces in order to cope simultaneously with more than the "one-and-one-half wars" (one major, one minor) that had formed the base of U.S. contingency planning in the 1970s. A new arms race appeared to be under way.

The Reagan administration accelerated these trends. In the 1982 budget it won an increase in military outlays of 17 percent (or about 10 percent, in constant dollars), an unprecedented peacetime jump at the same time that many domestic programs were being cut. Military pay was increased by 14.3 percent, and development of strategic forces was sharply speeded up, especially the B-1 bomber and MX missiles, along with a "Stealth" bomber for the 1990s, and more air- and sea-launched cruise missiles. A five-year, $96 billion program for building 133 new ships was begun, along with the new M-1 tank, new fighter planes, and new air- and sea-lift capability. The 1983 budget proposed a further 18 percent spending increase, which (even after congressional cuts) constituted a massive military build-up.[7]

Who Benefits from Defense

For us the question is which income groups benefit from military spending. Even if defense were a pure public good, with all Americans consuming exactly the same amount, the actual benefits of the consumption might be very different for high-income as opposed to low-income people. Moreover, the purchasing of so many goods and services to provide defense could alter the distribution of income in the private economy. Finally, defense is not in fact a pure public good but a rather impure one. Parts of it are consumed in quite different quantities by different income classes. For all these reasons military spending can have enormous effects upon inequality in American society. The trick is to sort out exactly what those effects are.

Even to the extent that defense is equally consumed by all who happen to find themselves behind U.S. national boundaries, the benefits of that consumption for any particular individual depend upon his economic position and ethnic ties and relation to American society. They also depend upon whom the guns are aimed at: who is defined as the enemy of the moment. German-Americans had less reason than others to fear the Kaiser in World War I. Jews had more reason to resist Hitler. New England merchants had little to gain from our quarrel with Britain in the War of 1812. Residents of the Southwest had the most at stake in our various skirmishes with Mexico. For any given enemy, some citizens may benefit greatly from defense while others benefit little and might even be better off with no defense at all.

Thus, in the post-World War II situation, with the world polarized between East and West, we cannot assume that all Americans gain equally from military expenditures aimed primarily against the Soviet Union. The owners of factories and banks and oil companies very likely have more to lose from a hypothetical total surrender and a Russian occupation (assuming the Russians sought such a thing) than would the average blue-collar worker. The capitalists' wealth would presumably be expropriated by a Soviet-imposed North American Socialist Republic. (Of course, it is not impossible that a vice-president of General Motors would end up running the People's Automobile Works and would keep his dacha in Vermont and his yacht in the Bahamas.) The factory worker, on the other hand, has less to lose economically and might conceivably come out ahead if the economy were socialized and his workplace publicly owned.

If American workers would, in fact, be better off under socialism, it is possible that their tax dollars spent on defense against international socialism do them harm rather than good. If so, military spending is fundamentally pro-rich. It reinforces American inequality. From this perspective, in the current period Americans may benefit from military spending in proportion to their wealth. Obviously, how one estimates the distributive impact of the military budget depends heavily upon what one thinks about socialism in general and Soviet socialism in particular.

This line of argument, like the more conventional view that arms expenditures are designed to protect all Americans' lives and territory and to deter attack from any quarter, focuses on the strategic aim of defending the homeland. But even a casual look at force levels indicates that more is going on than simple protection of U.S. territory from invasion.

The danger of Soviet tanks pouring down from the Arctic Circle or a flotilla of Chinese junks assaulting the West Coast is rather remote. If some megalomaniac in Moscow or Beijing were actually tempted to embark upon such a fantastic project, he would no doubt be deterred by an appreciation of what even a very small U.S. nuclear force could do to his home country. According to one estimate which takes account of the delayed effects of firestorms and fallout as well as immediate blast effects, the delivery of just 200 equivalent megatons of nuclear weapons on the Soviet Union could destroy two-thirds of her industry and one-fifth of her population. One hundred equivalent megatons could destroy the most critical Russian industries. (Indeed, the horrifying prospect of a single thermonuclear explosion of even one megaton over Moscow would presumably deter a sane leader from attacking the United States.) Yet, as of 1980, the United States had the ability to deliver some 6,000 equivalent megatons, of which at least 1,500 could almost certainly be exploded on the Soviets even after a surprise attack upon U.S. forces.[8]

A small number of Trident missile submarines, dispersed at sea and virtually invulnerable to surprise attack, would appear sufficient to deter any unprovoked assault upon the United States. Why, then, the vast U.S. nuclear arsenal? Why the triad of bombers and land-based as well as sub-launched missiles, with many thousands of independently targetable (MIRVed) warheads? Why air-launched cruise missiles (ALCMs) and heavy bombers and an MX missile system?[9] Why the alarming talk about "falling behind" the Soviets?

A traditional answer has been that in planning strategic forces, the utmost caution is appropriate: the United States should be ready for the worst possible case of surprise attack, for exceptionally complete destruction of U.S. forces on the ground and exceptionally successful defense against U.S. retaliation. It is curious, however, that the advocates of worst-case analysis do not attribute the same kind of thinking to their wily adversaries. If a potential attacker gave any thought to how easily a surprise attack could go wrong and some retaliatory capacity could survive, he would shrink from the risk and would be deterred by even a small and fragile nuclear force arrayed against him.

Furthermore, if the sole aim of our strategic forces were to deter nuclear attack or invasion of the United States, one would expect serious efforts at mutual disarmament and international peacekeeping. The possession and proliferation of nuclear weapons makes possible—even likely—the use of such weapons; and there is no certainty that any use—however "limited" or "tactical"—could stop short of a total thermonuclear spasm, in which every available bomb and missile was hurled at population centers. The resulting radiation, electromagnetic pulses, thermal pulses, blast waves, and fallout would destroy lives, communications, and structures over vast inhabited areas. Subsequent firestorms, worldwide fallout, dust-induced cooling of the climate, and possible destruction of the ozone layer (which protects us from the sun's ultraviolet radiation) would have incalculable consequences—perhaps throwing us back into a vicious iron age of mutated humans (as chillingly described in the novel *Riddley Walker*), or destroying the human species altogether, or even ending life on earth.[10]

The horror of a thermonuclear holocaust is sufficient to make questions of income distribution trivial by comparison. Not much income would be left, and it would not likely be distributed in orderly ways. Any friend of the human race ought to work for peace. But within the narrow confines of my present argument, the point is a slightly different one: that the United States, the leading nuclear power, has *not*, in fact, made much effort to mutually freeze and cut back nuclear weapons but rather has expressed scorn for disarmament and the United Nations, let alone world government, and has rushed to produce ever more and better tools of destruction; and that this armament splurge has had income-distributional consequences quite different from those of simple defense of the homeland.

One possible explanation for massive U.S. nuclear armaments is political. It asserts that unnecessary weapons are built because defense contractors and the military and its supporters get together in a military-industrial complex with enough political clout to buy arms regardless of need. (We will have more to say about this later.) A second explanation, not wholly inconsistent with the first, is that strategic weapons are not really intended to deter an unprovoked general attack on the United States. Rather, they are intended to back up a system of worldwide American influence. Many of the scenarios for possible use of nuclear weapons involve conflicts far from American shores—disputes over West Berlin or Yugoslavia or South Korea or the Persian Gulf—in which the United States might resort to nuclear arms in order to avoid a loss with conventional forces. Indeed, the magnitude of U.S. strategic forces and some aspects of military doctrine suggest that a "counterforce" first strike might be carried out in some circumstances to defuse Soviet retaliatory capacity and ensure that the will of the United States prevails.

Worldwide Influence

The nature of U.S. conventional forces also suggests an aim of enforcing worldwide influence rather than merely deterring attack (see Table 15). In 1980 about $52 billion, more than one-third of the military obligational authority, was devoted to general purpose forces, contrasted with only $11 billion (8 percent) on strategic forces. (Training, supply, research and development, intelligence and communications, and other such support functions took up the bulk of the budget.) Of the sixteen army and three marine divisions on active duty, about three-quarters were either stationed in Europe or pre-positioned for airlift to Europe, and most tactical air forces were oriented toward Europe as well. Despite some excessive alarmism in the 1970s and early 1980s, the great mobility and striking power of these forces, together with NATO allies, provided a fairly even qualitative balance with the opposing Warsaw Pact.[11]

While it may seem obvious to most Americans that the defense of Europe is in the U.S. national interest, plainly protection of Europe is not identical to the defense of American shores. The meaning of "defense" is itself ambiguous. What role would U.S. forces play if there were an effort to overthrow an elected communist government in Italy or France? In fact, what role might the United States play in preventing such an election in the first place?

TABLE 15 *U.S. Military Force Levels, 1979–1983*

	1979	1980	1981	1983 (est.)
Military personnel (thousands)				
Army	758	777	781	784
Navy	522	527	540	569
Marine Corps	185	189	191	195
Air Force	559	558	570	600
Total	2,024	2,050	2,082	2,148
Strategic forces				
Intercontinental ballistic missiles:				
Minuteman	1,000	1,000	1,000	1,000
Titan II	54	54	53	44
Polaris-Poseiden-Trident	656	576	520	568
Strategic bomber squadrons	25	28	25	22
General purposes forces				
Land forces:				
Army divisions	16	16	16	16
Marine divisions	3	3	3	3
Tactical air forces:				
Air Force wings	26	26	26	26
Navy attack wings	12	12	12	13
Marine Corps wings	3	3	3	3
Naval forces:				
Attack and multipurpose carriers	13	13	12	13
Nuclear attack submarines	72	74	81	93
Other warships	172	183	196	219
Amphibious assault ships	65	63	59	60
Airlift and sealift forces:				
C-5A airlift squadrons	4	4	4	4
Other strategic airlift squadrons	13	13	13	13
Troopships, cargo ships, tankers	47	52	60	63

SOURCE: U.S. Office of Management and Budget, *The Budget of the United States Government*, fiscal years 1981 (p.93), 1982 (p. 98), 1983 (p. 5–14) (Washington, D.C.: U.S. Government Printing Office, 1980, 1981, and 1982).

It is too simple to view defense of Europe as merely a way to stop an onslaught against the United States early and on favorable ground. The protection of U.S. markets and investments, and of kindred societies, is involved as well. This point is all the more clear outside Europe. A North Korean invasion and reunification with South Korea could hardly be seen as the first step on the way to California. Even dedicated believers in domino theories don't seriously suggest that after Thailand comes Hawaii. Yet the United States maintains twelve or thirteen aircraft carriers, which would be easy targets in a nuclear war but meanwhile are very handy for showing the flag or launching expeditionary forces into small countries. We have kept troops as "tripwires" (e.g., in South Korea) so that U.S. involvement in any conflict would be automatic. Other troops, equipped for counterinsurgency, are ready to be airlifted anywhere on the globe.

The thrust of U.S. foreign policy since World War II, in fact, has been to resist any military expansion by communist countries; to prevent leftist governments from coming to power anywhere in the world by revolution or civil war or even peaceful means; and, when prevention has failed, to use covert (and occasionally overt) means to overthrow governments of the Left. The United States spent large sums to prevent communist victories in the Italian elections of 1948 and subsequently. It helped defeat the leftist partisans in the Greek civil war; engineered the overthrow of the Mossadegh regime in Iran; intervened militarily in Korea, in what was arguably a civil war over an externally imposed boundary; provided the bulk of support for the French in Indochina; and organized the overthrow of the Arbenz government in Guatemala. The United States also intervened militarily in a revolutionary situation in Lebanon; covertly worked to overthrow the Sukarno government in Indonesia; organized the exile invasion of Cuba and after its failure attempted several times to assassinate Fidel Castro; and used marines to support a right-wing military coup against a mildly leftist regime in the Dominican Republic. It supported a coup against the Goulart regime in Brazil; intervened first covertly and then overtly against leftist revolutionaries in Laos, Vietnam, and Kampuchea; sponsored a coup by colonels against an elected government in Greece; resisted the election of the Allende regime in Chile, and then supported a coup against it and backed right-wing forces in Portugal and Angola.[12]

The Vietnam War, of course, was the biggest and least successful intervention against the Left, involving up to 500,000 troops, millions of tons of TNT, billions of dollars, and thousands of American casualties, to say nothing of the death and devastation inflicted on the Vietnamese.[13] Vietnam was a sobering experience for the United States. But it is striking that the same pattern of resistance to leftist regimes continued even while the Vietnam War was winding down, with the incursion into Kampuchea and overthrow of Sihanouk, and after the war, with the overthrow of Allende and interventions in Angola and Portugal. By the beginning of the 1980s, American leaders were ready to contemplate the use of force in Iran, Libya, El Salvador, and Nicaragua.

International Inequality

Who has benefited from such interventions? This question requires a brief digression. Like the issue of nuclear war, it makes our concern with inequality of income among Americans seem rather parochial, for U.S. military activity drastically affects the income and welfare of people throughout the world. Income is distributed far more unequally on a worldwide basis than it is within the United States. The poorest American (although this offers little comfort when he contrasts himself with his wealthier neighbors) is a prince compared with the average citizen of Upper Volta. At a time when the average per capita income of the top half of the world's population was over $1,300, the average income of the lower half was only about $100 per year.[14]

The very high degree of world inequality, in which the bottom half of the world's population gets less than 10 percent of world income while the top 10 percent gets 30 percent of the income, is open to all the same ethical objections outlined in Chapter 1. Human satisfaction is not maximized; conflict and instability are promoted; communal harmony, liberty, self-fulfillment, and equal opportunity are all stifled. The same is true of inequality *within* other countries, which (especially in the poorest ones) is often greater than within the United States.[15]

What impact, then, does U.S. military and foreign policy have upon the worldwide income distribution? Some short-run effects are obvious: like the rich man in the middle of a ghetto who lives in a fortress apartment with guards at the door, the United States uses its military might to keep the poor from taking any of its wealth and thereby preserves international inequality. In addition, its support of right-wing regimes throughout the world helps local landlords and capitalists keep their peasants and workers in line and thereby maintains extreme inequality within countries.

The long-run effects depend upon processes of economic development and the merits of socialism versus capitalism. If, as Americans tend to believe, economic development proceeds most quickly and efficiently under free market capitalism, then U.S. imposition of conservative regimes, even brutal and antiegalitarian ones, might be in the long-run interest of the people who suffer under them—assuming that they did encourage development and that the fruits of development were some day distributed in an equitable fashion. But some U.S. clients (Samoza, Diem) have specialized in repression *without* development, and the evidence concerning capitalist-style development is mixed at best. If, on the other hand, socialism can attain rapid development while at the same time increasing equality within countries, then U.S. opposition to the Socialist tide must be seen as antiegalitarian in the long run as well as in the short.

Impact on Americans

Within the United States itself, who benefits from military and foreign policy directed against leftist forces abroad? To some degree, clearly, American consumers gain. Anti-communist policies have effects similar to those of the Monroe Doctrine and the Open Door in early American diplomacy: the protection of markets to invest, to sell U.S.-manufactured goods, and to obtain raw materials—including oil. A neocolonial system of trade provides cheap goods for Americans to buy and income to buy them with. These things presumably aid Americans in proportion to their incomes.

At the same time, however, a disproportionate share of the benefits probably goes to the wealthy Americans who own multinational corporations. The subjection of workers abroad to low wage rates exposes American workers to fierce competition and puts a lid on the wages they can earn. (Only later does the rise of foreign capitalists, as in Japan and Germany, threaten the profits of U.S. capitalists.) One could argue that in the long run the chief American beneficiaries of U.S. foreign and military policy are the owners of capital who are protected in making investments abroad. If so, in calculating the distributional effects of military spending, the benefits ought to be allocated to income classes in proportion to their ownership of capital abroad. That is, the main beneficiaries are the very richest Americans.

The *process* of military spending and military policy also has distributional consequences. The draft, to take one example, is an in-kind tax on those who are forced to serve. Millions of men and women have fought and risked their lives for low wages that they would not voluntarily have accepted. Those suffering most tend to come from the low end of the income scale since children of the wealthy can often obtain student deferments or "essential" jobs at home or, at worst, can volunteer for officer and noncombat positions. The poor and the black of low education were drafted disproportionately during the Vietnam War, for example, and were more likely than their affluent high school classmates to be killed in action.[16] Thus, the draft tends to act as a regressive tax, taking proportionately more from the poor than the rich—even though the few high-income people who are inducted lose more when deprived of their civilian salaries.

A volunteer army, on the other hand, like that of the post-Vietnam years, helps those on the bottom of the income scale by providing jobs when no other work may be available. A peacetime volunteer army amounts to a huge (if not very productive) public service employment program. Similarly, wars themselves—while killing and destroying far more than they create—do tend to promote full employment and raise workers' share of the national income, at least in countries (like the United States so far in the twentieth century) lucky enough to escape devastation of their own territories.[17] It is hard to sort out which of these effects prevails, whether on balance the poor gain or lose from providing military manpower, but it seems unlikely that they gain any very large share of the vast military budget.

One aspect of military manpower policy that contributes to inequality is the high pay given to officers. In the past, officers were underpaid relative to comparable civilians. They were expected to give up money for the sake of patriotism and glory—with a few special perquisites (PX privileges, cheap food and housing, free medical care) to sweeten the sacrifice. But a movement to improve officers' pay took hold, and by the middle 1970s they surpassed their civilian brethren, particularly with respect to retirement pensions. A military officer could retire young (after only twenty years' service) and receive a generous pension, with nothing to prevent him from earning a full civilian salary as well. In 1980 the United States spent about $12 billion on retired military personnel—more than on either the pro-poor AFDC or Food Stamps program.

The procurement of military materiel also benefits the rich. This is most obvious in the case of sophisticated weapons systems, which are highly capital-intensive (thus increasing returns to capital as versus labor in the economy) and which increase the incomes of well-paid engineers and scientists. As Leontieff and others have shown, a dollar of military spending produces fewer jobs but more salary per job than does a dollar of civilian spending. Moreover, the money goes mostly to the richer regions of the country.[18] The widely publicized travail of defense contractors and engineers in the post-Vietnam military contraction was temporary and represented, after all, only a modest decline from the glorious days in which anyone who could manufacture a laser-guided bomb—or a "people sniffer" or a tear gas encapsulation system—was assured of rich financial rewards.

These pro-rich effects of weapons procurement would occur even if the government got full value for every penny it spent.

But they are accentuated by the fact that much military spending is wasteful and inefficient and offers great profits to fortunate contractors.

It is virtually impossible to establish a free market with competitive prices for large weapons systems because of the extreme uncertainty and the enormous capital involved in research and development of goods which only one customer (the U.S. government), if any, would purchase. Rather than simply offering to buy whatever missiles private entrepreneurs happen to produce or letting out bids at unrealistic fixed fees, it makes sense to specify what is wanted and pick a firm and help it through the development process, paying for any necessary but unexpected expenses incurred along the way. Other countries do this by nationalizing their leading defense industries. The United States, instead, tries to preserve the forms of private enterprise and—either officially or in effect—negotiates "cost-plus" contracts with private firms.

Cost-plus contracts with private firms have many defects. It is hard to ferret out actual costs when companies have an incentive to overstate them, and hard to prevent unnecessary costs from being incurred in order to busy idle plants or to inflate the base upon which a proportionate fee may be calculated. It would be difficult enough for zealous government inspectors to avoid cost inflation, but inspectors are also afflicted by mixed motives (what harm to allow some extra profits so long as they deliver the goods?) and by temptations to corruption. A contractor with billions at stake has a lot to offer a middle-income procurement officer: not just a crude suitcase full of cash, but an implicit promise of employment to come.

The result is that defense contractors often enjoy a businessman's utopia of virtually riskless work with rent-free use of government-owned equipment and liberal provision for cost overruns (or, in the case of Lockheed, bail-out from bankruptcy). Accurate figures on profits are not easily obtained, but in good times they appear to run very high indeed. According to Weidenbaum's estimate in the late 1960s, a group of large defense contractors averaged 17.5 percent profit on their investment, compared with an average of 10.6 percent for comparable civilian firms. (To be sure, part of this margin can be regarded as payment for the risk of lower profits in peacetime.) Most of the profits are collected by a few very large corporations owned by the wealthiest Americans.[19]

Moreover, many weapons systems do not work very well. The emphasis on sophisticated high technology leads to frequent breakdowns and unreliability—planes that won't fly, guns that jam, precision computer systems that malfunction, and huge natural targets like aircraft carriers that require their own elaborate defense systems. The supersophisticated M-1 tank turned out to require as nursemaids a battlefield bulldozer ("ACE") to dig holes for it to hide in and a special tanker truck to satisfy its ravenous appetite for gasoline. Such expensive systems are good for defense contractors but not necessarily for defense.[20]

Procurement of food, uniforms, vehicles, and the like is more susceptible to competitive bidding than are major weapons systems. Despite some conspicuous cases of profiteering, such procurement has become more competitive and more efficient in recent years. In addition, it involves goods that are less capital-intensive than weapons systems and probably does not divert income so heavily from labor to capital.

One final distributive aspect of military spending deserves mention. Since there is a tendency to regard total public spending as more or less fixed in the short run, money devoted to the military tends to come out of civilian programs. The losers are generally social welfare programs, especially education and health.[21] If pro-poor programs are curtailed by military spending—and that certainly seemed to be the case in the 1982 and 1983 budgets—then even defense money doled out in proportion to people's incomes is antiegalitarian.

Foreign Aid

In addition to the military budget, the United States spends some money—a little under $11 billion in 1980—on "international affairs." About half of this ($5.6 billion) goes to foreign economic and financial assistance, including multilateral development assistance, AID grants and loans, Public Law 480 food aid, and "security supporting assistance."

Foreign aid is a relatively small program, taking up less than 1 percent of the federal budget. Such a modest sum could not possibly make a dent in world inequality. In fact, if U.S. aid for 1980 were divided evenly among the 4 billion people living in other countries, it would amount to less than $1.50 per person. Of course, it might be unreasonable to expect rich nations like the United States simply to give their wealth away in an outright redistribution for the sake of world equality—more realistic, perhaps, to ask that they provide technology and seed money to help poor nations grow and develop their own economies. But $1.50 won't buy many seeds.

It is worth noting that the U.S. foreign aid effort is also small in comparison with that of many other wealthy countries when calculated as a proportion of national output. In 1980, U.S. net development assistance amounted to only 0.27 percent of our total national production, lower than that of twelve Western nations (the Netherlands gave a much larger 0.99 percent, Norway 0.82 percent, Sweden 0.76 percent, Denmark 0.72 percent, and France 0.62 percent); and far lower than that of five OPEC countries, all of which gave more than 2 percent of their production. (The U.S. figure had declined by about half since 1965.)[22] To be sure, none of these countries can be described as fulsomely generous, but—contrary to some Americans' self-images of profligacy—the United States was among the most stingy of the lot.

In any event, U.S. aid is not divided up equally among the poor of the world and does not necessarily promote economic development at all. Only about $1 billion in 1980 went for crucial programs of multilateral development assistance and another $1 billion for food aid. Some $2 billion was devoted to "security supporting assistance" (largely for Israel and Egypt) and another $900 million to military assistance. In addition, many billions of dollars' worth of arms were sold abroad, at low prices and on easy terms—taking the place of the outright military aid which was once a much larger budget item.[23]

In the post-war years, aid, economic as well as military, has been subordinated to the foreign policy purpose of resisting communism. The largest single effort, the Marshall Plan, was explicitly devoted to rebuilding European allies against the Soviet Union. During the 1950s and 1960s aid was focused on countries bordering upon Soviet and Chinese spheres of influence, especially Taiwan, South Korea, and South Vietnam. Most of the world's poor lived outside such countries and were hardly touched by U.S. aid. Nor is it clear that the poor in, say, Syngman Rhee's South Korea gained much from U.S. help.

Since foreign aid has functioned as a tool of foreign policy, its distributive effects must be analyzed in foreign policy terms. Again, the long-run effects upon world inequality depend upon whether feudal, capitalist, or socialist regimes could most effectively develop the economies of poor countries and distribute the proceeds. It is likely that U.S. aid for military dictatorships and landed aristocracies has reinforced inequality in the world. And again, effects within the United States depend upon considerations of international trade and investment. Although American consumers as a group have benefited from the cheap raw materials and manufactured goods obtained within the "free world," American workers have lost from the competition of cheap foreign labor and capitalists have gained lucrative investment opportunities. On balance the inequality of Americans' incomes has probably been increased.

Peaceful Public Goods

A number of domestic programs provide goods of a more or less public nature. For the most part these programs are small, especially in comparison with the huge expenditures devoted to the military. Their benefits are distributed in a variety of complicated ways.

Science and Technology

Science and technology, for example, clearly belong in the category of public goods. Information and knowledge are subject to great economies of scale: once produced, a new idea can be used by millions almost as cheaply as by one person. Moreover, it is difficult to exclude people from consumption. In the day of the telephone, television, and the Xerox machine, information travels fast. Consequently, it is difficult to sell new knowledge for its full value, and it would be underproduced in a purely free market economy. This is particularly true of basic research. A fundamental discovery may yield unforeseen applications and be used widely without commensurate reward to the researcher. Investment in such research is risky and returns only a portion of its fruits to the investor, so not enough of it is done by private entrepreneurs.[24]

Patent and copyright systems are designed to correct part of this market imperfection by granting government-enforced monopolies over certain uses of information for limited periods, but they cannot wholly eliminate external benefits, especially from basic research. Hence, governments also invest directly in the production of knowledge.

In 1980 the U.S. government spent about $5.7 billion, 1 percent of the budget, on general science, space, and technology. Of this only $1.6 billion went for basic research, including National Science Foundation programs and basic work under NASA and the Department of Energy. (In addition, however, basic research funded through other budget categories including the National Institutes of Health and the Defense Department brought the total to $4.7 billion, approximately 70 percent of all the basic research carried out in the nation.) The distributional effects of this spending are almost entirely unknown. Much of the money goes in the first instance to relatively high-income individuals—scientists at the most prestigious universities and laboratories in the richest states[25]—but the more important long-run impact of the research itself is quite obscure.

The money spent on space flight and space technology (over $4 billion in 1980) has since the 1960s dwarfed all other science programs, with only energy offering some competition in recent years. The achievements have been spectacular: orbiting astronauts and landing them on the moon, exploring the planets, establishing space laboratories and shuttles. Again the distribution of benefits is difficult to ascertain. The providers of the technology—engineers and the owners of capital-intensive electronics and aerospace firms—have received increased incomes due to government demand for their products. There are a number of military, and conceivably some civilian, spinoff benefits from the technology developed for space, with unknown distributional impact.

Perhaps the main point is that exploring space is akin to building the Egyptian pyramids. It is a glorious achievement of civilization, one that will be remembered after much else is forgotten. Yet it does not put much bread on anybody's table. Like fine art, it is a luxury good, wanted more by people with high incomes. The poor would prefer Food Stamps instead of space shots. This is not an argument against the space program but a plea that space enthusiasts should make up for it with pro-poor programs elsewhere in the tax and budget system.

Administration of Justice

Law and order is another classic public good. When a criminal is caught or deterred, all potential victims benefit; it is not easy to demand a fee for the service and exclude from protection those who won't pay. There are also economies of scale in providing law and order over a broad geographical area rather than turning particular shops or houses into security zones. Once again, private markets left to themselves would underprovide the good. Only large firms and wealthy individuals could afford private guards in the absence of courts and policemen.

In the United States, law and order are mostly provided by states and localities, which lay out more than 80 percent of the money and pay for most policemen, courts, and prisons. The federal government spends a modest amount on the administration of justice: about $4.6 billion, less than 1 percent of the budget, in 1980. Of the federal money, about half is devoted to law enforcement, including the FBI (about $600 million in 1980) and rapidly growing border enforcement by Customs and the Immigration and Naturalization Service (over $800 million). Another one-third of the federal spending goes to courts and litigation, with smaller amounts for assistance to states and localities[26] and, finally, for federal prisons.

It is not immediately obvious which income classes benefit most from law enforcement. Low-income people suffer more than others from assault, rape, murder, and other violent crimes and, therefore, gain more when such crime is reduced.

Lineberry found that in at least one community, San Antonio, poor neighborhoods got about equal police manpower and better than equal fire protection. A study of Boston found that the best police and fire protection went to areas with high business activity and strong political support for the mayor; predominantly black areas were not discriminated against on a per capita basis, but the "need gap" was not compensated for either.[27]

In any case, one could argue that the U.S. criminal justice system is not very serious about stopping the street crime that terrorizes low-income people, especially those stuck in ghettos or barrios, and their neighbors. As with health care, we try to act after harm is done rather than preventing the damage. In impoverished areas, jobs or other attractive alternatives to crime are scarce. Society is disorganized: no cohesive community (or no block warden, as in Cuba) keeps track of what people are doing and reports adolescents with arms full of loot to the police. In the name of liberty, we are casual about guns and avoid national identification cards or other means of keeping track of people; multiple aliases are easy to use, and marauders can disappear without a trace. Punishment is neither swift nor sure; criminal prosecution is treated as a game, an adversary joust in which the smart, the rich (who hire top lawyers), and the lucky can often get off. Yet poor suspects, innocent or guilty, are often ground down by the system.[28]

What our legal system probably does best is to facilitate business, through the enforcement and interpretation of contracts and tax laws and commercial arrangements, and to protect large holdings of private property. (The FBI, e.g., when not on political crusades, has long specialized in apprehending bank robbers. Embezzlers, price-fixers, and computer thieves do tend to be punished in the genteel fashion that their nonviolent behavior and middle-class status is taken to warrant, but it remains true that substantial effort goes into stopping big crime.) Some of this helps consumers and workers roughly in proportion to their private incomes. To the extent that the benefits of law and order accrue in proportion to property ownership, however, law enforcement programs are pro-rich.

Moreover, political uses of law enforcement machinery, as in the FBI's obsessive harassment of Martin Luther King, the Socialist Workers party, and various leftist individuals and groups, probably benefit the rich indirectly by discouraging serious consideration of egalitarian economic or political alternatives. Repression of the Left has been common in U.S. history, from the use of injunctions against the labor movement, to the Palmer raids of the 1920s, the Smith Act prosecutions of the 1940s and 1950s, and overt and covert actions against the New Left in the 1960s and 1970s.[29]

Government Operation

About 0.8 percent of the federal budget is spent on "general government." Roughly half of this ($2.3 billion in 1980) goes for tax collection. Much of the rest is spent on the operation of Congress, and lesser amounts go for management of federal property and personnel and records, for territorial and Indian government, and the president's executive office. Presumably the benefits of maintaining these government institutions are distributed in the same way as the benefits of the programs they fund and administer, except that many of the salaries go to people of upper-middle income.

Energy

As of the early 1970s, the United States had no energy policy at all—or a very perverse one.[30] After the OPEC oil boycott and price rises of 1973-1974 and 1979, we began to spend a small but rapidly increasing portion of the federal budget on energy. Outlays jumped from 0.5 percent of the budget in 1970 to 1.1 percent (over $6 billion) in 1980 (see Table 13). Some two-thirds of this was spent on energy supply, including research and development of nuclear, fossil fuel, solar, and other energy sources. In addition to the $6 billion in budget outlays, some $5.4 billion in tax expenditures—foregone revenues—were incurred in the name of energy supply, through generous tax treatment of private exploration and development costs. Smaller amounts were spent on emergency energy preparedness (mainly building toward a 1 billion barrel strategic reserve of oil), regulation, and conservation.

Energy outlays rose strongly once again, to $10 billion, in 1981; but then—as the crisis seemed less pressing and price increases began to improve conservation and production—spending dropped sharply to an estimated $6.4 billion in 1982, less than the 1980 figure in constant dollars. Priorities shifted (somewhat surprisingly) with relatively more emphasis on nuclear fission and synthetic fossil fuels, and less on solar and other renewable resources.

Private firms in search of profits have incentives to develop energy resources regardless of government help. The public goods arguments for government action are weaker than elsewhere, therefore, except in the case of energy-related basic research on new and uncertain technologies like solar and nuclear fusion.[31] The urgency is so great, however (despite periodic temporary "gluts"), and some technologies require such heavy capital outlay, that government assistance may be needed to make up for imperfections in capital markets. Also, only government (by building up oil reserves) may be big enough to cope with boycotts and threats by the oil cartel.[32]

In the short run, most energy subsidies probably increase the returns on private capital and benefit high-income individuals. (The oil depletion allowance has been a conspicuous example.) In the longer run, improved technology presumably benefits people in proportion to their use of energy, that is, roughly in proportion to income. Regulation of energy prices also has some important effects upon income distribution and will be discussed in the next chapter.

Environment

Natural resources and the environment plainly involve public goods. Clean air and water are hard to sell in private markets because it isn't feasible to exclude people from enjoying them without paying for the cleanup measures. Lacking any way to charge for the benefits, firms have little incentive to use clean technologies or pollution control devices. Unless government acts, pollution control is underproduced; dirty manufacturing and shoddy disposal processes are overused. The costs are transferred to downstream users of filthy water or to unfortunate neighbors who breathe dirty air and ingest toxic wastes.

Regulation and taxation have been the primary techniques for government action against pollution. Federal environmental regulations of the sort we will discuss in the next chapter proliferated during the 1970s. But in recent years, the government has also begun to spend substantial sums on cleanup efforts. During the 1970s, some $27 billion ($3.4 billion in 1980) went to provide 75 percent of the cost of municipal sewage treatment plants. The federal role in sewage treatment responds to externalities among local political jurisdictions: an upstream town may not bother to purify waste that flows into other towns and other states unless it is helped or coerced to do so. It is difficult to tell which income classes benefit and how much from environmental cleanup. Presumably, everyone gains equally from reductions in disease, but the aesthetic and recreational benefits are of more interest to higher-income people and are probably distributed roughly in proportion to income.[33]

Substantial sums ($4.2 billion in 1980) are also spent on water resources, including flood control, water supply, irrigation, waterways and harbors, hydroelectric power, and recreation. The public good character of flood control, together with alleged imperfections in capital markets and the difficulty of assembling necessary parcels of land without eminent domain powers, is used to justify government involvement in activities that could otherwise be carried on for profit by private enterprise. Many of the government projects conducted by TVA and the U.S. Army Corps of Engineers have been quite successful, but some are apparently inefficient and exist largely because they can be doled out in pork barrel fashion among congressional districts.[34] Once again the benefits going to different income classes are hard to estimate. Local contractors and skilled labor gain from the construction process, and in many cases agribusinesses reap the benefits of cheap irrigation.

The U.S. government also spends some money (over $2 billion in 1980) managing public lands, which take up about one-third of the total land area of the country. And a modest sum ($1.7 billion in 1980) goes to acquisition and operation of recreational resources—parks, recreation areas, wildlife refuges. In principle, parks could be provided by the private market, with fees for entry, but the immense capital required and the externalities involved (views of the Tetons or the Grand Canyon from miles away), together with land acquisition problems, the irreversibility of development, and the likelihood of greater future than present appreciation of unspoiled wilderness, have led since the time of Theodore Roosevelt to much federal ownership of recreational land.

The benefits to individuals of federal parks and public lands are probably proportional to income since even such mass entertainments as Yosemite Park are attended more by suburbanites with camper vans than by the urban poor. The more esoteric benefits of preserving Big Horn sheep and whooping cranes involve luxury goods of chief interest to the upper-middle class. Again, this is not to say that endangered species should not be saved but only that the income-distributional consequences of doing so are somewhat pro-rich.

State and local parks may benefit the poor more than federal parks do. Scattered evidence indicates that the location and quality of parks in some communities (Prattville, Alabama; San Francisco) have favored the well-to-do whereas in other communities (Philadelphia, Detroit, San Antonio) they have been equal or pro-poor in effect.[35]

Transportation

The government has a long history of involvement in transportation policy. Early in the nineteenth century state and federal governments began to subsidize canals and roads and waterways. Later huge subsidies, in the form of millions of acres of land, were given to railroads building transcontinental lines. State and local governments have had primary responsibility for road building, but in the 1950s the federal government organized a trust fund for grants to the states paying 80 or 90 percent of the cost of interstate highways. Many billions of dollars were spent over more than twenty years to establish a nationwide highway network.

Spending on transportation remains substantial—at 3.6 percent of the federal budget—$21 billion in 1980. The largest single part of that total, more than one-third of it, goes for highway construction. About one-sixth is spent on construction of airports, air safety, and airline operating subsidies. Somewhat smaller amounts go to mass transit and railroads (both growing in recent years) and to the Coast Guard and maritime subsidies.

The public goods rationale for much federal transportation spending is not beyond challenge. Unlike small streets, interstate highways could be operated as toll roads by private enterprise, with drivers paying according to use. Government could regulate the tolls if they became too high as a result of increasing returns to scale and the natural monopoly situation. So long as trucking is not excessively subsidized, railroads, too, could presumably flourish in private markets, with perhaps some regulation of their monopoly tendencies. Competition between trucks and rails might be sufficient to eliminate even the need for regulation. Air and maritime transportation, lacking monopoly-producing roadbeds or rights-of-way, would not seem to require regulation, let alone subsidy, except perhaps in the earliest days of air travel.

On the other hand, imperfect capital markets may have required government assistance in making the large fixed investments (with slow returns) in canals and rails and perhaps highways. Here, too, the problem of land acquisition probably necessitated government use of eminent domain powers: otherwise a stubborn landowner in the path of a highway could extort an exorbitant price or refuse to sell altogether. In addition—though probably less significantly—the interstate highway program was born amidst rhetoric about providing the public good of mobility for national defense. The result, in any case, has been an engineering marvel second only to the space program that has speeded and cheapened surface transportation.

Mass transit is a more clear case of a public good. Since automobiles produce public bads of pollution and noise and congestion, which drivers generally escape paying for, cleaner and more compact buses and subways provide social benefits not reflected in the prices that riders are willing to pay. Subsidies for mass transit (or high taxes on trucks and autos) make sense. Yet very little has been spent on mass transit: practically nothing before the 1970s, and only about 15 percent of the transportation budget in 1980. In fact the large subsidies to trucks and automobiles through the federal highway program, along with various regulatory decisions, have put mass transit and railroads at a great disadvantage. In the early 1970s, when increasing oil prices made public transportation all the more desirable, the United States was left with deteriorated roadbeds and rail equipment. Most railroads faced bankruptcy or required long-term subsidy. The new Amtrak improved passenger service greatly but was expensive; by 1982 its subsidies were cut. Many urban bus and subway systems remain inadequate.

But these matters involve efficiency, not equity. Our main concern is the distributional impact of transportation spending. Obviously, automobile owners benefit more than others from the highway program, and automobile owners, especially those who take long interstate trips, tend to be found in the upper-income levels. The same is true of the air travelers who gain from subsidies to airport construction and air traffic control. In addition, highway and airport construction has undoubtedly rewarded the high-income stockholders of firms in the cement, construction, automobile, oil and gas, and tire industries. (Contractors have especially benefited in areas—Chicago comes to mind—with rigged bids, sloppy work, and frequent repairs.)

On the other hand, consumers have enjoyed lower prices for goods carried by truck or other subsidized transportation. Cheap mass transit in urban centers is clearly pro-poor; but much transit money actually goes to commuter trains and suburban bus lines that subsidize the affluent.[36] All in all, the net benefits of federal transportation spending have probably been roughly proportional to the amount an individual consumes, which in turn is roughly proportional to income.

Local streets tend to fit the definition of public goods. But they, too, probably benefit people unequally in proportion to their income. Car owners gain more than nonowners. Levy and others found that in Oakland, California, most of the road construction money went to selected arterials. Resurfacing was done mainly in upper-income areas where residents were quick to complain about potholes.[37]

Agriculture

In farm policy, public goods rationales for spending are questionable. True, farmers are at the mercy of pests and changeable weather and must endure fluctuating prices and incomes. But if the problem is just instability of income, one would expect that private loans or crop insurance could be used to average out the fat years and the lean. Or if private markets were imperfect because of moral hazard or the difficulty of forecasting (and relying upon) farmers' future production, government might get into the pure loan or insurance business. It does so to some extent through the Federal Crop Insurance Corporation.

But, of course, the U.S. government has not merely smoothed out farm incomes; it has subsidized them in one of the biggest of all income transfer programs. For many years farm incomes have been supported through schemes of "loans" (often not intended to be repaid) with crops—valued at artificially high prices—taken as security and through payments for acreage restrictions, as well as by the consequent raising of market prices and by special tax breaks.

The amount of subsidy varies greatly from year to year depending upon world supply and demand. During much of the 1950s and 1960s the United States produced enormous food surpluses, and many billions of dollars were spent in supporting prices. The worldwide food shortages of the early 1970s ushered in a period of high world demand and less surplus production so that agricultural spending declined sharply from 2.6 percent of the budget in 1970 to below 1 percent in 1980 (see Table 13)—only $2.7 billion for price supports. (The decline would have been even greater except for restrictions on exports to the Soviet Union.) But renewed bumper crops raised subsidies again to $4 billion in 1981, and more than $6 billion in 1982.

The traditional justification for supporting farm incomes holds that the nation is better off with citizens of the vigorous, self-reliant character that family farming is said to produce. Contrary to the rationale of encouraging small family farming, however, the great bulk of farm subsidies has gone to the richest farmers and the biggest agribusinesses.[38] The reason is simple: the more land and larger production a farmer has, the more he gains from a given increase in the prices received for produce. Subsidies to big farmers have been so enormous that upper limits were put on the amount of any one subsidy payment, but such limits can be evaded by division of formal ownership.

In view of the Jeffersonian rhetoric surrounding the program, it is ironic that the money spent on agriculture has tended to make large-scale farming more and more profitable and productive and to accelerate the demise of noncompetitive small farming. (Of course, in the long run, consumers may have benefited from lower prices.) There is also some irony in the fact that during most of their history the pro-rich farm subsidies have been much larger than pro-poor income transfers like Food Stamps or AFDC, discussed in Chapter 3.

Commerce and Housing

The budget category of "commerce and housing credit" covers a grab bag of programs, mostly administered by the Commerce Department or the Department of Housing and Urban Development, that take up a little over 1 percent of the federal budget. It includes federal subsidies to the Postal Service ($1.7 billion in 1980, rapidly declining to an estimated $0.6 billion in 1982), which since 1970 has supposedly been run as a business, charging mail users for postal costs. (Now that national communications are well established, it is hard to see why the Post Office cannot operate on a businesslike basis, except insofar as it provides a useful place for subsidized public service employment.)

This budget category also includes small business assistance ($950 million in 1980), the gathering of economic and demographic statistics ($800 million in 1980, and much less in noncensus years), promotion of exports and tourism, and federal insurance of deposits in banks and savings and loan associations. The precise distributional consequences of these programs are obscure, but for the most part they appear to subsidize certain business activities and high-income individuals.

Housing credit and mortgage insurance through FHA, GNMA, and FmHA were previously discussed as income transfer programs. It can be argued that they also have public goods implications since the creation of attractive and safe neighborhoods benefits people in and around them as well as the residents of particular dwellings. As we noted in Chapter 3, housing credit programs shifted from a heavily middle and upper-middle class orientation to more concern with low-income housing in the late 1960s, but default rates were extremely high, and much of the benefits went to upper-income mortgage lenders and real estate speculators. When tax expenditures are taken into account, especially deductions for mortgage interest and property taxes, housing programs give more to high-income people than the poor get from public housing and housing assistance payments.

Community and Regional Development

Another grab bag set of programs that have grown rapidly in recent years is found in the category of "community and regional development." A little over 1.5 percent of the budget ($10 billion in 1980) goes to community development block grants; area and regional development, including Indian programs, regional commissions, and local public works as well as rural and economic development loans and grants mostly to private businesses; and disaster relief and insurance. The largest single part of this, nearly half, consists of community development block grants.

The block grants are allocated by need-based formulas to pay for public land, buildings, social services, planning, and management, that is, for virtually whatever local governments are doing. Distributional effects, therefore, depend upon the nature of local programs. The use of poverty rates and housing quality in the allocation formulas ensures that some of the money goes to the poorer communities, such as distressed urban areas. Often, however, the favored targets have been places with slow *growth* but relatively high income.[39]

Revenue Sharing

"General purpose fiscal assistance," too, covers many diverse programs. It, too, has been growing rapidly to replace categorical grants to state and local governments and now takes up almost 1.5 percent of the federal budget ($8.6 billion in 1980). Most of this money ($6.8 billion) takes the form of general revenue sharing, which is parceled out to some 39,000 units of government primarily on the basis of population—but with some preference toward those with fiscal problems. Use of the money is unrestricted except to require nondiscrimination and public participation. Here, too, the distribution of benefits depends upon the nature of local programs, but the targeting on governments with fiscal problems tends somewhat to increase income equality. A nonbudgetary revenue sharing program without such equalizing implications is the exemption of municipal securities from federal tax on interest income. This saves municipalities money by helping them borrow at lower interest rates but also subsidizes the high-tax-bracket purchasers of tax-free securities.

Interest

Payments of interest on the public debt depend for their distributional effects upon how the borrowed money is spent (i.e., upon the distributional impact of the whole federal budget) and upon the incidence of the taxes that borrowing replaces, as well as the distributional effects of any inflation that the federal debt may cause. In addition, government demand for money to borrow may raise the returns upon capital generally, thus benefiting high-income individuals. The net effects are unclear. Interest expenses rose substantially in the late 1970s as a result of inflation and high interest rates and took up an increasingly large part of the total federal budget—11 percent of it ($64.5 billion) in 1980, $82 billion in 1981, and an estimated $99 billion in 1982.

As we have seen, externalities and public goods can be invoked more or less plausibly in connection with many different sorts of programs. This includes several social welfare policies that we treated in Chapter 3 as mainly involving income transfers. Public health, for example, benefits not only those who are inoculated or get help with rat extermination but also those who are spared from epidemics of infectious disease. Public education provides a kind of basic job training for the young, which private employers could not undertake efficiently on their own (those they trained might work for other, free-riding employers), and parents might not be willing to pay full tuition at the cost of reducing their own consumption. In addition, education may produce a more intelligent and better informed citizenry, which makes life pleasanter for each individual citizen. To the extent that such public goods are provided, the distributional effects of social welfare programs involve complicated additional calculations of the sort discussed in this chapter.

The Net Impact of Taxes and Spending

Several scholars have attempted to figure out how the distribution of income is affected by all the government programs we have discussed, taken together: by taxes, social welfare spending, and spending on public goods. There are many difficulties and uncertainties in the way of getting a definite answer. But their work, when examined closely, indicates that the totality of federal, state, and local taxes and spending do not much, if at all, decrease the inequality of Americans' incomes.

These estimates of government's effects are based on a series of simplifying assumptions. The first step is to calculate a "pre-government" distribution of income among income classes, that is, to calculate what proportion of all Americans' income would have been received by the bottom 10 percent of the population, by the next higher 10 percent, and so forth, in the absence of government action.

Pre-government income is estimated from actual income statistics by excluding government transfer payments and adding back in any money paid out in taxes. But the hypothetical income that people would have received in the absence of government action should also include *indirect* taxes on property and corporate income and the like insofar as they are passed on to renters or consumers or employees and thereby raise their expenses and lower their real incomes. Because of uncertainty about tax incidence, it is hard to know how much higher the income of each group would have been in the absence of indirect taxes, so this factor is usually ignored. Also, it is usually assumed that wages and salaries and other private income would have stayed the same in the absence of government taxes and spending. Yet we have seen that taxation and spending alter the returns to capital and labor. It is unrealistic to assume that space engineers would be as highly paid without a space program. Actually to calculate how much income each family would have received without government activity would be a mind-boggling task.

Once a rough estimate of the pre-government income distribution has been made, the next step is to look at the amount of money collected by each tax or spent under each government program and figure out how much of it comes from or goes to each income class. This is done by means of "distributors," based on assumptions about the effects of the program and known characteristics of each income class. One might, for example, assume that a family benefits from government spending on transportation in proportion to the number of automobiles it owns. Then the distributor for the share of transportation money going to each income class is simply the proportion of automobiles owned by that income class. Or one might assume that families benefit from education programs in proportion to the number of school-age children they have. Then the benefits for each income class would be calculated by multiplying the total amount of money spent on education by the proportion of school-age children found in each income class.

The final step is to add to the total pre-government income of each income class its estimated share of the benefits from each spending program, and to subtract its share of each tax. The result is a "post-government" distribution of income. The net effects of government action are inferred by comparing the pre- and post-government income shares going to each income class. That is, if a scholar found that the bottom fifth of all American families got only 5 percent of pre-government income but got 10 percent or 15 percent of all the income after government taxes and spending were taken into account, he might infer that government was having an egalitarian impact. Or the comparison could be made in terms of Gini coefficients or other summary characteristics of the pre- and post-distributions. If the Gini coefficient of the post-government income distribution were much lower that that of the pre-, we could infer that government was substantially equalizing incomes.

Gillespie

One of the first comprehensive efforts of this kind was carried out by W. Irwin Gillespie. Using 1960 data, Gillespie concluded that both federal spending and state and local spending were strongly pro-poor and that federal taxes were progressive, approximately balancing the regressive effect of state and local taxes. He therefore found that the total net effect of federal, state, and local taxes and spending was to increase equality. According to his calculations government action added 55 percent to the income of the lowest (under $2,000) group and subtracted 13 percent from the income of the highest (over $10,000), leaving those in the middle about even.[40]

It is important to note, however, that a large percentage increase in the income of poor people does not necessarily imply a large decline in inequality because a big percentage of a pittance is still just a pittance. If one family's $2,000 annual income went up 55 percent to $3,100, for example, and another family's $40,000 went down 13 percent to $34,800, the high-income family would still have more than ten times as much as the low-income family. The inequality would still be very great. Gillespie's own figures, therefore, do not indicate that government had any strongly equalizing effect.

Moreover, some of Gillespie's assumptions probably tended to make government activity look more pro-poor than it really was. In his "standard case," military expenditures were assumed to be distributed in proportion to family income, but we have argued that in actuality the benefits go disproportionately to the very high income owners of property. Gillespie treated Social Security and unemployment and veterans' benefits on an annual basis so that they appeared to go mainly to the lowest income citizens, but we have seen that most such benefits accrue to people whose lifetime earnings are in the middle ranges. Gillespie's handling of education expenditures assumed, contrary to fact, that low-income students attend schools that are just as good as those high-income students attend. And throughout he assumed that a dollar spent (say, on hospitalization or housing for the poor) resulted in a dollar's worth of benefits and that government spending did not increase the pre-tax earnings of the middle- or high-income providers of the goods and services—doctors, defense contractors, highway builders, and the like.

To be sure, some of Gillespie's procedures, such as his focus on the "adjusted" (post-government) income base and his contention that the property tax was wholly shifted (one-half to renters and homeowners and one-half to consumers), actually tended to make government look less pro-poor than it was. But these probably were dwarfed by errors in the opposite direction. If appropriate adjustments were made in Gillespie's figures, the net impact of government would look more nearly neutral, not changing the income distribution much at all.

Musgrave

Musgrave, Case, and Leonard updated Gillespie's analysis using 1968 data and tried out a variety of assumptions about the incidence of particular taxes and spending programs. Naturally, their results varied according to which assumptions were made. They found, for example (in harmony with the Pechman and Okner results reported in Chapter 2) that federal taxes were progressive by any reckoning but much more so if corporate income taxes fell upon capital rather than being passed on to consumers, wage earners, or renters. The effect of state and local taxes depended heavily upon the incidence of the property tax. If the property tax was borne partly by consumers and renters, state and local taxes as a whole were regressive, but if the owners of capital paid all of the property tax, state and local taxes were slightly progressive. The overall effect of all federal, state, and local taxes, therefore, may have been either substantially progressive or slightly regressive. Under a "benchmark" set of assumptions, holding that only half the corporate income tax was borne by owners of capital and that residential property taxes were passed on to renters and half of commercial property taxes were shifted to consumers, the net effect of all taxes in 1968 was very nearly proportional, a constant 33 percent of total income throughout nearly all of the income scale.[41]

Musgrave and his collaborators calculated that "allocable" expenditure programs, including transfer payments and spending on education, highways, health, and agriculture, were strongly pro-poor at both the federal and the state and local level. In fact the poorest Americans (those with incomes under $4,000) got allocable benefits worth more than 100 percent of their total income whereas those in the highest income range got only 9 percent. The effects of "general" expenditures like military spending, however, depended once again upon what assumptions were made. If general expenditures were distributed in equal amounts to each family, the effect was pro-poor; but if their benefits were proportional to income, they, of course, had no effect upon inequality. Thus the total effect of all spending was pro-poor, especially at the federal level, and all the more so if general expenditures benefited families equally.

The net effect of all taxes and spending, according to Musgrave et al., depended once again upon the assumptions chosen. Under the "benchmark" tax assumptions, which appear as plausible as any, and the assumption that general expenditures benefited people in proportion to their income, the net effect was strongly pro-poor, especially at the lowest income level. The poorest Americans received some thirteen times their private incomes in net benefits while on balance the richest gave up about 12 percent of their incomes.

It would be a mistake to think that such redistribution would have much effect upon inequality, however. Private incomes that were minuscule to start with, averaging "near zero," remained small even if they were multiplied by a factor of thirteen. Thirteen times zero is zero. And a 12 percent drop in a $100,000 income would hardly be confiscatory. Even if these estimates of redistribution were correct, post-government incomes remained very unequal.

In any case, it is likely that the Musgrave et al. calculations, like Gillespie's, overstated government benefits to the poor. Social Security payments, which made up a very large part of federal expenditures, were treated on an annual basis so that they seemed to go to the very poor; but as we have seen, Social Security beneficiaries have lifetime incomes in the middle ranges, and on a lifetime basis the program is not very redistributive. The same is true of such other transfer payments as unemployment insurance. Education expenditures were treated as equally benefiting the family of each student even though the children of the wealthy tend to have access to better schools. The benefits of all programs were equated with their costs, thus overvaluing the benefits of medical care and probably a number of other programs. No account was taken of the increased private incomes which government spending brought to the owners of capital and to doctors, electronics engineers, highway contractors, bureaucrats, and other high-income people.[42] Military spending was taken to benefit people in proportion to their incomes, ignoring the role of military and foreign policy in protecting capital (especially capital invested abroad), which is mostly owned by the very rich. It would be difficult to make precise estimates taking all these factors into account, but their effect would clearly be to reveal a much less pro-poor impact of government.

Reynolds and Smolensky

Still another effort to estimate government's impact upon the distribution of income was made by Reynolds and Smolensky, using data from 1950, 1961, and 1970. Their calculations for each separate year resembled those of Gillespie and Musgrave et al. They relied upon similar incidence assumptions and similar series of distributors to estimate "pre-" and "post-fisc" distributions of income and came to similar conclusions. In 1970, according to Reynolds and Smolensky, private factor incomes were distributed very unequally, with a Gini coefficient of 0.446. Post-government income, under "standard" incidence assumptions, was distributed substantially more equally, with a Gini ratio of 0.339. In terms of simple arithmetic, therefore, the effect of government was apparently to reduce inequality by 0.107 on the Gini measure. Taxes were found to be roughly proportional; about half the decline in inequality resulted from transfer payments and much of the rest from general expenditures.[43]

These calculations very likely overstate benefits to the poor in the same ways and for the same reasons as the earlier studies did. Indeed, they probably overstate them even more by treating half of general expenditures as providing equal dollar benefits to each household. About one-third of the apparent equalizing effect of government disappeared when Reynolds and Smolensky instead considered all the benefits of general expenditures as distributed in proportion to income. If part of military spending were allocated according to property ownership, as we have argued it should be, the effect of government would appear still less equalizing.

Reynolds and Smolensky themselves did not put much stock in the year-at-a-time calculations. In fact, they strongly questioned the whole idea of trying to estimate the distributive effects of government by comparing "pre-" and "post-fisc" income distributions. They recapitulated all the problems and uncertainties earlier mentioned by Gillespie and Musgrave et al. and pointed out some new ones. They emphasized the indeterminacy of tax incidence, especially for the property and corporate income taxes; the fallacy of valuing program benefits as equal to their costs, but the extreme difficulty of measuring actual benefits; the difficulty of sorting out government effects on pre-government private income; and, indeed, the impossibility of ascertaining what a "pre-government" distribution of income would look like, whether it is conceived of as a pay-as-you-go Lindahl equilibrium with public goods or as income in the absence of government altogether. (For that matter, how could a twentieth-century industrialized economy function, and provide private incomes, without government?) Reynolds and Smolensky concluded that it is simply "not sensible" to try to discover the redistributive impact of government at one moment in time in the conventional way.[44]

Their agnosticism is well founded. We must probably abandon hope of ever answering with precision the question of who gets what from government. It is very likely impossible to find out exactly how much income inequality emerges from the private economy and to what extent (if any) it is reduced by government action.

As Reynolds and Smolensky pointed out, however, there is somewhat less uncertainty about what the final *post-government* income distribution looks like. This does not require sorting out how government does or doesn't affect the size of "private" incomes; it simply tells us what incomes people end up with after *both* public and private factors have played their part. And there may also be less uncertainty about *changes* in post-government distributions and government effects so long as measurement errors stay about the same at different times. We can at least get some idea of whether or not government action has made incomes more equal over time.

Table 16 displays Reynolds and Smolensky's findings about trends in pre- and post-government income inequality, as measured by Gini coefficients over the years 1950, 1961, and 1970. This small table contains a lot of information. As we noted, government appears to have had an equalizing effect in each year: every post-government measure of inequality is lower than the corresponding pre-government measure. But the apparent extent of redistribution depends heavily upon incidence assumptions. Under certain rather implausible progressive assumptions (line 5), the post-government distribution of income looks much more equal than the pre-. Under the more plausible assumptions of line 3 or 4, the amount of redistribution is rather modest. If we put our faith in something like Reynolds and Smolensky's "standard" incidence assumptions—or if we suspect pro-poor biases even in them—it is apparent that a very high degree of inequality remains after government has acted.

Table 16 is most persuasive on questions of change. For all the incidence assumptions except the "progressive" set (which unrealistically presumes that general expenditures benefit all households in equal dollar amounts and that part of the Social Security tax comes out of corporate dividends), post-government income stayed just as unequal—or got more unequal—over the twenty-year period. And under any of the incidence

TABLE 16 *Estimates of Income Inequality Before and After Government
Taxes and Spending, 1950–1970*

		Gini Coefficient of Inequality	
Distribution	*1950*	*1961*	*1970*
Pre-government			
1. Private factor income	0.436	0.436	0.446
Post-government			
2. Income after taxes and spending (standard incidence assumptions)	0.363	0.342	0.339
3. (Standard assumptions except general expenditures by income)	0.384	0.378	0.375
4. (Regressive assumptions)	0.394	0.388	0.384
5. (Progressive assumptions)	0.328	0.289	0.284

SOURCE: Morgan Reynolds and Eugene Smolensky, *Public Expenditures,
Taxes, and the Distribution of Income: the United States, 1950, 1961, 1970* (New York:
Academic Press, 1977), p. 67.

assumptions one cares to choose, the post-government distribution remained just as unequal in 1970 as it was in 1961. That
is, in the course of a decade that brought the War on Poverty and
a huge expansion of social welfare expenditures, there was no
increase at all in income equality.

The Reynolds and Smolensky data suggest that between
1961 and 1970 government had to run fast simply to stand still.
Private incomes apparently became more unequal, and pro-
poor government spending merely increased enough to make
up for the loss. At worst, the situation may be somewhat bleaker
than that: government activity may have partly caused the increase in private inequality if growth in unemployment insurance encouraged layoffs, welfare discouraged work, and Social
Security led to early retirement. (As we have seen in Chapter 3,
however, these effects were probably small.) More likely, government just held the line against an increasingly unequal private sector.[45]

It is not easy to summarize the complicated economic research reviewed in this and the previous chapters. But we can
reemphasize three points: (1) under plausible incidence as-

sumptions, the incomes of Americans remain quite unequal even after all government action is taken into account; (2) under the same assumptions (though with less certainty), post-government income in any one year looks only moderately more equal than pre-government; and (3) over time, greatly increased government activity has not led to more income equality. There is little indication that the U.S. government has done much net redistributing of income.

Cross-National Comparisons

All the difficulties that hamper U.S. studies of government effects upon income distribution apply to studies within other countries as well and warrant similar skepticism about the feasibility of assessing the impact of government. This is all the more true of efforts to compare one country with another when differing income concepts and data measurements and differing definitions of the public and the private defy comparability. (The elusive valuation of in-kind medical benefits is crucial, for example, when comparing countries that have socialized medicine with the largely private-medicine United States. And private U.S. pension systems must be factored in to any comparison with European countries that have larger Social Security systems.)[46]

Still, enough is known that we can be fairly sure that the post-governmental income distribution is substantially more equal in Great Britain and Sweden (with post-fisc Gini coefficients of 0.318 and 0.302 in 1972) than in the United States (0.403 by a fairly comparable measure in 1970). The same is almost certainly true of other Scandinavian countries (Norway, Denmark) and of the Low Countries (Netherlands, Belgium); it is probably true of Germany and Japan and possibly of other OECD countries as well. On the other hand, Canada looks about the same as the United States, and some other countries are more unequal.[47] In short, when all government taxing and spending and other action is taken into account, the United States is probably not the least egalitarian of Western industrialized countries, but it is very likely on the low end of the scale.

When it comes to socialist or communist nations, the difficulties of comparison are even more awesome because of the general lack of market price valuations for goods that are publicly provided. Yet there certainly is reason to believe that post-government incomes are substantially more equal in China, Cuba, the Soviet Union, and most of Eastern Europe than they are in the United States.[48]

Whether post-government incomes in communist countries are also more equal than those of the most egalitarian European social democracies and, if so, by how much; whether any of these countries approaches the full egalitarian possibilities of socialism; and what, if any, policy implications all this has for the United States: these are harder questions that we cannot hope to resolve but will touch upon further in later chapters.

The Politics of Public Goods

The policies we have lumped together under the rubric of public goods tend to share certain political characteristics. Compared with social welfare policies, they usually have lower public visibility, fewer conflicts along party lines, and more unchallenged domination by interest groups. There is also more room for technical expertise, deliberation, and executive leadership.

Weak Party Differences

The lack of party differences over public goods is especially conspicuous. By contrast, on social welfare policy and labor-management relations and civil rights, Republicans and Democrats have had some serious policy disagreements. The alternation of parties in power has brought zigzags in policy, from the expansive social welfare schemes of the Democrats to more restrictive policies (or at least a slowing of growth) under the Republicans. When it comes to military and foreign policy, however, or transportation, science, energy, or even the environment, party differences have been muted. There has been more bipartisanship, more apparent agreement on the national good, more policy continuity from one party regime to the next. In matters of public goods the parties act more like Downsian vote seekers, moving toward the center of public opinion (or at least toward similar positions), and less like "responsible parties" with distinct ideological attachments of their own.[49]

This contrast has much to do with the economic and social make-up of the party coalitions. The New Deal realignment brought together working people, organized labor, and religious and ethnic minorities like blacks, Jews, and Catholics under the banner of the Democrats while the Republicans mostly relied upon industry and finance, higher-income people, and white Anglo-Saxon Protestants. These party groups tended to agree among themselves and differ with the other party over social welfare policy, but they have been much less unified and less distinctive on most matters of public goods. On social welfare policy, leaders of the two parties have divergent policy preferences of their own and are also driven apart by the need to please their money givers, doorbell ringers, and other activists; but on most public goods issues they are free to move closer together, each trying to appeal to the median voter or to the same interest groups.

This has not always been so; it is just true of the current party alignment based (weakly) on class and ethnicity. In the nineteenth century the parties did differ over certain issues with public goods features, including economic nationalism as opposed to states' rights, slavery, the tariff, agriculture versus industry, and immigration. In fact the earlier party systems were organized around geographically based positions on these issues: northeastern commerce and manufacturing, southern slave-holding and cotton growing, western agrarianism. But in recent years, with a few exceptions, public goods issues have not touched regional interests or identifiable class or ethnic groups in seriously divisive ways, so that there has been no basis for organizing party structures around them. Information costs and transaction costs (the difficulty of getting together) make it hard to form enduring party alliances over an issue unless the alliances can draw upon existing social or geographical cleavages relevant to that issue.

The relative lack of party differences on public goods issues, in turn, tends to reduce public involvement in such issues. Without partisan debate, less information about the policies is available, and people are less aware of what the government is doing or what would be in their interest. Low-income citizens in particular tend to have less influence. Without a party to alert and mobilize them they tend not to form clear opinions or to participate much in politics. In Schattschneider's phrase, the "scope of the conflict" becomes narrow, with the participants overrepresenting wealthy individuals and interest groups.[50]

Interest Groups

Interest group activity tends to take a particular form. Curiously, many public goods, which are supposed to be indivisible, are provided in quite divisible fashion and parceled out in what Lowi calls a "distributive" manner among congressional districts. Local contractors and other interests seek concentrated private benefits from providing these public goods while the general public tends to be unaware of their diffuse costs. Hence, vote-seeking (and money-seeking) congressmen want pork barrel projects of post offices, military bases, dams, and the like for their districts, and bureaucrats happily allocate programs to expand congressional support.[51]

On a more national basis, too, relatively monolithic interest groups tend to dominate the policy-making process. Public goods (unlike, say, social welfare policy) do not usually divide business from labor or one economic sector from another. Practically all organized interests who care about the subject favor military spending, highway building, and space exploration. Thus such goods tend to be overprovided and to be provided in ways that are inefficient and excessively favorable to high-income people.

Another feature of public goods politics is an important role for executive leadership. Particularly in foreign affairs that do not immediately and directly affect domestic interests, Congress has generally deferred to the president. Policy is made largely within the executive branch. In addition, many public goods policies involve considerable expertise and analysis. Often goals are broadly agreed upon, but to attain them requires answering difficult technical questions about the measurement of costs and benefits (since the market mechanism doesn't provide useful price information about public goods) or the merits of alternative technologies or the likely impact of different strategies. Economists, natural scientists, and strategic analysts all play a part. There is room for extensive deliberation.

Variations by Policy Area

The characteristic features of public goods politics are more pronounced in some policy areas, and at some times, than in others. Military and foreign policy, for example, since World War II have offered a preeminent example of bipartisanship. Both parties have supported strong armed forces, resistance to communist or socialist regimes abroad, protection of American markets and investments, and the like. (If anything, the Democrats, on balance, have been slightly more aggressive.) Only in a few cases, such as the last years of the Vietnam War, when Democratic dovism emerged, have the parties disagreed substantially about tactics.

Similarly, foreign affairs have been marked by particular deference to presidential leadership, at least when things are going reasonably well. Only in the case of a catastrophe like the Vietnam War, with its domestic impact through battlefield deaths and taxes and inflation, did Congress and even the general public become actively involved, and congressional restrictions on the executive persisted through the early 1970s. (Matters involving Middle Eastern oil and close-to-home Central America may have a similar potential.)

Military spending has been a subject of especially strong lobbying activity by interest groups. The congressional armed services committees have served as dispensers of real estate, doling out military bases to favored districts. Defense contractors have used all the familiar lobbying techniques, including free entertainment to cultivate close personal relations, lavish campaign contributions, help with speeches and bills and research, employment of ex-generals and ex-congressmen, and publicizing the danger of "falling behind" the Soviets and the virtues of new weapons systems. It is quite possible that the military-industrial complex thereby succeeds in selling the United States far more arms than are needed.[52]

American public opinion may also have been manipulated on military issues. The post-Vietnam antagonism to arms spending gradually dissipated and then turned to support for spending increases during a decade of alarmist statements about growing Soviet power in official testimony and leaks and comments by organizations like the Committee on the Present Danger.

In 1981 the Department of Defense published a glossy, colorful booklet of facts and photos on Soviet armaments, neglecting to mention any of their weaknesses, or to point out the stable (not growing) production of most systems, or to offer serious comparisons with U.S. weaponry. President Reagan spoke of a "three-to-one or even six-to-one" Soviet nuclear advantage in Europe, apparently not counting British and French forces or U.S. submarines offshore. In 1982, resisting proposals for a nuclear freeze, Reagan alleged a Soviet "definite margin of superiority," a "great edge," which would have to be overcome before any arms halt—neglecting the clear U.S. advantage in number of deliverable warheads and in missile accuracy (though not in number of launchers or payloads) and ignoring the question whether indeed nuclear "superiority" had any meaning or relevance in an era of mutually assured destruction.[53]

On the other hand, more fundamental explanations of U.S. foreign policy may involve the structure of the economic system and/or the dynamics of international relations. Given a capitalist economy, it may be in the interest of workers as well as capitalists to promote investments abroad and encourage trade.[54] To go a step further, fostering friendly governments elsewhere has been the policy of practically all big nations, including socialist ones. Much of military spending is probably dictated by the structural fact of nation-state anarchy. That is, when other countries are free to arm and conduct military adventures as they wish, no one country can afford to disarm on its own. It is a prisoner's dilemma situation, in which all would be better off with internationally enforced disarmament, but none has an individual incentive to disarm on its own, and cooperation is difficult.[55]

The failure of the United States to redistribute its wealth on an international basis is easily accounted for by an interest-group type of analysis. Foreign aid is an orphan program, without any substantial domestic constituency except those who want to sell their goods abroad. Only a few idealists care about world inequality. The foreign poor have no vote in Congress. It is a simple matter of selfishness that few Americans are willing to lower their living standard in order to help the needy of the world so long as we think, perhaps mistakenly, that our island of affluence can safely ignore the unrest of the impoverished.

Whether because of racism or elitism or simply matters of cultural proximity, white middle-class Americans also tend to worry less about poverty—or even death—among brown and black people in the Third World than they do about Europeans. As Arthur Hoppe has noted, we suffer more for a jailed Pole than for a thousand butchered Kampucheans; we are more outraged by the killing of four Dutch journalists than of thousands of peasants in El Salvador.[56]

The space program, which takes up the bulk of U.S. spending on science and technology, seems to have responded to military pressures and the dynamics of international competition, with, no doubt, some extra impetus from the manufacturers of space hardware. Certainly the program has flourished through periods in which the general public was unenthusiastic and favored cuts in spending. On the other hand, pure scientific research, lacking any powerful interest group constituency, is very likely underprovided by the political system.

Energy policy appears to have been strongly influenced by interest group activity. The many years of very favorable tax treatment of oil companies, with depletion allowances, foreign tax credits, and deduction of exploration outlays as current costs rather than investments, may well have reflected corporate influence upon the tax committees of Congress. Even the partial abandonment of the percentage depletion allowance represented a largely symbolic concession.[57] There is also some room for structural explanations of these and other energy policies. High profits and investment incentives may be necessary to get private enterprise to develop energy resources, and, as we have noted, only government can cope with OPEC or fund certain kinds of basic energy research.

Energy politics changed after 1973, at least for a time. When the OPEC price rises hit U.S. consumers of gasoline and heating oil, energy policy became much more visible and more a matter of public concern, taking on some of the features of high-visibility social welfare policy rather than the usual low salience of public goods. It can be argued that so long as private companies and their stockholders own the U.S. energy supplies, only high prices and profits can persuade them to produce and sell energy. Similarly, perhaps only high prices can efficiently enforce conservation. But the windfall profits brought by higher prices were so huge, and the gains to some of the richest Americans so obvious, that redistributive aspects of energy policy became an explicit issue. Conflicts over price controls and rationing and profits taxes reached the general public. Some partisan differences appeared, with Republicans mostly content to let the profits stay where they fell while Democrats sought ways to keep prices to consumers down or to tax away profits and return them to the citizenry.

By 1981, however, a perceived "oil glut" had defused the energy issue and restored interest group politics as usual. The windfall profits tax was largely repealed. As Office of Management and Budget Director David Stockman remarked: "The hogs were really feeding."[58]

The environment, like energy, moved much more into public view in the 1970s. Traditionally, dams and other public works had been of interest chiefly to local contractors and labor unions and the Army Corps of Engineers and had been quietly doled out to favored congressional districts in pork barrel fashion. The coal companies devastated Appalachia with little protest. National forests and public lands were turned over to lumber companies, mines, and cattlemen for exploitation.[59] Industries freely polluted air and water. Low-visibility interest group politics predominated over public goods concerns for a clean, healthful, and attractive environment.

Beginning at the end of the 1960s, the environmental movement began to win public attention. "Public interest" groups like the Sierra Club helped counterbalance business lobbying, and a considerable amount of restrictive legislation was passed.[60] It is noteworthy, however, that many environmental regulations were postponed or diluted, especially when they conflicted with energy production, and that much environmental spending subsidized private business, as when sewage treatment plants were built to handle industrial waste. The environmental movement itself has an upper-middle-class cast. It is plausible to argue that even at its height, environmental policy was still much influenced by interest groups overrepresenting the wealthy; and that was certainly true of the rollbacks of the late 1970s and early 1980s.

Transportation policy in the United States, since the 1950s, has clearly been influenced by organized interests. The automobile and gasoline companies, concrete and steel manufacturers, construction workers, and contractors succeeded in establishing the huge interstate highway program, paid for through a virtually autonomous trust fund.[61] But the genuinely public goods concerns of avoiding air pollution and noise and congestion were neglected because no organized groups championed them. Indeed, the promotion of automobile as opposed to rail travel actually helped produce public bads. Even after the "urban crisis" was recognized, mass transit—with its pro-poor implications as well as its efficiency as a public good—lacked the organized backing to pry much money loose from the highway fund.

Agriculture, again, shows signs of interest group influence. The public knows and cares little about price supports and is probably unaware of how supports and acreage restrictions and marketing orders cost consumers higher prices. But rich farmers care, and the rich farmers are organized. In fact, much of agricultural policy involves self-government through local committees dominated by the wealthiest and most successful farmers, especially members of the American Farm Bureau Federation.[62]

Chapter 3 indicated that social welfare policies are not free from interest group influence. Realtors and mortgage lenders shaped some housing programs. Doctors came to dominate the payment systems of Medicare and Medicaid. Teachers and social workers have had much to say about education and public aid programs. But on issues falling more nearly into the public goods category, visibility to the public tends to be lower and interest group influence even higher.

In passing, I have noted some ways in which public goods programs tend to be inefficient (e.g., in providing too much defense and not enough mass transit or scientific research or clean air) and have suggested some political explanations. But our main focus is on equity. The chief point is that the provision of public goods in the United States undermines any redistribution of income from rich to poor in two ways. First, public goods, which are not generally pro-poor, take up a very large part of the budget. Insofar as people want to limit the total size of the budget, each dollar spent on public goods takes a dollar away from what could be spent on more redistributive transfer programs. (Granted, this is an odd way to view the budget since pure transfer payments would involve no real costs—only a reshuffling of incomes—but most people do view budgets this way and impose a trade-off between public goods and transfers.) Second, public goods are actually provided in particular ways that are more pro-rich than necessary. Again and again, the money goes in large part to technicians' salaries and corporate profits and matters of special upper-income concern rather than to the citizenry as a whole.

Structure Versus Group Struggle

We have suggested two types of political explanation for these facts, one based on interest group power, the other on the structure of the economy and the international system. Interest group analysis argues, for example, that spending on the military and space and highways is so great because interest groups bring it about. It also points to group influence as the reason the spending takes its particular pro-rich form. The wealthy and well-organized channel the benefits to themselves.

Common sense observation of politics practically compels one to accept such interest group explanations, at least in part. There are many cases in which groups that are active in politics subsequently benefit from policy. It is the most natural thing in the world to infer that the groups bring the benefits about. Furthermore, some persuasive theories of collective action, like Olson's, indicate that just such group influence should be expected.[63]

At the same time, however, the attribution of causality is always open to question. The pattern of group benefits following group activity is usually consistent with alternative processes: epiphenomenal (unnecessary) action, information providing, or even extortion by politicians. No experimental evidence of interest-group influence is available. There is always doubt. We have said "seems" or "appears" more often than we would like. And even on the reasonable premise that some interest group influence occurs, it is hard to say exactly how much.

A structural explanation of the large magnitude of public goods would emphasize that in any capitalist economy (perhaps in any market system) it is a functional imperative that government provide goods that the market fails to provide efficiently. Otherwise everyone loses. And the more advanced and industrialized the economy, the more externalities there are likely to be—the more smoke and garbage and noise and congestion; the more people and things to defend from attack, and the fancier technology for doing so; the more sophisticated scientific research; the more interdependence in every sphere of life—hence the more spending needed on public goods (and, if people believe in limited budgets, the more money diverted from possible redistribution).

Similarly, the structure of the capitalist economy may partly account for the particularly pro-rich form that public goods spending takes. In such an economy, if government ownership and entrepreneurship are rejected, private incentives must be offered in order to get people to work and save and invest, just as with private goods. Aerospace corporations want profits and space engineers want high salaries if they are going to produce rockets. So long as public goods are provided by private enterprise, they will probably reinforce economic inequality.

Still another sort of structural influence results from competition among political jurisdictions. States, and especially cities and other localities, must specialize in public-goods-type spending to the virtual exclusion of redistribution and must tax and spend in particularly pro-producer ways in order to attract the industry and the high-income residents needed for revenue. A city that really tried to redistribute income from high-income citizens to low would probably suffer a massive out-migration of the wealthy and immigration of the poor—defeating the policy.[64]

Finally, we have suggested that the structure of the international system, with its anarchistic competition among self-interested nations, has much to do with determining high levels of military spending. Nations that don't arm don't always survive.

In order to test structural explanations or to distinguish among them (to tell, e.g., whether it is only a capitalist economy, or any market economy, or any economy relying upon material incentives, that imposes particular structural constraints upon policy), it is necessary to compare political systems. This is particularly difficult in the case of international relations since we have only one world to observe. Nor is it easy for national economies. Many important kinds of alternative systems—for example, market socialism, or communism without material incentives—do not exist in pure form to be compared. Insofar as systems do differ, comparison is hindered by the way differences cluster together. Socialist countries lack corporate interest groups, and it is hard to tell to what extent contrasts with capitalist countries result from differences in economic systems and to what extent from differences in interest group configurations.

We are left, then, with some persuasive arguments indicating that interest groups and also a variety of structural considerations play a part in the antiegalitarian character of public goods in the United States. We cannot be sure which type of explanation is more important, and we cannot definitively demonstrate the impact of either. But, in any case, the whole range of U.S. taxing and spending policies does not achieve a high degree of equality in the post-government income distribution, and the public goods spending component is not helpful.

5

Law and Regulation

Taxes and spending are not the only policies that affect income distribution. Government also influences how much money people get and what prices they have to pay for goods and services through a multitude of laws and regulations. Professional licensing, rate setting, quality and safety standards, antitrust measures, minimum wage provisions, macroeconomic policy, the law of property and contracts, even constitutional provisions: all play a part in determining the distribution of "private" money income, which, as we have seen, is very unequal. They also affect nonmonetary income, from such public goods as safety and air quality. And by altering the market prices of other goods and services, they affect what people can buy with their money and thereby change the distribution of real net incomes.

The impact of these measures is even harder to assess than that of public goods spending. But on balance government laws and regulations have probably contributed to, or at least not reduced, income inequality. In this chapter we first discuss regulations dealing with the price or quality of goods, then macroeconomic policy, and, finally, the legal and constitutional framework of the U.S. economy.

Regulation of Price and Quality

In theory, economic regulation is mostly aimed at dealing with problems of public goods. The same sorts of arguments about externalities, natural monopolies, lack of information, and market imperfections that come up in connection with spending programs are also invoked on behalf of regulation. Regulation, in fact, can be viewed as simply another tool for providing public goods, a tool with particular advantages and disadvantages, such as the politically relevant fact that most of its costs do not appear in government budgets.

The public goods arguments for regulation are often compelling. Laissez faire, or unhampered free enterprise, would produce some inefficient outcomes. Yet the results of regulations, in some cases, have turned out to benefit the regulated rather than the general public and actually to create inefficiencies.

Occupational licensing, for example, is touted as protecting consumers against charlatans who might do irreparable harm before they were found out. Most states and localities require licenses for doctors, lawyers, druggists, opticians, architects, realtors, contractors, plumbers, and electricians; and indeed, for barbers, morticians, and taxicab drivers. Even if such licensing restrictions succeed in raising the quality of service provided, however, it is inefficient to forbid work of lower quality (hence lower price) which some consumers might want. Lack of reliable information about quality is presumably the central problem. If so, why not provide the information directly (perhaps by requiring prominent display of credentials or test scores) rather than interfere with supply?

In any case, closer scrutiny gives reason to doubt that quality control is really all that is at stake. Much licensing is based on criteria irrelevant to skills, and some licensed occupations pose little if any hidden or irreparable hazard to the public: hair grows back from a sloppy haircut, and bad eyeglasses can be replaced.

The chief effect of licensing, in fact, may be to restrict the supply of services and thereby to force consumers to pay more for those available, that is, to raise the incomes of the licensed. There is evidence that the practitioners of professions do much better with licensing than without.[1] And many (though certainly not all) practitioners of the licensed professions already enjoy very high fees and salaries so that increases in their incomes increase inequality.

One of the most conspicuous cases is that of doctors, who are licensed for practice by their American Medical Association brethren and who (since the 1910 Flexner report) graduate from only a few accredited medical schools and are forced to serve long internships before competing for fees. With entry to the profession so tightly controlled, the financial rewards are correspondingly enhanced.[2] In recent years, the use of paraprofessionals and foreign-trained physicians has somewhat loosened the supply but barely enough to keep pace with the bonanza of increased demand that government induced with Medicare and Medicaid. American doctors, often vehement opponents of socialism or government "interference," have done very well by government.

Lawyers have not emulated doctors' restrictions on training—a law degree of one sort or another can be obtained fairly easily—but American Bar Association-administered state bar examinations restrict the supply of attorneys actually allowed to practice and thereby bolster lawyers' incomes. Competition from realtors and others is vigorously suppressed. Architects, too, strictly control entry into their profession through apprenticeship requirements and examinations.

While the extra income that licensing brings to barbers, beauticians, and taxi drivers (all in the lower-middle-income range) does not much affect the shape of income distribution, the benefits for doctors, lawyers, architects, and other high-income professionals clearly make the distribution more unequal.

Bans or limits on advertising (e.g., for drugs and eyeglasses or by doctors or lawyers) have been reduced in recent years, but in the past they substantially curtailed competition and raised prices and income. Curiously, such regulation, in the name of "professionalism," directly contradicts the market imperfection arguments for regulation, which urge that more information be provided to consumers, not less.

Quality standards often tend to cause inefficiency. Local building codes, for example, frequently require excessive labor or costly materials not needed for any practical purpose except to raise the income of construction workers, contractors, and suppliers. Of course, the purchaser of a home could be at a severe disadvantage in trying to find out what is inside the walls without some kind of help from government regulation or information provision. Again, the problem is with the form regulation takes, not the principle of regulation.

State and local governments engage in some direct regulation of prices, particularly for telephone service and electricity. Here, too, the argument for regulation seems strong: that parts of these industries are natural monopolies. With increasing returns to scale, a firm that once sets up a network of local phone or gas or electric lines can sell service to additional nearby customers for very little, drive out competition, and then charge monopoly prices unless government steps in to protect the consumer. But it is not clear that the consumer has in fact been protected. The firms do not make it easy for regulators to learn their true costs; technical difficulties stand in the way of setting rates that would encourage efficient use of resources (marginal cost pricing would not cover total costs); and the "public utilities" often get state and local government approval for private monopoly profits. It may be that here, as in some other areas of regulation, there exists no ideal solution that is economically and politically feasible. The question may be which is worse: inefficient regulation or unhampered monopoly.[3]

Federal Regulatory Agencies

Over the years the federal government too has come to regulate a variety of economic activities. The Interstate Commerce Commission (ICC) was established in 1887 and given power over railroad rates. The Federal Trade Commission (FTC), overseeing general trade practices, and the Federal Reserve Board (FRB), regulating bank assets, were set up in 1914. Many new agencies were established during the New Deal of the 1930s, including the Civil Aeronautics Board (CAB), Federal Communications Commission (FCC, absorbing the Federal Radio Commission of 1927), the National Labor Relations Board (NLRB), Securities and Exchange Commission (SEC), and the Federal Power Commission (FPC). Others were added later: the Atomic Energy Commission (AEC, subsequently transformed into the Nuclear Regulatory Commission [NRC]), the Consumer Product Safety Commission (CPSC), the Environmental Protection Agency (EPA), and the Occupational Safety and Health Administration (OSHA). Much regulating is done by agencies within regular executive branch departments, such as the Antitrust Division of the Justice Department and the Food and Drug Administration.

Several of the old-line regulatory commissions, although created amidst populist rhetoric and concern about the public interest, have brought inefficiency and have favored those supposedly regulated. The oldest of them, the ICC, provides a classic example. Much of the agitation for the regulation of railroads came from Western farmers—trapped by the railroads' monopoly over transportation of their grain to Eastern markets—who sometimes had to pay more for short hauls than long and who could not get the rebates that were extracted by big shippers. (As it happens, early pressures for federal regulation also came from New York shippers and from Pennsylvania oil interests outraged at the rebates given to Standard Oil.) In 1887, with practically universal political support, the ICC was set up and given a mandate to end rate discrimination among customers or between long and short hauls.

Scholars agree, however, that the ICC became a protector of the railroads. The only question is when this happened. Bernstein argues that the ICC passed through a regulatory "life cycle," with a vigorous idealistic youth fading to a cynical, interest group-dominated maturity. Kolko, on the other hand, has shown that some railroads favored federal regulation from the beginning in order to avoid worse restrictions by the Grange-dominated states and to get legal sanctions to replace the private cartels and pooling agreements that were trying to set high rates but had kept degenerating into rate wars and instability. The ICC did take some pro-railroad actions right at the start (referring shippers to private conciliation, for example, and acting on very few formal rate protests). But in any case there was increasingly pro-industry behavior over time, culminating in the Transportation Act of 1920, which granted railroads an exemption from the Clayton Antitrust Act, legalized pooling agreements, guaranteed a "fair" profit, limited entry into the railroad business, and mandated federal enforcement of rates set (presumably at monopoly levels) by agreement among the railroads themselves.[4]

Recent econometric work by MacAvoy and others has confirmed that competition was fierce in the 1870s and 1880s, with repeated failures of cartel rate agreements. Chicago Board of Trade quotes on the cost of shipping grain East were generally much lower than the railroad cartel's officially posted rates because of "secret" rebates, and the low effective rates are further evidenced by the small differences between the Chicago and the Eastern prices of grain. According to MacAvoy, the ICC, while cutting some short-haul rates, immediately benefited the railroads by increasing long-haul rates (at least until the Supreme Court undercut its powers in 1897 and 1898), thereby, in effect, enforcing the cartel's monopoly pricing and increasing railroad profits. Similarly, Spann and Erickson call ICC regulation a "fiasco" from the start. They offer the rough estimate that for the crucial Chicago-East Coast trunkline area in 1890 the ICC brought savings of $8.7 to $17.4 million for short hauls, but that these were far outweighed by losses from excessive long-haul rates in the $13 to $36.5 million range, for a net loss to shippers and consumers of $4 million to $19 million in a single year—at a time when a dollar was a dollar. (On the other hand, Zerbe points out some apparent errors in Spann and Erickson and estimates a net *gain* from regulation of about $9 million.)[5]

By 1920, if not before, the ICC was very effectively protecting railroads against their consumers. During the 1920s and 1930s the growth of unregulated automobiles and trucks gradually undercut railroads' monopoly position, but the Motor Carrier Act of 1935 opened the way for the ICC to limit that threat by regulating trucking as well. After 1935, the ICC effectively dampened competition both within and between transportation modes (including waterways and pipelines as well as railroads, buses, and trucking) to the disadvantage of travelers and shippers and consumers.

One of the earliest Ralph Nader exposés, directed by Robert Fellmeth, describes in disturbing detail how the ICC regulated transportation during the 1950s and 1960s. At that time trucking regulation involved a crazy quilt of highly restrictive operating certificates, permitting particular truckers (often only one or two of them) to carry particular goods between two particular points by a particular route. Rapid Freight, for example, might be authorized to carry peaches, but not pears, to and from Tempe, Arizona, and San Jose, California—but no points in between—by specific highways. Operation without a certificate was illegal. Certificates were granted sparingly—only upon a showing of public "need," for which lack of adequate existing service had to be demonstrated and excessive existing prices were *not* considered. The result was a patchwork of miniature monopolies, which extracted high prices from shippers by means of routine ICC approval of tariffs drawn up by cartel "rate bureaus." In theory a trucker who had operating authority could independently post a lower, competitive rate; but the rate bureaus automatically protested any such reduction to the ICC as upsetting rate stability and promoting cutthroat competition, and the ICC upheld a high proportion of the protests. The threat of protests and delays and high legal costs was sufficient to deter rate cutting and let the rate bureaus, in effect, set government-enforced monopoly prices.[6]

While it was cutting down competition within modes of transportation, the ICC also restricted competition between modes. On long hauls (perhaps anything over 200 miles), railroad transportation is thought to be inherently cheaper than trucking, even despite government subsidies to the interstate highway system. But the ICC set long-haul freight rates for trains so high that trucks got a lot of inefficient long-haul business. Moreover, it set rates especially high for high-value goods, which tend to have inelastic demand for transportation (i.e., nearly as much of them will be shipped at high prices as at low) so that high profits can be extracted without loss of business. At the same time it forbade abandonment of useless rail lines and ruled out abandonment of—or higher prices for—unprofitable passenger service, which the railroads then allowed to deteriorate in quality. Indeed, the ICC seemed to set prices as high as traffic would bear wherever modes didn't compete, and as high as the higher-cost mode where they did. The consequences included more transportation than the nation needed and many inefficient runs with near-empty trucks or train cars. Free competition would clearly have been preferable.

The Civil Aeronautics Bureau (CAB) provides a similar example. Founded with the aim of subsidizing an infant industry, it erected formidable barriers to entry (it did not authorize a single new trunkline carrier between 1938 and 1978) and set rates high. This pattern continued long after the infant industry reached middle age. While unregulated intrastate carriers in California and Texas flew passengers at cut-rate prices, the CAB enforced tariffs set by the industry cartel. In 1969, for example, according to Douglas and Miller's estimate, total fares were between $336 million and $538 million higher than free market competition would have dictated.[7]

The Federal Communications Commission (FCC) may offer the clearest case of all in which regulation benefited the regulated. In 1927, amidst widespread concern over chaotic interference among broadcasters on the same frequencies, the Federal Radio Commission was given power to license exclusive use of radio frequencies. From the beginning, however, it was mandated to give away, rather than sell, these valuable rights—even though (as Coase and others have argued) it would be more efficient for the FCC to auction off frequencies, letting the market efficiently allocate spectrum uses and recapturing the value of broadcasting rights for the public. The result has been windfall profits for broadcasters. In addition, the FCC for a long time protected existing broadcasters by restricting the use of cable or subscription television, satellite communications, and regional networks, thus reducing the amount and diversity of available programming.[8]

Similarly, since the Banking Act of 1935 the Federal Reserve, the Comptroller of the Currency, and especially the Federal Deposit Insurance Corporation have severely limited the number of new banks chartered or insured—and hence, presumably, have inflated the profits of existing banks. Peltzman estimates that without regulation the number of new banks established between 1936 and 1965 (2,272 of them) would have at least doubled.[9]

Other agencies apparently benefiting the regulated include the old Oil Import Administration in the Department of Interior, which for many years (oddly invoking a national security rationale to "develop," i.e., use up, domestic oil before foreign) set restrictive import quotas that raised oil prices and pleased the domestic petroleum industry; and several agencies in the Department of Agriculture like the Agricultural Stabilization and Conservation Service (responsive, to be sure, to the secretary and the White House), which set marketing quotas and acreage controls that kept farm prices high.[10]

During most of American history, protective tariffs and quotas have been imposed upon a variety of imports, often in a very restrictive fashion, sometimes by act of Congress, and sometimes by executive agreement or treaty or ruling of the Tariff Commission. Among recent targets for exclusion have been Argentinian beef, Italian shoes, and Japanese steel and automobiles. The effects are a shoring up of particular domestic industries (often inefficient ones) with complicated impacts upon profits, wages, and jobs and higher prices for consumers.

The regulatory picture is not always so simple, however. The Federal Power Commission (FPC) has had a history of some pro-industry actions, including allowing high rates of return (above the marginal cost of capital) for power transmission; yet the chief complaint against the FPC has been that for many years it set the price of natural gas *too low*, inducing overconsumption and shortages. Similarly, the Atomic Energy Commission (AEC, now NRC) neglected safety and environmental concerns, permitting careless disposal of nuclear waste and excessive exposure to radiation and suppressing information about some of its lapses; but its promotion of commercial nuclear energy has also been criticized as half-hearted and misguided (fixated on selling the light water reactor) rather than pro-industry.[11]

Indeed, certain relatively old-line agencies have long had distinctly pro-consumer or pro-worker orientations. The Wagner Act of 1935, which established the National Labor Relations Board (NLRB), reversed more than half a century of government repression of labor unions through court injunctions, criminal prosecutions, and the use of police and militia to break strikes. It set forth a national policy in favor of collective bargaining, which the NLRB has enforced with fairly specific and well-reasoned guidelines for union and industry behavior. This favoring of unionization has undoubtedly raised the incomes of most American workers (at the cost of some featherbedding and inefficiency) and has probably thereby increased income equality, although some marginal, nonunionized workers at the bottom of the income scale have been left out.

The Securities and Exchange Commission (SEC)—aside from some deviations such as its long-time sanction of high fixed brokerage commission rates—has policed the stock exchanges and helped investors by making much more information available about securities trades and corporate finances. If the prices of stock exchange seats can be trusted as an indicator, the SEC has been no boon to brokerage houses: the price of seats fell 50 percent in one month in 1934 when the SEC legislation was first considered, and that loss appears never to have been recouped.[12]

Similarly, the Food and Drug Administration (FDA) in the Department of Health and Human Services, while not exactly a regulatory tiger most of its life, has set requirements of truth in labeling and (since 1938) has kept new drugs off the market until there is reasonable evidence of their safety. The 1962 requirement of drug *effectiveness* was not very seriously enforced at first but was later applied with a vengeance. The Federal Trade Commission (FTC), also less than a firebreather during most of its existence, has nonetheless restricted a number of deceptive trade practices and has occasionally taken up its antitrust responsibilities. The SEC, FDA, and FTC share a focus on crucial informational problems faced by the unaided consumer and therefore have a particularly strong public goods justification.[13]

Since the passage of the Sherman Antitrust Act in 1890 and the Clayton Act in 1914, official government policy has opposed monopolistic control of industry. The chief enforcement responsibility lies with the Antitrust Division of the Justice Department. To the extent that antitrust enforcement has been successful, it has presumably eliminated the inefficiently high prices and low production that result from monopoly and has lessened inequality by cutting the monopoly profits that go to owners of capital.[14]

It is hard to know just how successful the somewhat sporadic enforcement effort has been. A few corporate giants have been broken up, and many mergers have been prevented; yet corporate sales and assets are more concentrated now than ever before. In the early 1980s, antitrust enforcement seemed to drop to a new low. But since competition often works through substitutable goods (tin cans and plastic bottles compete with glass, aluminum competes with steel), there is no easy way to define markets or compute market shares, no easy way to tell just how competitive or monopolistic American industry actually is or how different it would be without antitrust.

The "New" Regulation

In the late 1960s and early 1970s there was a great upsurge of consumerist and environmental regulation. The FDA and FTC were revitalized, ferreting out and banning potentially dangerous food additives, unproven drugs, and deceptive advertising. The NRC began to take safety and environment more seriously. Even more important, the Environmental Protection Agency (EPA), the Occupational Safety and Health Administration (OSHA), and the Consumer Product Safety Commission (CPSC) joined the regulatory army, with large and fast-growing staffs and many new rules for industry to heed.

The EPA deals with a classic problem of public goods, where action is needed to prevent pollution of air and water by firms that impose negative externalities on their neighbors. To be sure (as Coase tells us) if information and transactions were costless, a simple specification of property rights (the right to pollute at will or to be free of pollution) might be sufficient so that polluters and pollutees would get together and negotiate an efficient outcome: for example, compensation to those suffering from pollution, if the pollution were necessary to produce goods more valuable than the harm suffered; or payment to industry to stop production or clean up the discharges, if that could be done at less cost than continued pollution.[15] (Of course, it could make a considerable difference to the income distribution who started out with the legal rights.) But information and transactions are costly. Millions of city dwellers with sore eyes cannot easily figure out which factories are spewing how much sulphur dioxide into the air and then get together to dicker with them. It is probably more efficient to have government step in.

The EPA did so, on a large scale, by setting standards specifying just how much of a given pollutant could be discharged or what methods had to be used to abate it. This particular regulatory technique was controversial since most economists believe that a tax on pollution equal to its social cost or the sale of negotiable pollution rights would be more efficient; industry could then adjust precisely, eliminating pollution only when the cost of doing so was less than the amount of harm caused by the pollution. (Increasingly, trading of rights was in effect permitted. One could argue that extreme regulations were useful at the outset to mobilize the public behind a clear cause and to spur the development of antipollution technology.)

More to the point for us, the distributional consequences of standards and other environmental regulations, while hard to ascertain, are probably regressive. The direct health benefits of cleaner air and water might constitute a higher fraction of income for the poor than for the rich and hence be pro-poor in their effect. But this would not likely be true of the aesthetic and recreational and conservationist benefits, which are luxury goods of more interest to the rich.

Moreover, environmental improvements must be paid for, somehow: more likely in the form of higher prices for manufactured goods than in lower profits, so the consumers of goods end up paying. And low-income people pay proportionately the most because they consume a larger fraction of their incomes. Furthermore, if environmental standards are sometimes so burdensome as to prevent profitability, that reduces employment, again hurting workers. On balance, the regulation of stationary air pollution probably has antipoor effects, as does the control of automobile emissions. (The costs of control devices are proportionally higher for cheap cars than for expensive.) Dorfman offers the "untrustworthy" estimate that in 1976 pollution control gave each high-income family a net benefit of about $59, based on costs and willingness to pay, whereas low-income families bore an excess burden of about $61. The EPA's actions have apparently favored the upper-middle parts of the income scale.[16]

Once again, the point is not that it's a bad idea to clean up the environment but only that to do so is not generally pro-poor. An egalitarian should seek ways to compensate through other policies.

Workplace health and safety, like environmental protection, raises compelling arguments for government action. To be sure, in a perfect labor market with fully informed and mobile workers, there would be little problem: people would refuse to take risky work unless a wage premium outweighed the expected losses from injury. Employers would have to pay higher wages for any accidents or diseases suffered in their workplaces, so they would improve health and safety measures whenever the total benefits of doing so exceeded the total costs, which is precisely what society presumably wants done. In order to spread the risk, workers could buy insurance. But no such perfect market exists. Workers do not have full information about risks, especially unknown hazards or long-term dangers like those once faced from asbestos or Beryllium, so they don't know that they should demand higher pay. Furthermore, workers (say, in a one-industry town) sometimes lack the mobility or bargaining power to insist on wage premiums for risk even when they know about the risks. And individually purchased insurance would be overpriced because of adverse selection and moral hazard.

One possible form of government intervention would be strict employer liability, enforced in the courts, but this would provoke expensive litigation and would not solve the problems resulting from delayed harm: stale evidence and vanishing employers. In any case, the U.S. legal system has severely limited employer liability by means of the fellow servant rule, the doctrine of assumption of risk, and Workmen's Compensation, which provides fixed amounts of compensation for injuries in lieu of tort liability. In theory Workmen's Compensation reduces litigation costs and guarantees restitution, but in practice the payments are very low, a distinctly antiworker form of regulation, which means that employers don't bear the full costs of injuries and therefore underprovide safety. (Risk-graded premiums paid by employers for the compensation insurance could restore employers' incentives, but risk-grading has been very imperfectly arranged.)[17]

An especially efficient kind of government action would be to provide information about risks—subsidizing research, publicizing hazards, reporting firm-specific injury rates. It might also set up a Swedish-style board and safety-steward system to educate workers and to encourage labor-management cooperation. Government could then make up for remaining failures of the market process by fining firms for each injury. Ideally, these fines would be returned to injured workers in the form of full compensation for injuries: the equivalent of an equitable, risk-graded workmen's compensation scheme. Only as a last resort would specific standards for a firm's behavior be imposed—in the case of long-term health hazards like asbestos, for example, where there would be no observable "accident" to fine and the employers at fault would be hard to track down when a worker got sick twenty or thirty years after employment. Only in such cases would the government move to forbid (or, perhaps better, heavily tax) dangerous conditions or equipment or procedures.

A rather different tack was taken—at least initially—by the 1970 Occupational Safety and Health Act (OSHA), administered by an agency (with the same acronym) within the Department of Labor. OSHA quickly laid down some 4,400 specific standards for employers to follow, covering everything from power tool design to portable ladders to safety helmets. Moreover, the emphasis was on safety rather than health—just the opposite of what was most needed—and little information was provided. Almost certainly the effect of OSHA was to require more safety measures at lower wages (since risk premiums go down and the safety costs are largely imposed on workers) than workers wanted, thus lowering their total incomes. According to one estimate, if the 90 dBa noise standard were strictly enforced, it would have cost $13.5 billion, with only $2.6 to $6.5 billion worth of benefits in increased comfort and decreased hearing impairment.

It is slight comfort that enforcement efforts by OSHA were feeble and penalties so slight that there was little incentive for employers to comply: this bred disrespect for law and disadvantaged the obedient. Apparently, injury rates did not even change much at first though some improvements appeared later. But to the extent that OSHA has had any effect, it has not always been the straightforward pro-worker impact that the casual observer might expect. Again, this is not an argument against government regulation of workplace health and safety but against the peculiar American version.[18]

Rather similar considerations apply to the Consumer Product Safety Commission (CPSC), established in 1972, which relied on standards rather than information-provision or taxes and which may have cost consumers more in high prices than it gained them in safety. There were some embarrassing cases like the fireproofing of infants' sleepwear, which was first required and then banned as toxic. There is little reason to believe that the CPSC has helped low-income people.

Several other regulatory programs ostensibly intended to help working people or the poor have had negative, or at least ambiguous, effects. The minimum wage, for example, is supposedly designed to ensure a decent wage level for all workers by forbidding any wage payments below a certain hourly rate. But those hoping for an egalitarian result fail to take account of how employers respond to the minimum wage: they simply refuse to hire anyone who cannot produce more than the minimum wage's worth of work. Those who have jobs get paid the minimum, but many other jobs are abolished. Unemployment in certain industries (e.g., retail trade) and among those with low skill levels (e.g., many black teenagers) rises alarmingly, and the poor are probably worse off than they would be without the law. Furthermore, workers earning wages around the minimum level actually tend to have high family incomes (e.g., teenagers from wealthy families often work part time) so that even if the minimum wage actually raised their earnings, inequality would not be reduced.[19]

Similarly, rent control sounds like a way to help low-income people get cheap housing. But in New York and other places where it has been tried, the actual effect of controls has been irregular, with many high-income people as well as low benefiting from controlled rents. The main winners are whoever gets into low-rent housing first and stays put. Optimistic expectations for rent control, like the minimum wage, fail to take account of how the market reacts. The landlords of rent-controlled apartment buildings won't invest more money in losing propositions; they often let the apartments go to seed or get out of the business altogether (sometimes via insurance fires), thus reducing the supply of housing. Tenants illegally sublet at exorbitant rents. And new investors shy away, further restricting the supply of housing and forcing uncontrolled rents to rise. It is not clear that the poor gain anything.

The many antidiscrimination and affirmative action rulings by courts and HEW and other agencies are probably a different matter. Beginning in the mid-1960s, blacks and other minorities won enormously improved access to voting, education, public accommodations, and certain employment opportunities, especially with the federal government. Without question, minority citizens took great steps toward legal equality. Yet in the 1980s, housing and schools remained largely segregated. And the net effects on the income distribution were not entirely unambiguous: blacks of high educational and income levels flourished while the earnings gap between low-education blacks and whites actually widened. It is conceivable that antidiscrimination regulations led some employers, using various subterfuges, to avoid the initial hiring of low-skill blacks in order to escape pressures for later raises and promotions. "Equal opportunity" may not contribute as much as expected to income equality.

To further complicate any overall assessment of the regulatory picture, the 1970s saw the beginning of a strong movement toward deregulation. Among the early targets were the most obviously inefficient old-line agencies, the ICC, CAB, and FCC. The CAB experimented with allowing various discount air fares and then, after the Airline Deregulation Act of 1978, opened up routes and fares to widespread competition. The SEC in 1975 eliminated fixed brokerage commissions, whereupon fees fell significantly. The FCC authorized more television channels, reducing scarcity and increasing competition; it increased competition between AT&T and other companies over data processing and long-range telephoning; it removed many restraints on cable television and AM radio stations. The ICC, particularly after receiving its 1980 legislative mandate, granted more liberal trucking authority with broad discretion over routes and commodities and some discretion over rates. It largely deregulated the notorious home moving business and took steps to make collective rate setting illegal. For railroads it eased restrictions on piggybacking, line abandonment, individually tailored contracts, and rate adjustment, moving toward an end to collective rate setting. During the same period the EPA and OSHA granted delays or relief from particularly stringent environmental and safety standards.[20]

The Net Distributional Impact of Regulation

It is not at all easy to summarize the distributional effects of the whole range of government regulatory activity. Many complicated regulations push in different directions, so it is hard to add them up and calculate the net result. In fact, it is difficult to be sure even about the impact of any one set of rules. Many affect nonmonetary incomes (safety, clean air, quality of television programming) that are hard to measure. And most affect prices, wages, investments, and the like in ways that reverberate through the economy with unexpected impacts.[21]

We have seen that some of the most apparently pro-poor regulations may, because of market reactions, actually have antipoor, antiegalitarian effects. The same is true of "pro-consumer" regulations. But by the same token, some of the most apparently pro-industry kinds of regulation may not, in fact, really increase industry profits, or enrich the already wealthy, or increase inequality. To be sure, occupational licensing rather clearly benefits upper-income earners. Similarly, the FCC has profited networks and station owners, and the ICC, at least in some periods, has plainly increased the profits of railroads and truckers. Yet in recent years, railroading has proved no great bonanza for stockholders, and CAB protection did not lead the airlines to high profits.

The CAB regulation of airlines, which has been studied with considerable sophistication, illustrates how "pro-industry" actions may not actually benefit the regulated. Douglas and Miller found that when the CAB limited entry of new carriers and set high fixed fares, the airlines competed for customers in terms of *quality* of service, especially the frequency of flights. They flew far more often, with expensive half-empty planes, than they would have in a free market. Thus, the airlines competed away most of their CAB-produced profits. Of the $366-538 million in excess fares charged in 1969, Douglas and Miller estimate that about $248-356 million was deadweight loss to society, that is, pure waste. Much of the rest went to passengers in reduced waiting time. Airline profits between 1955 and 1970 averaged only a moderate 6.5 percent return on capital.[22]

Thus, we cannot be sure of the overall effects of price and quality regulation upon the distribution of income. It plainly has not brought about any great increase of equality, and it may have had the opposite effect. Quite possibly there has been little net impact on the income distribution.

Regulatory Politics

Regulatory politics practically demand an interest group interpretation. Most regulation takes place in very low-visibility settings. Much of the subject matter is technically complex, even arcane, remote from the daily concerns of the average person. Information costs are high. The average American feels little need to know precisely what formulas are used in regulating his electric utility rates and would find the formulas very hard to understand if he tried. Hence the public is particularly prey to symbolic politics. (Edelman's ideas about symbolic politics were first worked out in a regulatory context.) Moreover, there are barriers against organizing collective representation of the diffuse interests of numerous consumers. If organized at all, they tend to be underrepresented compared with producer interest groups.[23]

Thus, the general public ordinarily plays little part, either directly or via group representation, in regulatory matters. The scope of conflict is narrow. The field is left to organized groups, especially those with the most concrete material interests at stake, namely, corporations and others who are supposed to be regulated. They exert influence through all the familiar channels. They testify and litigate and provide information to agencies. They interact socially with regulators, make ex parte contacts, and offer special favors. In extreme cases this amounts to bribery, but more often it is just friendly socializing, with sometimes perhaps a tacit promise of later employment. Groups influence who is appointed to regulatory positions, often promoting candidates from the ranks of the regulated—on grounds of expertise. And they work through elected politicians, especially congressmen on the relevant oversight committees, lobbying and giving campaign contributions. The relationship

among regulators, the regulated, and congressional committees is sometimes referred to as an "iron triangle."[24]

It is difficult to prove exactly how much impact interest
groups have upon policy, but the nature of policy outcomes,
together with active group efforts at influence, permits the in-
ference that group impact is substantial.

Schattschneider's classic description of frantic pressure
group activity and the doling out of group benefits concerned a
regulatory policy, the tariff of 1929-1930, when Washington was
overwhelmed with industries each getting theirs. (Subsequent
congressional lobbying over tariffs has been quieter, but there is
reason to believe that the Reciprocal Trade Acts mainly just
shifted interest group activity to the executive branch and the
Tariff Commission.)[25]

Another well-studied case of interest group influence concerns the Interstate Commerce Commission. Long ago Huntington described railroad pressures on the ICC, noting U.S.
Attorney General Richard Olney's early letter to a railroad
friend urging that he "use" the ICC rather than oppose it. Kolko
and others have shown that the railroads were active from the
beginning of federal regulation, even drafting some legislation.
More recently, the Nader research group compiled evidence of
cozy ICC ties with industry, including partying and industry
funding of speeches and trips by commissioners; a common
flow of personnel between the agency and industry (six of
eleven commissioners in a row who retired from the agency got
rail or motor carrier jobs); and at least one fairly clear instance of
corruption.[26]

There may be predictable changes over time in the extent of
interest group influence. According to Bernstein's notion of a
regulatory "life cycle," new agencies begin with active public
participation and reformist goals but later fall prey to industry
influence. To put it in our terms, at the outset strong grievances
and extensive publicity cause a temporary lowering of information costs for ordinary citizens. There is relatively high public
attention; the scope of conflict is broad, and the general public
tends to get its way. But with the passage of time people become
satisfied with symbolic redress, public attention wanes, the
scope of conflict narrows; the regulated come to dominate the
process. Bernstein's evidence suggests that such a cycle has oc-

curred in several regulatory agencies, with periodic renewals of reformist zeal and then relapses to serving the regulated.[27]

Similar reasoning indicates that the power of the regulated tends to be especially great at the state and local level where constituencies are small and visibility very low. Selznick's showing of powerful elite influence upon the TVA at the grassroots and McConnell's similar analysis of agricultural county agents, both of which tell much about local program implementation in general, apply with particular force to state and local boards that deal with such matters as zoning, tax assessments, racetrack regulation, or liquor licenses. Contrary to traditional American rhetoric about decentralized government being close to the people, when functions are scattered among obscure minor agencies, only organized groups of those directly affected pay close attention and insist on a voice in decisions. The point is all the more true in cases of self-regulation, for example, when professions are delegated the power to license themselves.[28]

The idea that regulated industries and groups tend to dominate the regulatory process, long familiar to political scientists and sociologists, has more recently been adopted by some economists as "the" theory of regulation. Considerable work has been done to show that the regulated do in fact prevail and to derive mathematically the conditions under which industries will seek and obtain particular kinds of regulation.[29]

But even if scholars' claims of producer dominance accord with the evidence of pro-producer policies by many (though not all) old-line regulatory agencies, how are we to account for the rise of consumerist and environmentalist regulation? Surely business interest groups did not promote the EPA, OSHA, or CPSC. Does the existence of those agencies contradict the analysis and require a fundamentally different theory of regulation?

I would argue that there is no real contradiction. For the most part interest group domination of regulatory politics has continued simply with a modified lineup of groups playing the game. The Sierra Club, Friends of the Earth, Common Cause, and many other new "public interest" groups entered the scene. They changed the balance of forces to some degree, and, at least for a time, they were able to enlarge the scope of conflict through publicity. The public became more aware of air and water pollution, automobile defects, workplace hazards, toxic chemicals, dangerous products, and the like and demanded action. The new groups were able to influence legislation and regulatory standard setting. And in many cases (as in the alliance of the Sierra Club with Eastern coal producers), they soon adopted the techniques of old-fashioned interest group politics.[30]

Not all the reasons for these groups' emergence are clear, but one should not underrate the importance of individual publicists and entrepreneurial organizers like Rachel Carson, Ralph Nader, and John Gardner. Carson's *Silent Spring* and Nader's automobile safety reports alarmed and alerted the public. The pro-consumer shift in the FTC depended significantly on the Nader-Cox exposé of that agency. Common Cause was essentially Gardner's one-man creation. Once people were aroused and groups formed or activated, selective benefits like the Sierra Club's trips kept memberships up, with politics a by-product. (Hardin argues, however, that political contributions actually ended up subsidizing Sierra Club hikes rather than vice versa; and Common Cause kept going with few if any selective benefits for members.)[31]

Three observations should be made about the new groups. First, even at their peak, public interest lobbies were not nearly as well financed or as numerous as corporations and groups representing industry. Consumers and ordinary citizens remained very much underorganized. Second, as the public clamor died down, Bernstein's cycle asserted itself, and the traditional interest groups tended to regain dominance. Third, and most important for our purposes, these public interest groups generally did not (and do not) represent the poor. Most of their members have come from the middle or upper-middle class. With the exception of organized labor—the principal backer of OSHA—they seek upper-class goals, technocratic, aesthetic, and preservationist. As we have seen, the results have not been pro-poor. The wealthy got their scenic landscapes; unionized workers got safety standards (if not always efficient ones); but low-income people got very little from the new regulations.

If the new forms of regulation are explicable in interest group terms, what of deregulation? On the surface, at least, deregulation would seem either to contradict the argument that past regulation resulted from interest group influence or to signal a drastic shift in the balance of group power—a reversal of the pro-business bias in the pressure group system. I would argue, however, that the correct interpretation is a somewhat different one.

In the first place, the deregulation movement demonstrates how much political impact economic theory can have when it is skillfully disseminated. During the 1960s there was an outpouring of empirical and theoretical work on the inefficient effects of regulation, which appeared first in academic journals like the *Journal of Law and Economics* and the *Bell Journal of Economics* and in monographs from the American Enterprise Institute and the Brookings Institution; eventually it found its way into the popular press. There can be little doubt that this new evidence convinced many people of diverse political persuasions that regulation had often been wasteful and counterproductive.

The new information produced an unusual consensus of Left and Right. Many liberals lost their illusions about what regulation was doing for ordinary citizens. Nader with his exposés and Edward Kennedy with his CAB hearings joined the deregulatory vanguard. These activities broadened the scope of conflict and mobilized the general public. At the same time, on the basis of the new economic evidence (e.g., the finding that under apparently pro-producer price regulation, monopoly profits tend to be competed away) some business groups began to question whether they were, in fact, benefiting from their friendly regulators. United Airlines, for example, apparently concluded that it would do better in a free market than under CAB rules.[32]

This analysis applies to deregulation by the old-line agencies concerned with transportation and communications. But even more important has been the counterattack by business against environmental and safety regulations. Taking advantage of economic arguments about inefficiency, small businesses rose up against what they saw as harassment by OSHA, and big pollution-producing businesses like the steel, auto, paper, and chemical industries fought against costly EPA cleanup orders. Much of the political impetus for deregulation came from these business groups. In the Reagan administration, especially, efforts were made to cut back or abolish OSHA, EPA, CPSC, the FTC, and the like rather than to make their work more efficient.

In many cases, then, the same kinds of political forces that had earlier brought about or captured the traditional regulatory process later worked for deregulation—even in cases where inefficiency was not the real issue—and delayed or reversed many of the new environmentalist and consumerist regulations. It remains to be seen, of course, how far the deregulation movement will proceed and to what extent the general public will pay less attention and interest groups assert more complete dominance. Already in the early 1980s, at the very time the "new" regulation was being cut back, the FCC and ICC showed signs of resisting further deregulation—in response to industry pressure and the appointment of new pro-network and pro-trucking (and pro-Teamster) commissioners.

Macroeconomic Policy

Inflation, unemployment, economic growth, and such aggregate economic phenomena can have substantial effects on the distribution of income. They are affected by many policy choices involving overall levels of government spending and taxation, the size of surpluses or deficits, modes of financing debt, the structure of the tax system, the amount of money printed, and the level of interest rates. Taken all together these choices constitute macroeconomic policy, a particular kind of economic regulation.

Compared with other advanced industrial countries, the United States has had relatively high rates of unemployment and relatively low inflation. During every five-year period between 1960 and 1979, for example, U.S. unemployment was substantially higher on average than unemployment in Japan, Germany, France, or (pre-Thatcher) Great Britain (see Table 17). At the same time, inflation was generally lower in the United States than in the other countries. Only Japan (in one of the four periods) and Germany (in two of them) enjoyed lower inflation rates.[33]

As the anti-inflation crusades of the 1970s and early 1980s remind us, this unusual mixture of high unemployment and low inflation has reflected deliberate policy decisions. The money supply has been curtailed, interest rates raised, government spending cut, and "voluntary" and even compulsory wage and price controls imposed, all in the name of fighting

TABLE 17 *Unemployment and Inflation in Selected Countries*
            (percentages)

	United States	Japan	West Germany	France	Great Britain
Unemployment (average rate)					
1960–1964	5.7	1.4	0.6	1.5	2.6
1965–1969	3.8	1.2	0.8	2.1	2.8
1970–1974	5.4	1.3	1.0	2.8	3.3
1975–1979	7.0	2.1	3.6	5.1	5.5
Inflation (total change in CPI over period)					
1960–1964	+4.7	25.6	11.0	18.6	13.4
1965–1969	16.2	21.1	8.9	17.4	17.5
1970–1974	27.0	54.2	27.1	36.6	48.5
1975–1979	34.9	27.0	15.5	44.8	65.8

SOURCE: Calculated by the author from U.S. Office of Management and Budget, *Economic Report of the President, 1981* (Washington, D.C.: U.S. Government Printing Office, 1981), pp. 354-55. Unemployment rates from other countries are adjusted to be comparable with the U.S. unemployment concept.

inflation. Some of these measures are of dubious effect: the connection between deficits per se and inflation is tenuous, and wage and price controls—which distort economic allocations—probably do little in the long run to restrain inflation. Restricting the growth of the money supply, on the other hand, undoubtedly works to slow inflation, but it has the nasty side effect of slowing economic activity. One need not believe in a long-term Phillips curve trade-off between inflation and unemployment to note that, in the short run at least, anti-inflationary measures slow down the economy and increase unemployment.[34]

The obsession with deficits and with holding down government spending proceeds from a false analogy with families and local small businesses—implying that the government will go "bankrupt" if it cannot pay its bills with tax revenues—and from a grain of truth: if deficits grow too much faster than the GNP, they must either be "monetized" and lead to inflation or the money supply must be restricted. But spending and deficits per se need not affect inflation at all; they are not in fact related either across nations or over time. Moreover, the United States has had fairly steady deficits and a *declining* national debt as a percentage of GNP (recently around 35 percent). Indeed, U.S. debts and deficits have been quite low relative to other advanced economies. And it is worth noting that the very concept of a national "debt" proceeds from an odd accounting procedure that would not be followed by any business: counting only liabilities and not assets. Using a more sensible balance sheet approach, Eisner calculated that, as of 1980, the federal government had a low net debt (liabilities minus liquid assets), and its total assets of gold, loans due, land, buildings, equipment, and the like far exceeded debt obligations and gave it a net worth of perhaps $270 billion—more than $3,000 for each American household.[35]

The anti-inflationary thrust of U.S. policy is not new; it has persisted through most of American history. Sound money was a keystone of the Constitution, which took the power to print money away from inflationist states like Rhode Island and centralized it in the more conservative federal government. Strange as it sounds to the modern ear, the United States actually went through long *de*flationary periods, in which a dollar was worth more each year. While that was a blessing to wealthy creditors (whose assets appreciated in value), it was a curse to debtors, who had to pay back more valuable dollars than they borrowed. This was particularly burdensome for small farmers who typically had to borrow between planting time and harvest; in the late nineteenth century their resentment of deflation fueled populist demands for inflationary coinage of silver. The United States stuck with gold, however; only the discovery of new gold ore in Alaska counteracted the strong deflationary trend. Much later (in 1932) the abandonment of the gold standard symbolized a somewhat less rigid attitude toward monetary growth, but the United States has nonetheless remained very inflation-averse.

Unemployment, on the other hand, has been more readily tolerated. In fact, it was long considered no business of government at all. Cycles of boom and bust were allowed to run their natural course. "Panics" and depressions, which threw millions of unemployed workers and their families into desperate circumstances, were accepted as inevitable. In reaction to the Great Depression of the 1930s, the New Deal and Keynesian economic theory introduced a new orthodoxy: that government ought to fight economic downturns by countercyclical stimulation, increasing spending, cutting taxes, incurring deliberate deficits, and expanding the money supply. In the early 1970s, the New Deal practice of direct funding of public service jobs also enjoyed a modest revival. Still, the United States has lagged behind most other industrial countries by permitting high "normal" levels of unemployment (see Table 17) and provoking even higher levels in order to combat inflation.[36]

It is important to understand that this kind of macroeconomic policy has antiegalitarian effects. The net income-distributional impact of inflation may be slight—perhaps, somewhat anti-rich; but the effects of unemployment are very harmful to those of low income. The result of preferring unemployment to inflation, then, is to hurt the poor.

The Impact of Inflation

Economic theorists agree, with virtual unanimity, that inflation as they define it—a *general* increase in wages and prices—if it were fully anticipated, would not hurt anyone. With such inflation, prices would rise, but by definition wages would rise at the same rate; everyone would have to pay more dollars for a pound of hamburger, but everyone would have more dollars to spend and would be no worse off. So long as inflation is fully anticipated (e.g., if it proceeds at a steady rate and everyone knows the rate and acts on his knowledge), then no one should be hurt at all. Wage raises or cuts are added to or subtracted from an automatic raise that counterbalances inflation; savers get a normal interest rate plus the amount needed to offset the decline in value of their capital; prices, as usual, move up or down relative to each other, but all such rises and falls are tacked onto a basic inflation rate. Inflation changes nothing except the arbitrary measuring rod, the dollar, which shrinks relative to everything else; but this doesn't matter since everyone gets more dollars. There is no need to carry cash in wheelbarrows either, since the government can simply raise the denominations of bills from time to time.[37]

Fanciful though this exercise in economic theory may seem to the beleaguered housewife trying to pay her grocery bills, it has some genuine relevance. To the extent that what we call inflation really *is* a general rise in wages and prices and to the extent that it *is* fully anticipated, it does no harm. Once inflation has been going on for a while, the problem of fixed incomes shrinking relative to rising prices tends to disappear. Employers adjust wages; new contracts are entered into; pension schemes are revised. Soon after inflation reached a high level in the 1970s, Social Security payments were indexed to keep up; indeed they were *over*indexed so that they rose faster than the actual prices paid by the retired. Likewise, savers, after first seeing the value of their assets decline, were able to invest in Treasury certificates and money market funds and certificates of deposit that yielded high interest rates well above inflation. The "bracket creep" by which some people feared that progressive income taxes would take a bigger percentage bite as nominal incomes rose was easily remedied: Congress adjusted the tax rates for inflation on an ad hoc basis. Cuts in tax rates on capital gains and corporate profits compensated for the taxation of illusory profits from inflated inventories and capital. (To be sure, indexing would have been more effective.) And for the most part, wage and salary changes took inflation into account. College professors and others who fell conspicuously behind were suffering from weakened demand for their services, not from inflation.[38]

A good deal of the harm popularly attributed to inflation in the 1970s and early 1980s actually resulted from large *relative* (rather than general) price increases: especially rises in the cost of food and in OPEC-controlled oil—which, in turn, raised the cost of many other goods relative to wages. People's real incomes declined. The damage fell especially heavily on the poor, who spend a high proportion of their income on food and energy. Tight macroeconomic policies used to attack this kind of "inflation" were ineffective (tightening the money supply did nothing to break up OPEC); they compounded the suffering of the poor by imposing unemployment on top of the price rises.[39]

When, however, *general* inflation is not anticipated—as it often is not—it, too, has important short-run income-distributional consequences. When inflation unexpectedly increases, some owners of capital take a big initial loss: for example, bonds with fixed dollar interest payments and redemption values fall in market value until their yields overtake the inflation rate. Common stock values fall as well unless companies' earnings are expected to rise faster than inflation. The wealthy are hit hard.[40] Debtors get a big break—they can pay off their debts with cheap dollars. Homeowners, for example, see the value of their houses escalate while they pay only fixed-balance and fixed-interest-rate mortgages. (Eventually, when inflation is anticipated, new mortgages either reflect the new high interest rates or are written to accommodate varying rates.) Fixed income pensioners are hurt until indexing begins. Small savers lose out—if government regulation keeps bank and savings and loan interest rates low—until adjustments are made.

The short-term effects of unanticipated inflation go in many cross-cutting directions so that Piachaud, based on a thoughtful review of evidence from Britain, concluded that "there were no simple effects of inflation on income distribution." Some other scholars agree. Certain effects, like the bother of planning and adjusting in the face of uncertainty, cause trouble for everyone. But probably the very wealthy (owners of capital) are hurt most, to the benefit of middle-income people who get the homeowner windfall. (Oddly enough, many U.S. homeowners seemed more vexed by their increased property taxes than pleased with their much higher property values.) Thus inflation, insofar as it affects the income distribution at all, probably tends to equalize it somewhat. Minarik's simulation, using a broad "balance sheet" concept of income to include capital gains and losses, indicates a fairly strong equalizing effect.[41]

By the same token, any unanticipated decline in the inflation rate is a boon to the groups that were initially hurt, especially the wealthy. As this is written, the 1980s seem to promise just such a bonanza for the rich, with stock and bond prices surging (after the 1981-1982 recession) in response to disinflation.

Effects of Unemployment

Unemployment, on the other hand, plainly and unambiguously hurts those at the bottom of the economic heap. The wealthy are not much troubled by it; in fact, the existence of a reserve army of unemployed tends to depress wages and raise the returns to capital, that is, profits, relative to wages.

Marginal, low-wage workers are the most often out of work. Unemployment compensation cushions the blow somewhat, but payments are limited in amount and duration; many people, especially the unskilled, stay out of work beyond the expiration of benefits. As we have noted, unemployment insurance mainly helps unionized middle-income workers who are subject to cyclical layoffs. Moreover, unemployment insurance can involve unpleasant and degrading bureaucratic encounters after long waits in line. But most important, nothing can compensate for the shame and distress and psychological damage of not being able to produce or to support oneself.[42]

Unemployment at a rate of 5 to 10 percent, which may sound low to the untouched upper-middle class, affects many millions of low-income, jobless people and their families and dependents and friends for part or all of every year. It is also a fearful psychological sword hanging over the heads of those who are presently employed but in danger of joblessness at any moment. And the official figures do not reflect additional millions of people without work who have become discouraged and dropped out of the labor force—they are no longer counted as unemployed.[43]

The character of unemployment has changed somewhat in recent years as more women and teenagers and part-time workers have entered the labor force. Many of the jobless now fall into those categories. But this does not mean that for them unemployment is somehow painless. Most of the unemployed are still chief wage earners for their families; most are involuntary job losers. They average about four months out of work and express dissatisfaction with their income and family situation and life as a whole.[44]

It is little comfort to the unemployed that much of their joblessness may be "frictional," that is, a necessary result of search processes that eventually match the complex multidimensional characteristics of workers and jobs.[45] Even if a high normal level of unemployment is dictated by the efficient working of the marketplace, that makes it no less painful for the workers and no less within the power of government to help—as many countries do. Moreover, a substantial portion of unemployment is probably not frictional. Some unfortunates, especially minorities and those with limited skills, find themselves persistently and repeatedly out of work. Among black teenagers, for example, the average unemployment rate in 1980 was 35 percent—and it had stayed at that level for about five years.[46] In such cases, the market is not working efficiently either because of private market imperfections (e.g., discrimination) or government interference (e.g., the minimum wage). Efficiency as well as equity considerations would seem to call for a remedy.

The Politics of Inflation and Unemployment

The politics of macroeconomic policy involves some party differences, with Democratic administrations trying harder to reduce unemployment whereas Republicans have accepted somewhat higher unemployment and worked harder to cut inflation. The Eisenhower administration, for example, markedly reduced inflation from the Truman levels while letting unemployment rise (see Table 18). Under President Johnson, with a stimulative tax cut and the deficit-financed Vietnam War, inflation increased. (The Kennedy administration, however, which included a Republican secretary of the treasury and a Republican chairman of the Federal Reserve Board, does not fit the pat-

TABLE 18 *Party Differences in Unemployment and Inflation, 1949-1980*

Party—President	Years	Unemployment (average % of labor force)	Inflation (average annual % change in CPI)
D—Truman	1949–1952	4.3	3.3
R—Eisenhower I	1953–1956	4.2	0.6
R—Eisenhower II	1957–1960	5.5	2.1
D—Kennedy	1961–1963	6.0	1.1
D—Johnson	1964–1968	4.2	1.8
R—Nixon	1969–1972	5.0	4.5
R—Nixon, Ford	1973–1976	6.7	7.4
D—Carter	1977–1980	6.5	9.9

SOURCE: Calculated by the author from U.S. Office of Management and Budget, *Economic Report of the President, 1981* (Washington, D.C.: U.S. Government Printing Office, 1981), pp. 267, 289.

tern; it held inflation low and let unemployment rise.) Under Nixon and Ford, unemployment went up. Despite their clamping down on the money supply and their use of price controls, the OPEC oil price shock and the delayed effects of Vietnam produced substantial inflation, but not as much as under the subsequent Carter administration. The Reagan team, for all its conflicts among supply-side stimulators, monetarists, and budget cutters, drastically curtailed money supply growth at the outset and pushed harder to stop inflation than unemployment, which rose to a post-war record of more than 9 percent in 1982.

Party differences on macroeconomic policy, like those concerning social welfare, follow from the nature of the New Deal party coalitions. Organized labor, a key adherent to the Democratic party, is naturally much more concerned about unemployment than inflation whereas the opposite is true of corporations, businessmen, and professionals who back the Republicans.

At the same time, as a close look at Table 18 makes clear, the party differences are limited in magnitude. Under postwar Republican administrations unemployment averaged 5.4 percent, barely above the Democrats' 5.3 percent; and inflation averaged 3.7 percent, barely below the Democrats' 3.8 percent. Only if the anomalous Kennedy administration is set aside do the differences look a bit more substantial: the remaining Democratic administrations averaged only 5.0 percent unemployment and a hefty 4.7 percent inflation. The annual data reveal that most of the party differences can be attributed to the Korean and Vietnam wars under Democratic Presidents Truman and Johnson, which cut unemployment and boosted inflation. To be sure, Hibbs's work indicates that the party differences persist even with statistical controls for the effects of wars and the business cycle, but they are not very large.[47]

U.S. party differences on macroeconomic policy look still weaker when they are compared with those in other countries where parties of the Left keep unemployment low (without necessarily driving inflation high—perhaps because they can enforce wage restraint). The United States has no socialist party to push for full employment. This results from the lack of a strong, Left-oriented trade union movement, which in turn probably stems from a series of historical factors including the nonfeudal origins of the country and its middle-class, "Lockean liberal" nature, as well as the abundance of land and resources that encouraged a capitalistic individualism and unusually sharp ethnic and racial divisions among workers.[48]

The absence of any socialist or social democratic movement has also had indirect political effects through its impact upon public opinion. Workers and the general public have been greatly confused—in some cases perhaps deceived—about the nature of macroeconomic problems and appropriate solutions. During the 1970s, Americans' real incomes stagnated (and, for a time, actually fell) largely because of sharp rises in food and energy prices relative to wages. The public, echoing politicians and pundits, identified this problem as "inflation" and repeatedly cited inflation as the most important problem facing the country. Economists, in turn, offered their standard remedy for inflation: tightening the money supply. Politicians followed their advice and thereby provoked or exacerbated recessions, throwing people out of work and lowering Americans' real incomes still further—and making low-income people pay the most.[49]

During this period, culminating in the recessions of 1980 and 1981-1982, virtually the whole country accepted a misleading rhetoric about inflation, emphasizing its alleged evils (many of them actually due to relative rather than general price increases) and urging drastic measures designed to solve a different problem. Many Americans were persuaded to favor policies contrary to their own interests. One might reasonably infer that the wealthy and the well organized, who had little to lose from unemployment and much to gain by stopping inflation, manipulated public opinion.

Economic Growth

Economic growth, another target of macroeconomic policy, has always played an important part in the American vision of the future: a future of abundance, an ever-expanding economic pie with continually larger pieces for everyone. From the earliest years, government policy has sought to promote economic growth. In the nineteenth century there were state and federal subsidies for the infrastructure of trade and Western settlement (roads, waterways, railroads, land grant colleges) and protective tariffs to encourage domestic industry.[50] More recently there have been general tax cuts to stimulate consumer demand and special tax expenditures (accelerated depreciation allowances, investment tax credits, lenient treatment of capital gains) to encourage the supply side, investment and production.

The unhappy fact, however, is that many of the policies put forward to promote growth have strongly regressive effects on the distribution of income. Cuts in corporate income taxes through investment credits and accelerated depreciation, which allow businesses to deduct the cost of equipment earlier than it is really used up, increase corporate profits, which go disproportionately to the wealthiest Americans. Direct cuts in corporate or capital gains taxes clearly benefit the rich. As we saw in Chapter 2, a large part of the gap between the highly progressive nominal income tax rates and the much less progressive effective rates comes from the very low taxes that the wealthy pay on capital gains.

To some extent the politics of economic growth, like inflation and unemployment, involve party differences. Republicans tend to push for ever-greater subsidies to capital investment whereas the Democrats and their labor allies deplore these "trickle-down economics" and seek growth through Keynesian-style stimulation of demand, increasing the purchasing power of ordinary citizens. Thus, it was Andrew Mellon and the Republican Harding and Coolidge administrations that sharply cut income taxes in the top brackets and began special treatment of capital gains. The Democratic Roosevelt regime first incurred stimulatory deficits; the Eisenhower administration greatly accelerated depreciation allowances; Nixon, Ford, and especially Reagan pushed for tax cuts for business and high-income individuals, and Lyndon Johnson's administration cut taxes across the board.[51]

Yet, at the same time, growth is a uniquely bipartisan issue. Everyone is for it; the parties differ only in relative emphasis on the supply or demand side of the economy. Over the years the Democrats, too, have been persuaded that if the economy is to grow, capital must be allowed its profits. Despite their grumbling about Mellon's regressive tax changes of the 1920s, the Democrats grudgingly went along and altered things rather little when they took power in the 1930s. Franklin Roosevelt quickly abandoned the idea of a heavy tax on wealth. It was the Kennedy administration that introduced the investment tax credit in 1962. And after a series of increases in tax progressivity with Republican presidents in 1974, 1975, and 1976, the Democratic Carter administration abandoned its promises of progressive tax reform and in 1978 sharply cut the taxation of capital gains.[52] Many Democrats later joined in the Reagan administration's proposals for still easier treatment of capital gains, and key Democrats actually sweetened the further acceleration of depreciation allowances in 1981 in the great orgy of concern over capital formation and growth.

Indeed it can be argued that if we take a capitalist or free enterprise system as given, it is truly in the interest of workers and the poor to let the capitalists have large profits (i.e., to tolerate a high degree of inequality) for the sake of economic growth. Only capitalists, the argument goes, are able to accumulate large savings and invest them in highly productive uses, which will yield higher wages in future years. To be sure, the capitalists enjoy some luxurious consumption along the way, and workers could get higher incomes any given year if the profits were paid out in wages instead; but such a short-run improvement would only come at the cost of giving up big income gains in the future. Even to a Marxist, the solution to a game in which rational workers and rational capitalists divide up the fruits of production may grant a very large share to capital.[53]

This constitutes a structural explanation for inequality. It asserts that inequality is inherent in capitalism, that reformist tinkering and redistributional schemes are of no use because it is actually in the interest of the poor as a class to stay relatively poor. With the passage of time their lot—in absolute terms—will keep improving faster than it could in any other way even though they remain at the bottom of the heap. (Of course, this argument assumes that absolute income levels are all that matter. We have suggested that relative deprivation is important as well; the poor might prefer equality at a modest income level instead of a slow, trickle-down rise in their standard of living with everyone else staying ahead of them.)

Within its own terms the structural argument raises two crucial questions. First, why don't the workers revolt and establish a different economic system, a socialist one, in which they own the means of production and get economic growth without giving the capitalists extra income and power? Second, just how tight are the structural constraints? How much inequality is in fact dictated by a capitalist system?

One possible answer to the first question involves false consciousness among workers, inculcated by capitalists and their agents, and "American exceptionalism" including the unusual ethnic divisions and other characteristics of the U.S. working class. This line of argument takes us back to interest group analysis: workers don't revolt because as a group they are confused or disorganized or outmanned by other groups.[54]

A different answer is more in harmony with the structural analysis. Even if an omniscient observer were certain that a superior economic system could be constructed (and there may be some doubt about that), the average worker or poor person faces considerable uncertainty about the virtues of the untried socialist utopia. And there would likely be great costs in trying to attain it. Revolutions tend to be violent and destructive; even a peaceful transformation might bring disorder and disruption for a time while capitalists were dispossessed and reeducated and a new society was built. The economy could go downhill into a valley of transition before it began to rise again. The present-day worker who revolted and suffered might ultimately help only his descendants, not himself. So why give up a satisfactory present for an uncertain future?[55] Whatever the reason, whether American workers are deceived or whether they make correct self-interested calculations, they have shown little inclination to rebel against capitalism.

The second, and harder, question is how much inequality capitalism actually dictates. One way to approach this question is to observe the degrees of inequality among existing capitalist countries, as we did briefly in Chapter 4. The most comprehensive available study of income distribution in advanced Western (OECD) countries, compiled by Sawyer, does not attempt to take account of in-kind transfers and public goods spending, but it does offer estimates of the shares of pre- and post-tax money income going to different income groups. This study confirms that none of the leading capitalist economies comes at all close to completely equal distribution of money income. In those countries, the top fifth of households (as of the early

1970s) got 37 to 47 percent of the post-tax income in every country while the bottom fifth got only 4 to 5 percent. It is also true, however, that several capitalist countries appear to have achieved substantially more equality than the United States, with little or no loss of economic growth (see Table 19).

As we have seen, precise cross-national comparison is very difficult because data are collected differently, incidence assumptions affect the results, and it would be hard to calculate the value of in-kind incomes across different nations. But Norway and Sweden, for example, seem to have maintained vigorous economies over long periods with a relatively high degree of equality in income (though not in wealth, which is highly concentrated). Even Japan, that paragon of post-war economic success, apparently has a more equal income distribution than the United States. Evidence about Germany goes both ways; Smolensky found substantially more equality there than in the United States.[56]

Much more reliable international comparisons will be needed before we can be sure about structural constraints. At present it appears that there probably *are* definite limits to

TABLE 19 *Income Inequality in OECD Countries (Post-Tax Household Money Income, Standardized for Household Size)*

		Income Share (%)	
Country	Gini Coefficient	Bottom Quintile	Top Quintile
Netherlands	0.264	9.1	36.3
Sweden	0.271	7.3	35.0
Norway	0.301	6.6	36.9
Great Britain	0.327	6.1	39.3
Japan	0.336	7.1	41.9
Canada	0.348	5.2	40.5
Australia	0.354	4.8	40.9
United States	0.369	4.9	42.1
Germany	0.386	6.5	46.3
Spain	0.397	4.2	45.0
France	0.417	4.2	47.1

SOURCE: Malcolm Sawyer, "Income Distribution in OECD Countries," *OECD Economic Outlook: Occasional Studies*, July 1976, p. 19.

equality under capitalism but that these are somewhat looser than one might suppose. The experience of existing economies indicates that there is a degree of flexibility in capitalist systems; that the United States is not now up against structural limits. It is also quite possible that no existing capitalist economy has actually attained the full measure of equality that would be compatible with a capitalist structure.

Even less is known about income distribution in socialist or communist countries where data (hard to compare, at best) are sometimes unavailable. The evidence that exists indicates that incomes are somewhat more equal than in capitalist countries. But the contrast is not extremely strong. The Soviet Union is apparently only about as egalitarian as Sweden or Great Britain, and perhaps a bit less so. The more homogeneous countries of Eastern Europe have more equal money income distributions than the U.S.S.R., but only a little, if any, more equal than Britain. (See Table 20, which achieves more comparability than usual in East-West comparisons by presenting per capita figures.) China has achieved an exceptionally high degree of equality among its urban citizens—probably the highest in the world—and substantial equality within rural communities as well, but the differences between rich and poor villages and the huge urban-rural gap probably raise inequality among its whole population to about average for developing countries. Thus socialist countries, too, maintain significant degrees of inequality for the sake of promoting productivity and growth. This suggests that structural constraints upon equality may extend more broadly than just to capitalist systems; probably they are inher-

TABLE 20 *Income Inequality in Selected Eastern and Western Countries (Post-Tax per Capita or Equivalent Unit Money Income)*

Country—Year	Gini Coefficient
Czechoslovakia—1973	0.207
—1965	0.240
Hungary—1969	0.236
Poland—1973	0.240
Great Britain—1974	0.250

SOURCE: Harold F. Lydall, "Some Problems in Making International Comparisons of Inequality," in *Income Inequality: Trends and International Comparisons*, ed. John R. Moroney (Lexington, Mass.: Heath, Lexington, 1979), p.33.

ent, to some unknown degree, in any economy that uses material incentives to get people to work. By the same token, of course, one could argue that no existing socialist country has come very close to its full egalitarian potential because none has transcended material incentives.[57]

A different approach to the question of limits involves examining the internal workings of our own economy. The conclusions are rather similar. In the first place, economic growth is not very well understood. Intuitively, it seems obvious that increased investment (if accompanied by adequate consumer demand) must lead to growth, but empirically the connection does not look very robust. Other factors, such as technological innovation (itself having an unclear relationship to profits and inequality) may be more important. Furthermore, as we noted in Chapter 2, the specific links between government actions (e.g., tax incentives) and investment are also murky. Investment tax credits probably do stimulate investment, but there is disagreement even about that. Accelerated depreciation allowances are more doubtful in effect and require giving up more government revenue for a given increase in investment. And lenient treatment of capital gains, which aids speculators in gold and antiques and real estate as well as productive investors, is the most pro-rich and least effective of all at encouraging capital formation. Such measures very likely produce more quick gains for the rich than long-term wage increases for the poor.[58]

In short, there is no compelling evidence that strong economic growth is actually incompatible with more progressive taxation, more pro-poor welfare measures, and more equality. Indeed, some antiegalitarian policies advanced in the name of growth, focusing upon investment and production, may actually *retard* growth by taking money out of the hands of consumers and shrinking demand for the goods that are produced.

In the political process, *beliefs* about what sorts of policies favor growth are often more important than the facts of economic structure, which, after all, remain largely unknown. Almost certainly, therefore, some of the politics of economic growth involve interest group (particularly corporate) power and deception or manipulation of public opinion.

Beginning in the mid-1970s, the Business Roundtable and a number of corporations launched a major campaign for policies that were supposed to aid capital formation, especially accelerated depreciation and easier treatment of capital gains. They recruited experts to testify before Congress about an alleged "capital shortage"; they subsidized publications by conservative think-tanks; they ran newspaper and television ads urging that the energies of the free enterprise system be unleashed. Some of the economic theory they popularized was highly questionable, but it plainly convinced many Americans and had much to do with the regressive tax changes of 1978 and later.[59]

A particularly striking example of opinion confusion or manipulation concerns the "Laffer curve" idea, an extreme manifestation of supply-side economics, which held that tax cuts for corporations and the wealthy could so strongly encourage work and investment and production that government revenues would actually *increase*. Tax rates would be lower, but there would be much more income to tax. This notion had great electoral appeal in 1980, and it apparently helped convince President Reagan and Congress and much of the country that it was possible to cut taxes sharply, and at the same time pour more money into military spending, without worrying about excessive deficits.

Long before the debacles of the 1982 and 1983 budgets, however, mainstream economists and the Wall Street financial community agreed—with virtual unanimity—that Laffer-style policies would not work. True, tax rates set at either zero or 100 percent would presumably produce zero revenue; the maximum amount of revenue would come with tax rates somewhere between zero and 100 percent. True, in theory some sort of curve could be drawn depicting these facts. But most leading economists agreed that: (1) the actual shape of the curve and the location of the maximum revenue point were unknown, and (2) U.S. taxes were not so high that revenue could be increased by lowering them. (That is, the United States was not, as Lafferites claimed, located on the far right-hand side of the hypothetical curve, with very high taxes and low revenues.)[60]

Indeed, the Laffer idea was scorned as "voodoo economics" by (later Vice-President) George Bush and as "a relatively sophisticated form of fraud" by John Kenneth Galbraith. Distinguished economists like Robert Solow compared it to "snake oil." Nordhaus hoped that it would turn out to be the relatively harmless quack cure Laetrile rather than the crippling Thalidomide.[61]

How could such a notion, ridiculed by experts, be embraced by millions of Americans, including the president and (apparently) a majority of congressmen? Part of the answer, no doubt, is that the hope for simple solutions springs eternal. How nice, after the grim 1970s, if people could pay less in taxes and still get more from government. But also crucial was a large-scale propaganda campaign.

Right-wing foundations like Smith-Richardson spent hundreds of thousands, perhaps millions, of dollars subsidizing Lafferite publications, many of them by journalists (and, alas, political scientists) untrained in economics. The ideas of Arthur Laffer, himself a marginal academic economist, were picked up by master publicist Jude Wanniski, who wrote frequent *Wall Street Journal* editorials (and, eventually, a book) and converted Irving Kristol of *The Public Interest*. Gradually, the whole *Wall Street Journal* editorial page was won over. Ambitious Congressman Jack Kemp, and then Ronald Reagan, climbed aboard. More orthodox economic analyses of tax disincentive effects on work and investment (e.g., by Feldstein) lent the crusade an aura of respectability. Wealthy conservatives, who didn't quite believe in a free lunch but wanted to cut taxes and limit government, encouraged acceptance of Lafferism. Reagan was elected, and the gospel according to Gilder was enacted into law.[62]

Many economic growth policies, which at first seem structurally determined, therefore, probably result instead from the power of organized business groups, which influence policy directly and also affect policy by manipulating public opinion. If the structure of the economy plays a part in such processes, its role is in giving rise to corporate political power, which in turn is used to create false beliefs about which policies are mandated by the economic structure.

The Constitution and the Legal System

The legal structure that supports the economic system, even more than macroeconomic policy or regulation, fundamentally affects inequality among Americans' "pre-government" or "private" incomes. Government provides legal underpinnings that are essential to the workings of a capitalist economy. Government, for example, provides a medium of exchange by printing money and declaring it legal tender. It creates and enforces all rights to real or personal property. It enforces contracts of sale, employment, and investment. It empowers corporations to act as legal persons. Through the Constitution, it even limits the extent to which government itself can interfere with the private economy.

The U.S. Constitution plainly envisions a free enterprise economy. Many of the federal legislative powers enumerated in Article 1, Section 8, are designed to support such an economy: the power to lay and collect import duties and to regulate commerce with foreign nations and among states; to establish a uniform bankruptcy law; to coin and regulate money, fix standards of weights and measures, and punish counterfeiters; to grant patents and copyrights (i.e., to create a form of property in writings and inventions); to provide for calling forth the militia if needed to suppress insurrections (the framers had in mind Shays's Rebellion of 1786, in which debtors had tried to prevent mortgage foreclosures and obstruct court enforcement of debt repayments); and to make all laws necessary and proper for the execution of those powers.[63]

In contrast to the weak Articles of Confederation, the new Constitution was intended to establish a national market with uniform currency and without trade restrictions among the states. The federal government was to protect commerce from interference by foreign nations or Indian tribes and was to stand behind sound money, assume the debts of the Confederation, and make sure that private property and contracts were not abridged. Beginning with Alexander Hamilton's legislative program in the 1790s, Congress acted upon these objectives.

The Constitution also imposed restrictions on state governments, a few of which were feared to have radical tendencies. According to Article 1, Section 10: "No state shall . . . enter into any treaty, . . . coin money, emit bills of credit; make anything but gold and silver coin a tender in payments of debts; [or] pass any law impairing the obligation of contracts. . . ." There was to be no printing of greenbacks, as Rhode Island had done to inflate the currency and relieve debtors; no release of debtors (mostly small farmers) from contractual obligations. And, under Article 4, Section 4, the United States guaranteed to every state "a republican form of government," which presumably barred any dictatorship of the proletariat at the state level.

After the Civil War, the Fourteenth Amendment further restricted the states: "nor shall any state deprive any person of life, liberty, or property, without due process of law." Even setting aside the Supreme Court's most extreme efforts to champion private property under the doctrine of substantive due process, the due process clause plainly gives property rights an exalted status. A requirement of just compensation whenever property is taken for public use would apparently rule out any massive redistribution of wealth or income by the states. A state can confiscate millionaires' assets for distribution to the poor only if it compensates the millionaires with equivalent assets, undoing the intended effect of the confiscation.

Certain constitutional restrictions on federal government action also limit interference with the capitalist economy. Under the Tenth Amendment, all powers not specifically granted to the federal government are reserved to the states or to the people. Most important, under the Fifth Amendment no person can "be deprived of life, liberty, or property, without due process of law; nor shall private property be taken for public use without just compensation." Thus, even before such a restriction applied to the states, the federal government was constitutionally barred from any major redistribution of wealth—except perhaps through the taxing power, which was itself limited until the Sixteenth Amendment of 1913 authorized a progressive income tax.

The Supreme Court and Private Property

The Supreme Court over the years has elaborated upon these constitutional provisions. The court first established its power of judicial review over both federal law and state law—in the process overturning Virginia's revolutionary war confiscation of British-owned lands. Then, in *McCulloch v. Maryland* (1821), it upheld the constitutionality of the Bank of the United States, giving broad scope under the "necessary and proper" clause to Congress's legislative power to facilitate a national economy. In the *Dartmouth College* case (1819) it held that a state was bound, under the contract clause, by a charter it had issued. And in

Gibbons v. *Ogden* (1824) it construed federal power under the commerce clause very broadly, striking down New York's grant of the Livingston steamboat monopoly as in conflict with a federal coastal licensing statute.[64]

During the early nineteenth century the court continued to encourage economic competition and to define federal powers broadly, thus assisting in the nationalization of the economy. In the *Charles River Bridge* case (1837), for example, it struck another blow at state-sponsored monopoly by construing a bridge charter narrowly, as not barring operation of a rival bridge nearby. And in the *Cooley* case (1851) it further defined the exclusive implication of the commerce clause as forbidding state regulation of matters "in their nature national." During most of this period, however, it did little directly to protect private property. It had only limited tools to restrict action by the states (in *Barron* v. *Baltimore* [1833] the Fifth Amendment and the rest of the Bill of Rights were held to apply only against the federal government), and the federal government had not been inclined to interfere with property.

In the late nineteenth century, with the rise of industrial capitalism and of government efforts to regulate it, the Supreme Court set out to preserve laissez faire against both state and federal incursions. It used the commerce clause to forbid state tonnage taxes on freight or the establishment of telegraph monopolies or various regulations of business. The 1886 *Wabash* case effectively prevented state regulation of interstate railroad rates. Then, slicing with the other edge of the same sword, the court held that the commerce clause did not justify application of the federal Sherman Antitrust Act to manufacturing because manufacturing was not "commerce" (*U.S.* v. *E. C. Knight Co.* [1895]). Similarly, in 1896 it construed the Interstate Commerce Act narrowly as not permitting ICC fixing of railroad rates.

In 1918 the court overturned the federal child labor law. And in 1935 and 1936, making a last desperate stand against the New Deal, it overthrew the National Industrial Recovery Act, the Bituminous Coal Act, and the Agricultural Adjustment Act, using arguments based on the tax clause, the Tenth Amendment, separation of powers, and the due process clause as well as the commerce clause.

In addition, after emasculating the Fourteenth Amendment of its intended protections for former slaves, the court gradually turned the amendment's language of "due process" and "equal protection" into barriers against state government interference with property. In the 1890s it developed a doctrine of substantive due process and overturned railroad regulatory commissions (*Minnesota Rate Cases* [1890]), minimum wage and hours laws (*Lochner* v. *New York* [1905]), and a total of some 184 state laws between 1899 and 1937—especially in the 1920s.[65] There can be little doubt that in the late nineteenth and early twentieth centuries the Supreme Court contributed to a distribution of income more unequal than it would otherwise have been.

To be sure, the court eventually retreated in the face of political pressure. In 1937 it essentially abandoned the battle, upholding a state minimum wage law and approving key elements of the New Deal—the Social Security Act and the National Labor Relations Act. From that time on, both state and federal powers to regulate the economy have been construed very broadly.

It is also true that in the twentieth century the Supreme Court—especially the Warren court of the 1950s and 1960s—has taken the initiative in making a number of decisions with egalitarian effects. The rights of accused criminals—who are usually poor—have been broadened markedly; coerced confessions and illegal searches have been discouraged, and in *Gideon* v. *Wainwright* and subsequent cases indigents have been granted the right to free legal counsel.[66]

The equal protection clause of the Fourteenth Amendment has been restored to its original purpose of helping blacks and other minorities. *Brown* v. *Board of Education* (1954) established the right of black children to attend formerly all-white public schools. Later decisions (with the help of federal legislation and administrative action) eventually enforced desegregation in most of the South and some of the North although the court's hesitancy to order metropolitan-wide desegregation (together with the workings of the private housing market) meant that many suburbs stayed lily-white and schools in big northern cities remained black and de facto segregated.[67]

The antidiscrimination principle of *Brown* was also extended to most kinds of government action (access to parks and beaches, hiring of government employees) and, in a more limited way, to private hiring, housing, and the like. Such measures had some definitely egalitarian effects.

Nonetheless, it is more important that the Constitution as interpreted by the court still upholds private property and freedom of contract as fundamental legal rights. It still prevents any drastic government interference with property, and it provides for government promotion of free markets. The Constitution strongly favors, if it does not actually mandate, private ownership of the means of production, that is, capitalism.

Common Law and Capitalism

After the American Revolution, the new states "received" the British common law, which was itself distinctly protective of property—but chiefly solicitous of the inheritance and quiet enjoyment of land by the aristocracy. British common law also had an overlay of equity jurisprudence, involving doctrines of substantive fairness; and it permitted such mercantilist interference with commerce by the state as the granting of monopolistic charters.[68]

By the end of the eighteenth century American courts had begun to modify the received common law, to be more conducive to commerce and economic growth in an emerging capitalist economy. They undermined its rationale as God-given natural law, adopting explicitly functionalist bases for decision. Absolute rights to undisturbed enjoyment of real property, so important to the English gentry, gave way to new, more productive utilization of land. The rule protecting "natural" (or prior established) uses of streams was for a time turned to the purpose of subsidizing investments in dams and mills and the like, giving them precedence over latecomers who wanted water. The same technique was, and still is, used in the West to encourage risky settlement and development. Then, in most of the country, established uses lost out. The courts let streams be obstructed or diverted for "reasonable" new uses of water. Mill acts limited the damages due for flooding caused by millponds. "Good faith possession" statutes and limits on the doctrine of waste encouraged the tenants on land to make improvements.

Eminent domain powers were used to run turnpikes and canals and railways through private lands with only limited compensation. Damages for such fallout of economic growth as railway-sparked fires were restricted by doctrines of proximate cause and scope of risk; damages were assessed by judges rather than juries and were transformed from punitive penalties into a cost of doing business. Old prohibitions against "nuisances," which had obstructed the noises and smells of industrial development, were modified. Rules of strict liability were replaced in ship collision cases by the concept of negligence, which required only reasonable care.

At first, economic development was encouraged by the granting of monopolistic charters for utility and transportation ventures. But as technology progressed, competition was fostered (as in the Supreme Court's *Charles River Bridge* case) by narrow construction of the charters' provisions. New bridges and canals and railroads were allowed to compete side by side with old chartered ferries and turnpikes.

Commerce was facilitated by development of contract law that was tied to the intent of the parties rather than to the courts' conceptions of fairness. Damages were calculated in terms of actual losses (including expectation, e.g., foregone profits on stock or commodity sales) so that breach of contract called for businesslike restitution rather than moralistic punishment. Commercial custom was used as a legal guide to intent and became a guarantee of certainty and predictability of contract terms. Tort rules like common carriers' strict liability were made modifiable by contract. Employers' liability for employee injuries was restricted by the fellow servant rule and the doctrine of assumption of risk.

A whole new commercial law came into being, created in part by federal courts using the *Swift* v. *Tyson* (1842) concept of a federal common law. Negotiability of financial instruments, which is extremely important to the smooth working of commerce, was established: an endorsee could recover against a remote endorser without need of a special contract between them; and original defenses were not held valid against a good-faith holder. Insurance was facilitated by striking down old defenses against claims and by developing actuarial conceptions of risk.

Bankruptcy laws arose to protect businessmen from disaster. Usury laws were weakened by lessening penalties and increasing permissible interest rates, thus freeing financial markets.

The importance of these legal developments is not primarily that they subsidized the emerging commercial and industrial classes and thereby increased income inequality in the nineteenth century. Very likely they did so; but some of that effect has subsequently been reversed—businesses' liability to customers and employees and neighbors, for example, has been broadened. The most important point is that the new laws facilitated the building of a capitalist economy. These rules were not just a sop to dominant economic groups. They formed a rational, logical part of an economic structure based on private enterprise.

A preeminent example is that remarkable legal invention, the business corporation. The corporation's powers as a legal "person" to contract and to sue or be sued, the limits on the individual liability of its stockholders, and the transferability of its stock, greatly encourage productive risk taking and the assembling of large amounts of capital in a market economy.

At the beginning of the nineteenth century, the few corporations that existed in the United States mostly held special charters from state legislatures to carry out narrow tasks involving large amounts of capital and risk—building a particular road or bridge, for example. Usually they were forbidden to expand their activities beyond the specified task. Often they were given monopoly privileges, which encouraged their initial risk taking but then severely hindered competition and innovation within the privileged sphere. Soon, however, states began to authorize easy incorporation for general purposes. New York, for example, allowed general incorporation for manufacturing firms in 1811 and added banks in 1838 and railroads in 1850.[69]

By the late nineteenth century, incorporation was a simple matter of routine in most places, and corporations chartered by the most lenient states (e.g., Delaware) were, under federal law, empowered to do business everywhere in the country. Now, of course, gigantic corporations are the most prominent feature of the American economic scene. Legal policy permitting incorporation must be taken as one of the most fundamental underpinnings of modern capitalism.

The contemporary legal system is primarily devoted to facilitating the private economy. The civil rights and civil liberties that so excite students of constitutional law occupy only a tiny fraction of courts' and lawyers' attention. Even criminal justice—which serves as the ultimate protector of private property (not, of course, that stealing would be a desirable mode of redistribution)—is a relatively minor part of the legal system. Most legal thinking and work and money goes into regularizing economic relationships and transactions. The heart of the law concerns real property, contracts, corporations, trusts, estates, and taxation. Its chief purpose is to promote economic efficiency.

Since the constitutional and legal provisions we have discussed are so inextricably linked to the workings of the private economy, their income-distributional effects must be judged in terms of the effects of capitalism as a whole. As we have seen, capitalism—while it does not require the extreme degree of inequality presently found in the United States—does almost certainly impose serious limits upon the degree of equality that can be attained. The U.S. Constitution and the legal system, in that sense, significantly contribute to inequality.

Constitutional and Legal Politics

One might ask two important questions about the politics of the Constitution: how the document came to take its original form and why it has persisted with little change over the years.

Charles Beard shocked many Americans when, in 1913, he argued that the Founding Fathers were not detached political craftsmen but were self-interested elites who fashioned a Constitution that profited themselves financially. He pointed out that the members of the Constitutional Convention were not small farmers or craftsmen or laborers, like most Americans of that day, but rather were large land (and slave) owners and land speculators, money lenders, merchants and manufacturers, and, of course, lawyers. All these groups benefited directly from the constitutional provisions protecting property and facilitating commerce. Moreover, Beard said, forty of the fifty-five were owners of public securities issued under the Articles of Confederation, which would be much increased in value by the Constitution's provision that the new government, with much greater revenue resources, would assume the debts of the old. All in all, Beard declared, five-sixths of the convention delegates had a direct personal interest in the Constitution.[70]

Subsequent scholarship has corrected Beard on several factual points. (For example, he overstated the delegates' ownership of public securities at the time of the convention.)[71] But the main thrust of Beard's assertions remains compelling. The framers undeniably tended to be rich and well born, not just able. The landowners and merchants and other upper classes from which they came certainly did benefit from the Constitution. Moreover, rather few ordinary Americans participated in the process of ratification; women and blacks and the unpropertied were excluded from voting, and many others sat it out. Thus, there is substantial warrant for interpreting the Constitution in interest group terms, as manifesting the power of the propertied landowners and the commercial and manufacturing classes.

But Beard's critics have pointed out that the framers could well have had the public interest chiefly in mind even if it happened to coincide with their private interests. Thus, an alternative explanation for the Constitution is a structural one: that a strong national government, protection of private property, and opening of national markets would benefit everyone. The emerging capitalist economy, which promised rich fruits for all, required the proper political and legal infrastructure. Reflection upon this claim makes clear, once again, just how hard it is to sort out structural from interest group explanations since the power of particular groups is fostered by economic structure while the existence of the structure itself (in this case its legal foundations) can plausibly be attributed to the actions of those same groups.

The persistence of our basic constitutional provisions unchanged for some two centuries is due, in part, to inertia and to the document's self-perpetuating design. Under the Constitution's own provisions, amendment is exceedingly difficult; since the addition of the Bill of Rights it has been accomplished hardly more than a dozen separate times. An additional explanation, fitting with the Beardian account of constitutional origins, would be that the same powerful groups that enacted the Constitution, later swelled by its workings and the growing economy, have protected it all along. (The awe and respect felt by ordinary Americans could be ascribed to mystification that keeps them from seeing the Constitution's pernicious features.) On the other hand, the Constitution can be seen as supported by the structural logic of the economic system. In this view it persists, with the help of its inherent flexibility to bend with changing circumstances, because it is needed for the flourishing of the free enterprise economy that benefits everyone.

The Supreme Court's evolving interpretations of the document might be taken as the predictable responses of judges who are appointed through a highly political process that reflects the power of interest groups. Or one might emphasize the judges' roles as far-sighted experts, adapting the law to fit optimally with the dictates of the changing economy.[72]

Again, the system of commercial and corporate law could be seen as the product of free enterprise lawyering, in which the best legal guns for hire naturally work for clients with the most money and thereby shape legal doctrine to accommodate the rich and powerful. It is no secret that top law school graduates tend to flock to Wall Street, that landlords get better legal representation than tenants, or that Standard Oil has better lawyers than Joe's Garage. At the same time, legal doctrine does often embody economic rationality.[73] Whether this results from the workings of the adversary system and the legal market or from judges' public regardingness and expertise is difficult to figure out. In the area of legal and institutional arrangements, perhaps more than anywhere else, structural and interest group explanations are particularly hard to untangle.

6

Conclusion: More Equality

We do not know, and probably cannot know, exactly who gets what from government. So many government actions affect the income distribution in such complex ways that it is virtually impossible to pin down precisely to what extent the U.S. (or any other) government contributes to—or lessens—income inequality.

Even the most straightforward sort of government action, like sending a Social Security check in the mail, turns out to be not so simple in its impact. We cannot just observe what the distribution of private incomes looks like (finding this out is itself a formidable task), learn how many people at each income level get what amount in Social Security checks, add those amounts to their private incomes to compute a post-transfer income distribution, and identify the difference between pre- and post-transfer inequality as an effect of government. Beyond that, we should consider lifetime income streams and try to discover whether or not those who receive Social Security are actually poor on a lifetime basis. If not, the transfers may equalize an individual's income over his own life cycle (an important accomplishment) but not equalize the lifetime incomes of different individuals with each other, which is perhaps even more important. Lifetime incomes are not easy to measure. Moreover, we should try to figure out whether the existence of Social

Security changes people's private incomes over the life cycle, perhaps leading to earlier retirements and reduced savings and thus merely replacing income that would have been generated in other ways. Even sophisticated studies cannot answer these questions with certainty.

In-kind government transfers like Medicaid or public housing raise the additional problem of figuring out how much they are actually worth to those who get them. We cannot simply divide up budget dollars and assume they are parceled out among the recipients of services because the value to recipients may be less than what the programs cost. Furthermore, the government's purchasing of goods and services from doctors, building contractors, social workers, and the like may have indirect effects on the income distribution that offset the direct effects of the in-kind transfers. Such effects are difficult to measure with any precision.

The benefits of public goods are by their very nature hard to divide up and assign to individuals. Since few, if any, goods are purely public, different income classes tend to consume different amounts of them, and it is hard to find out how much. But even to the extent that public goods are really public and consumption by everyone is equal, the value of that consumption (i.e., its contribution either to total utility or to dollar-equivalent incomes) would ordinarily not be equal. The value of the armed forces to different groups in society, for example, depends upon who is the foreign enemy at the moment. We cannot hope to be very precise about such matters; we must rely on rough estimates that the benefits of a particular public good are, say, about the same for everybody, or proportional to income, or proportional to wealth. Which of these estimates we choose strongly affects what we will find to be government's total income-distributional impact. Moreover, we must again worry about the indirect effects of government purchases upon the private incomes of defense contractors, space engineers, and the like.

The income-distributional effects of laws and regulations are even more difficult to untangle. There are many of them, affecting every area of life, and they work in complex ways. Every one of the countless governmental-induced changes in wages or prices or quality affects the distribution of income. Merely to gauge any one rule's effect is a serious scholarly task, and to try to add them all together is mind-boggling. Further, to assess the impact of the Constitution and the legal system as a whole requires understanding what effect a capitalist economic system has upon the income distribution, which in turn necessitates both microlevel and cross-national studies of the effects of economic structure, studies that are difficult to design or execute.

One thread of argument running through these comments, and through the book, concerns the need to think in what economists call a *general equilibrium* fashion. It is not adequate to view government actions as tacked onto the private economy, simply adding to or subtracting from what the market does. Government actions themselves affect the "private" behavior of individuals and firms as they make choices about work, savings, production, investments, and even living arrangements and family life. These choices, in turn, affect other "private" choices and reverberate throughout the economy so that the net long-run impact of a government policy may be quite different from its apparent short-run effect.

Taxes provide a number of examples. The personal income tax, which on the surface looks like a relatively simple subtraction of income from individuals, actually changes people's incentives and behavior all through the economy by means of its marginal rates and its special exemptions and deductions. Capital gains rates affect savings; mortgage interest deductions encourage housing ownership and construction; municipal bond exemptions subsidize state and local governments. Each of these provisions has complex indirect effects on the income distribution as well as the direct effects of eroding progressivity and benefiting the rich.

Similarly, payroll taxes drive a significant part of the economy underground where it is not taxed or measured. The "employer's" share of payroll taxes results in lower wages for workers and, perhaps, higher prices. Still more complicated are the effects of the corporation income tax, which is conceivably shifted forward to consumers in higher prices or backward to employees in lower wages or is borne by the owners of corporate stock or by the owners of capital generally—or some combination of these. And the property tax may be paid by the owners of land and buildings, or shifted to consumers and renters, or borne by all owners of capital. It makes a good deal of difference to the income distribution which of these things happens, but it is not easy to tell empirically what is going on.

A special difficulty in assessing the effects of government is that effects must be calculated relative to some counterfactual, some baseline model of what the world would be like without the government action. That is fairly manageable if we just want to judge the impact of a single tax or spending program: we can compare what the income distribution is like when the program is in place with what it would be like without the program, assuming everything else remains the same. (This is called "absolute incidence"; "differential incidence," relative to some similar program, is actually somewhat easier to compute.)[1] But when we want to consider the impact of all programs at once, we are compelled to imagine a "no government" counterfactual—a patent absurdity. It makes no sense to try to conceive of a modern industrial society functioning with no government at all because government is so closely interwoven with every economic activity.[2]

For some purposes it might be useful instead to compare the status quo with a "Lindahl equilibrium" counterfactual, in which incomes are determined by a perfect private market and public goods are paid for by each individual according to his marginal evaluation of them. But this is not a real possibility either, since individuals' exact preferences for public goods are unknown and probably unknowable. (Nor do we know what incomes a perfect private market would produce.) To use the Lindahl equilibrium as a base for comparison also accepts as given the income-distributional consequences of its particular scheme for providing public goods, which may or may not be normatively appealing. And it takes for granted, that is, ignores, the important effects government has through supporting the private market itself.

For many purposes, therefore—especially when we try to assess the impact of the legal underpinnings of the capitalist system—it is desirable to compare the U.S. or capitalist economies as a group with a socialist (or some other alternative) economic system. But since no existing economy very closely approximates ideal socialism (or, for that matter, ideal capitalism), we are forced into a speculative exercise concerning how the American reality differs from some hypothetical alternative.

The problem is twofold: (1) how to choose among different kinds of counterfactuals, and (2) how to specify the details of the chosen one so that it is not altogether unrealistic. Together with other problems of data and theory and method we have already mentioned, this makes it essentially impossible to be sure how government affects the income distribution or even to specify precisely what we mean by "affects."

Still, all the uncertainty should not be taken to mean that nothing of interest can be said about connections between government and inequality. The most severe difficulties come in trying to figure out a counterfactual "pre-government" or "nongovernment" income distribution to compare with the actual distribution. It is more nearly feasible to calculate a "*post-*government" or actual income distribution by which we can judge how much income inequality there is *after* all government action has been taken into account—without trying to sort out precisely what part of it is due to the private market (or would be present in some other baseline model) and what part is caused by government action. Using an estimate of the post-government income distribution we can at least judge whether or not, after the government has acted, an acceptable degree of equality is achieved. And we can make comparisons over time to see whether equality has increased or not subsequent to various government initiatives.

The answers are reasonably clear. In the United States, after the government has regulated the economy, imposed taxes, and provided social welfare programs and public goods, the total distribution of income is quite unequal. Based on Reynolds and Smolensky's "standard" incidence assumptions (but with general expenditures allocated proportionally to income rather than equally), the post-fisc Gini coefficient for 1970 was a very substantial 0.375.[3] And, as we have seen, even this is probably too optimistic an estimate. If some public goods (e.g., defense) were apportioned partly according to property ownership rather than income and if social welfare benefits like medical care and public housing were valued at their worth to recipients rather than their cost to the government, the distribution of income would look still more unequal.

Moreover, post-government income has not, during the period studied, become more equal. Reynolds and Smolensky's Gini coefficients (under the same incidence assumptions, with general expenditures apportioned according to income) stayed at virtually identical levels for two decades: 0.384 in 1950, 0.378 in 1961, and 0.375 in 1970. The Great Society and the War on Poverty, at least in their early years, either made no difference at all in the distribution of income or only offset other factors that were tending to increase inequality. (Some gains in equality during this period may have been concealed by changes in family structure. It is also quite possible that equality increased somewhat in the early 1970s, but this was probably reversed by the regressive policies of the late 1970s and early 1980s.) After all the government's actions are taken into account, then, income inequality in the United States is very great and has shown little or no sign of decreasing.

Because of the methodological uncertainties, we cannot be sure just how big a part government has played in causing or moderating these results, only that it has failed to overcome them. But our examination of particular government programs helps indicate how it is that government action permitted such high and stable levels of post-government inequality.

Taxes in the United States have done little or nothing to redistribute income. The federal income tax, supposedly very progressive, is undermined by exclusions and exemptions and deductions—especially the mild treatment of capital gains—that chiefly benefit the rich. Highly regressive payroll taxes have provided a larger and larger share of federal revenue. The corporate income tax, whatever its incidence, has virtually vanished. On balance, therefore, federal taxes are only moderately progressive. State taxes, on the other hand, are probably quite regressive, especially if substantial parts of the property tax are passed on to renters and consumers. State and local sales taxes, a large source of revenue, are very regressive because low-income people have to buy necessities and pay out a big part of their income in taxes on them.

Social welfare policies, though taking up a large part of the budget, have had surprisingly little redistributive effect. The bulk of the money goes for Social Security and other retirement insurance plans that smooth out people's lifetime incomes but do not greatly increase equality across individuals. Much the same is true of the biggest health program, Medicare. Programs (like AFDC and Food Stamps) that are more sharply targeted for the poor are quite small by comparison and have been the first to lose out in budget cuts. Medicaid, which mushroomed in the 1970s, has genuinely helped the poor but not nearly as much as its cost would indicate; much of the money has gone to doctors and hospitals in the form of inflated fees.

Public goods are not particularly intended to help low-income people, and they generally don't. The biggest—defense—does provide some public service jobs for people near the bottom of the income scale; but it also subsidizes the high incomes of engineers and scientists and the owners of high-technology corporations. In its central role of backing up U.S. foreign policy, military spending probably most greatly helps the most wealthy, owners of property, and especially owners of capital invested abroad. Many other more or less public goods probably benefit people roughly in proportion to their overall incomes. This may be true of highway programs (which help automobile drivers and the consumers of trucked merchandise), spending to clean up air and water pollution, energy production, and science and technology, including the space program. That is, nonmilitary public goods spending probably tends to provide more dollars' worth of benefits to a high-income person than a low, but the amount is roughly proportional to other income and, therefore, does not (assuming a "no-government" baseline model) much alter the income distribution.

A number of government regulations protect producers; some of these presumably increase the profits of the wealthy, but much of the excess revenue is probably competed away and results only in inefficiency not pro-rich income transfers. Regulations promoting environmental concerns are probably somewhat favorable to those of middle and upper income. Some regulations, like minimum wages and rent controls, which purport to help low-income people, are of dubious effect and, in addition to being inefficient, may actually hurt those on the very bottom of the income distribution.

Finally, the Constitution and the legal system clearly provide foundations for a capitalist economic system. Thus, the income distributional effects of that system are themselves products of government action. Capitalism does appear to put significant limits on the degree of equality that can be attained.

Why So Little Redistribution

Besides trying to ascertain *how* government affects people's incomes, this book has also been concerned with *why* government has the effects (or lack of effects) it does. This is a central question for political scientists and for anyone who wants to influence policy.

I have discussed two kinds of political explanations for why government has apparently done so little to bring about income equality. One, a type of interest group analysis which points to biased pluralism or imperfect political competition, sees corporations and organized groups with an upper-income slant as exerting political power over and above the formal one-man-one-vote standard of democracy. The other, a structuralist view, asserts that inherent features of a capitalist economy compel rational actors, even those of low income, to accept inequality for the sake of more material goods for everyone.[4] Either type of explanation could accommodate the fact of public acquiescence to inequality, one accounting for it in terms of ignorance or deception, the other in terms of correct calculations of self-interest.

There is some substantial evidence for each type of explanation. It is not possible to judge with complete confidence how true either one is, and important political and economic research about this remains to be done. But enough is known to conclude that both have some validity.

A capitalist system clearly imposes some bounds upon redistribution unless society as a whole is willing to sacrifice a great deal of consumption for the sake of equality. In such a system, if all the income of the wealthy is taxed away (or if incomes are somehow made equal in the first place), the formerly wealthy will presumably not save or invest as much, nor work as hard, nor innovate and produce as much. If everyone is guaranteed an equal income regardless of effort, some will undoubtedly choose not to work at all and will live off the largess of the tax-payers. There is no denying that even modest guaranteed in-comes would somewhat reduce the work effort of the poor. And high taxes probably have at least a moderately negative effect on the savings, if not the work, of high-income people.

As Okun put it, there is a trade-off between equity and effi-ciency. At some point, increased redistribution would so cut production that even the worst-off group would lose rather than gain from it. Particularly to the extent that the worst off are con-cerned with their absolute income level rather than with their relative standing (of course, we should not assume that this is always the case), such a point can be called a "limit" imposed by the system: further redistribution would be unanimously op-posed because it would make everyone worse off.[5] Different so-cial welfare functions would define different degrees of equality as limits. The general point is that the structure of a capitalist economic system interacts with virtually any welfare criterion (including any plausible voting scheme) to define some limit to redistribution—or, more precisely, to define costs that would eventually offset the benefits of increased redistribution.

The evidence from existing capitalist economies supports the argument that there are limits to redistribution. Comparable data are hard to come by, and we should not in any case leap to the conclusion that more equality would be impossible just be-cause we don't presently observe it; but certainly no industrial-ized free market economy now or in the past has come very close to complete income equality. Even the Scandinavian countries, models of social democratic capitalism with elaborate welfare state policies, retain highly unequal distributions of wealth and income. In Sweden, for example, in the early 1970s the top fifth of families got about 37 percent of all the post-tax money income while the bottom fifth got only 7 percent.[6]

Yet we should not exaggerate the tightness of structural lim-its on redistribution. The fact is that other capitalist nations, including Sweden, Great Britain, Japan, the Low Countries, and (probably) Germany, have much more equal incomes than the United States has. And this is true not only of countries with weak economies where it might be argued that redistribution was pursued beyond rational limits and the country had to pay the price; there are several vigorous capitalist economies in which productivity has grown rapidly along with a relatively high degree of equality.

Internal evidence from the United States bolsters this point. Income maintenance experiments show that rather little production would be lost by providing a moderate guaranteed income for everyone. Taxes could be made substantially more progressive without serious disincentive effects. For those able to work, guaranteed jobs, at good wages, would cost less than guaranteed incomes and would probably increase total production as well as increasing equality.

It seems clear that the United States has not in fact run up against limits imposed by its economic system. With very little, if any, loss in efficiency or production, it would be possible to have considerably more income equality. *Beliefs* and rhetoric about economic structure, not just the structure itself, have been important in restricting the redistributional effects of government. For an explanation of those beliefs and that rhetoric and for an explanation of why so much government action takes strange and inefficient forms, we must turn to an interest group analysis.

Interest groups are an inescapable part of the American political scene. Their role in policy making is almost certainly a great one. True, it is hard to demonstrate the extent of group influence with scientific rigor. Much that goes on is unobserved, and visible group activity can sometimes be explained away as harmless information-providing or the transmission of intense public opinion. But the shape of public policy is scarcely explicable in other than interest group terms, and specific policy results often correspond closely with activity by well-organized groups.

The patchwork of regressive tax loopholes, from depletion allowances to consumer interest deductions to tax shelters for Park Avenue "farmers," hardly makes sense as a rational economic design, but it does correspond to lobbying efforts by the wealthy and well organized. Expensive weapons systems with cost overruns and hefty profits undoubtedly have to do with the political power of defense contractors as well as with objective foreign policy needs. Large subsidies for the interstate highway system surely reflect the clout of truckers and road builders and the automobile and oil industries, just as price supports and payments to big farmers no doubt result from their political importance. Why would regulation, supposedly in the public interest, so often be designed to benefit the regulated—except that the regulated have political power beyond their numbers?

By the same token, the small size and peculiar shape of programs to redistribute income to the poor reflects the lack of organization by the poor themselves and the weight of conservative groups (which block redistribution) and organized service providers (who divert government dollars to their own pockets). Why should a program to help house the poor take the form of guaranteed mortgages that led to quick foreclosures and abandonments—except that the home loan industry wanted it? Why did urban renewal for so long mean black removal unless it was that white city dwellers and construction companies had more clout than the blacks whose housing was torn down? The public housing disgrace would seem to reflect more solicitude for builders than occupants.

Similarly, Medicare's and Medicaid's pouring of money into private fee-for-service medicine can only be understood in terms of the immense power of organized doctors and hospitals. Even Food Stamps, a successful redistributive transfer program, owes its odd in-kind (rather than cash) nature to the power of agricultural interests, who thought, mistakenly, that it would increase food consumption. The low level of cash transfers or jobs for the poor and the U.S. preference for bricks and mortar and in-kind services make sense only as a sign that corporations and the wealthy and service providers have more influence than the poor themselves.

About one central fact there can be no doubt: the system of organized groups is heavily biased toward the wealthy. Schattschneider's epigram that the chorus in the pluralist heaven "sings with a strong upper-class accent" puts it rather mildly.[7] By any relevant measure—the number of groups, or the extent of lobbying activity, or the amount of money spent—business corporations and professional groups overwhelmingly dominate the interest group universe. This is true despite the important presence of organized labor—weaker than business, and prone to neglect the interests of the very poor in favor of its own middle-income membership—and despite the emergence of a few dedicated "public interest" lobbies, which tend to be antibusiness but upper-middle class in orientation. Only occasionally do pro-poor social movements become significant political actors.

As Olson and others have shown, there are good reasons why the poor and ordinary consumers and taxpayers with diffuse interests do not usually get organized. The costs of communicating and getting together, that is, information and transaction costs, are simply too great relative to the potential gains. Each individual is tempted to act as a free rider and let someone else pay the money and do the work, so no one does it. Rational self-interest imposes a major barrier against organizing the poor into a political force whose numbers might partly counterbalance the money of business corporations.[8]

The techniques of group influence on policy are many. The blatant Watergate- or Abscam-style bribery that occasionally comes into public view may be more common than we would like to think, but it is certainly not the chief method by which groups get the public policies they want. The more important techniques are open, legal, and in themselves apparently innocuous: providing information to congressmen and regulators when little competing information is offered on the other side; using media campaigns to change the opinions of the public; cultivating personal relationships with politicians; electing friends and winning "access" with campaign contributions; tempting politicians with the prospect of future private jobs; recruiting regulators from within industry itself.

The most important channel of group influence is probably the most legal and innocent of all: recruiting and electing friendly politicians, who are predisposed to favor a group's goals long before they get into office. Campaign money and manpower can work wonders at helping sympathetic politicians in both parties (but especially Republicans) emerge as candidates, win nominations, and prevail in general elections. The grateful winners are then open to information-providing, personal contact, and the other techniques of lobbying. But more important, their true personal convictions are in line with what the interest group wants. Bribery is quite unnecessary. In fact, such a sincere ally is far more reliable than a venal politician whose loyalty is temporarily purchased with cash.

Interest group influence is greatest when political visibility is low, when the public is unaware of what is going on, and when politicians have little to fear from direct policy-related voting by ordinary citizens. On some matters of social policy, visibility tends to be high, the scope of conflict is broad, and the general public tends to prevail over organized interests—at least concerning the broad outlines of policy although the specific implementation may go awry. (The elderly get help with medical care, but doctors control the system of payment.) On other policies, especially those involving technical or apparently minor matters, the scope of conflict is narrow from the start, and interest groups often get their way unhindered. Examples include special tax provisions, highly sophisticated weapons systems, and Army Corps of Engineers dams. The most extreme case is regulation by little-known commissions or implementation of small programs at the local level when, as McConnell put it, special interests sometimes completely capture a government agency.[9] Interest groups tend to do best at the state and local level and with independent agencies, next best with Congress, least well with the president.

The main point, however, holds true at every level. Because money can influence elections and public opinion, money can influence policy. Interest group processes transmit economic inequality into political inequality, which in turn thwarts government redistribution and perpetuates economic inequality.

The United States is probably unusual in the extent to which corporations and professional groups influence policy because of the absence of leftist trade unions or a socialist party that could raise the visibility of distributive issues and mobilize the poor and the working class. American unions are oriented toward short-run bread and butter rather than broad political goals. The Democratic party, while somewhat more pro-redistribution than the Republican, is only a shadow of a vigorous European socialist party. In the United States there is relatively little counterweight to the influence of business and the wealthy.

In relying upon an interest group analysis to account for much of the government's failure to redistribute income, however, we notice that the analysis blends rather subtly back into a discussion of economic structure. In fact it becomes clear that it is somewhat artificial to separate the two. For very likely in *any* capitalist system with liberal democratic political institutions, interest groups with an upper-income bias will wield disproportionate political power.

Inevitably, under capitalism, a few individuals and corporations seem to hold large shares of wealth; usually they are well organized and (as a by-product of organization for other purposes) are well equipped to seek political ends. It is difficult to see how any capitalist society, so long as it permits free speech and free association, can prevent the turning of money and organization into political power. There are simply too many channels through which money can influence public opinion and policy makers. If this is so, the configuration of interest group power is itself to a substantial extent structural. It is quite possible, therefore, that a degree of egalitarianism that would in theory be perfectly compatible with the structure of capitalist economies is in fact ruled out by the political forces inevitably unleashed by those economies.

What Is to Be Done?

Those who favor a more egalitarian distribution of income and want to do something politically to reduce inequality in the United States would do well to consider the political causes of past failures to accomplish redistribution, which have important implications for future action. One should proceed rather differently, for example, depending on whether interest group or economic structural explanations are more nearly correct.

To the extent that structural constraints prevent equality, a serious egalitarian must face up to the prospect of working toward an alternative economic and social system. This means exploring the experiences of other times and places and thinking imaginatively about alternatives. It means thinking the unthinkable, even inquiring whether communist systems like those of Yugoslavia or China or others have any useful ideas to offer us.

If the chief problem is private ownership of the means of production—particularly if property income is the main source of income inequality—a solution worth thinking about is a democratic socialism which preserves many of the allocative virtues of markets (basing investment decisions on social profit and offering wage incentives for work) and which retains democratic politics and civil liberties while providing more equal earnings and welfare benefits. Such a system might look similar to a Swedish-style model of welfare state but with a crucial difference: private capital would be replaced by public.

If, however, the structural problem is really that of material incentives—of the need to provide highly unequal wages to encourage work—then to achieve substantial equality would require a fundamental change not only in the ownership of capital but also in incentive systems. Presumably the world could be a much more pleasant and more egalitarian place if people worked for the sake of helping others and for intrinsic self-fulfillment—or even patriotism—instead of material greed. (On the other hand, competition for prestige or status would not be a very attractive substitute for materialist striving. Unequal status can entail as much or more suffering and degradation than does unequal money. If, as some sociologists seem to believe, it is the only workable alternative, egalitarians are in grave trouble.)[10]

Of course, any basic change of incentive systems would mean a major tranformation in the way people think and act and live, a transformation that could come about only with radical changes in child raising and education and social organization. Here societies like China, which have tried to build a new socialist person, undoubtedly have some lessons (both positive and negative) to teach us.

Pessimists about human nature are quick to point to the failure of past utopian experiments and to the increasing resort, even by countries like Cuba and China, to the use of material incentives for the sake of increasing productivity.[11] Perhaps they are right, and no very egalitarian society is feasible; perhaps the poor will be always with us, and inequality is the lot of man. But at the very least, the matter deserves close attention. Careful scrutiny of past experience and future possibilities is called for. The vision of a cooperative, unselfish, egalitarian world should not be lightly abandoned.

Of course, any assessment of alternative social systems must take account of all the relevant costs and benefits. While we may be repelled by the high degree of inequality that capitalism brings and the base motives it cultivates, we must also acknowledge the marvelous efficiency that can be achieved by self-interested actors in decentralized markets. Capitalism is perhaps a dismal failure at distribution, but it has been a spectacular success at production. Any substitution of planning for markets would lead to serious problems of communication and organization. And nonmaterial incentives may be less flexible, less precise or finely graded, than material. Issues of personal liberty are also relevant.[12]

Transition costs must be considered as well. To change a functioning system is disruptive and expensive and should be undertaken only if there is a high probability of real gain. Evolutionary and peaceful methods of transition add greatly to the feasibility and attractiveness of change. One such idea is pension socialism, as in the Swedish Meidner plan, by which workers' funds would gradually purchase their own firms.[13]

Assuming that major social and economic changes are desirable, clearly there are formidable barriers in the way of achieving them. In America, radicals have little to work with, neither a militant labor movement, nor a large core of activists, nor a vigorous intellectual Left. The experience of the 1930s, when one would have thought capitalism most vulnerable, is sobering. Yet the economic and political shocks of the 1970s and 1980s and the excesses of the Right may help overcome Americans' complacency and create a climate more receptive to thinking about alternative futures.

The foregoing arguments depend heavily upon the extent to which capitalism, or material incentives, actually limit equality. But the facts about capitalism and material incentives and the workings of other incentive systems are not yet really known with any confidence. One important task on the egalitarian agenda, therefore, is to investigate them thoroughly. This means experimentation, econometric work, and, especially, comparative studies.

I have argued that interest groups as well as structural factors significantly contribute to inequality. Thus, it may be possible to do much within the current system. It makes sense to pay attention to specific government policies and to urge mild reforms of the sort congenial to American liberals. It is worth raising a hue and cry over each regressive tax or pro-rich subsidy, trying to increase the public visibility of its distributive effects and thereby to change the equation of political forces. Egalitarians should try to counteract right-wing propaganda; they should educate the citizenry about who pays for and who benefits from various government programs, as well as how much more redistribution is structurally possible, so that people will demand the increased equality that is in their interest.

It is worth trying to get rid of pro-producer (and inefficient) regulations and subsidies, to change ineffective medical and housing and other in-kind programs into effective ones or into direct income transfers. Most important of all, for those who can work, are *jobs*, to help them gain productivity and self-respect as well as income. Jobs could be produced by less harsh macroeconomic policies, more rational regulation, and public service employment.

The United States should also be able to provide genuinely equal educational opportunities for the poor, to promote residential and school integration of blacks, to devise systems of preventive medicine and community clinics without exorbitant fees, and to increase workplace democracy.[14]

In working for such programs, well-crafted policy proposals can have an impact, particularly if they are packaged and publicized attractively, so that they increase visibility and broaden the scope of conflict. (The call for "universal" rather than "means-tested," or income-tested, benefits is one possible example.)[15]

Beyond policy proposals, however, a central task is to arouse and organize people of low income to attain political effectiveness matching their numbers. This means organizing consumers and welfare clients and workers and blacks. It means constructing national lobbies as counterweights to business groups. Ultimately it may mean transforming a political party or forming a new one. None of this is easy, but policies are unlikely to change much without a change in political forces.

A related line of effort involves reforms to reduce the political power of money as much as possible by severely limiting private campaign contributions, prosecuting bribery, preventing conflicts of interest, fully disclosing politicians' sources of income, eliminating tax deductions for business lobbying, and the like.

The central point is that, over the long term, egalitarian results require *political* changes, changes in the forces that affect policy.

Of course, one should have no illusions about the ease of making even modest changes of this sort. The problems of information costs and transaction costs that inhibit organizing the poor and the general citizenry will not simply vanish. (Institutional rearrangements of incentives can encourage organization, however; the U.S. government's belated but effective facilitation of labor unionization should not be forgotten.) Interest groups and the wealthy will do much to resist reform and maintain their power. The ineffective 1971 and 1974 efforts to reduce the role of money in elections provide an unhappy example: only the forms (contributions to "PACs" instead of candidate organizations) changed; reality stayed the same or perhaps even got worse.

As I have suggested, the ability to translate wealth into political power may be a structural fact in a capitalist democracy. Even if money were somehow displaced from its pervasive role in the electoral process and in lobbying and legislative policy making, it would still affect what sort of information is and isn't transmitted to the public and thereby affect what policies the public favors and, indirectly, what politicians do.

To the extent that inequality of income and wealth is perpetuated by this interplay between the economic and political systems, the persistence of inequality must once more be attributed to fundamental structural conditions. Once again we are led to consider alternative social and economic systems but with no simple way to construct them. Only time and effort will reveal whether serious egalitarian reforms are possible.

Notes

Chapter 1

1. Arthur Cecil Pigou, *The Economics of Welfare*, 4th ed. (London: Macmillan, 1948; originally published 1932), p. 89.

2. Jean-Jacques Rousseau, *The Social Contract*, ed. and tr. Charles Frankel (New York: Hafner, 1947; originally published 1762), p. 47.

3. R. H. Tawney, *Equality*, 4th ed. (New York: Capricorn, 1961; originally published 1931), pp. 34, 84. Recent discussions of equality include Joseph H. Carens, *Equality, Moral Incentives, and the Market* (Chicago: University of Chicago Press, 1981); and Douglas Rae et al., *Equalities* (New Haven: Yale University Press, 1981).

4. Even Milton Friedman, *Capitalism and Freedom* (Chicago: University of Chicago Press, 1962), pp. 164–65, does not accept an ethical argument for marginal product wages but favors them on grounds related to freedom and incentives.

5. Imagine the opposite, that the optimal distribution involves some inequality. Then at least one person would have more than the mean income and at least one would have less. By the assumptions of identical utility functions and declining marginal utility, transfer of one unit of income to the low- from the high-income individual would increase the happiness of the one more than it decreased that of the other, thus increasing aggregate happiness. The original supposition of inequality in the optimal distribution of income is contradicted.

6. Some of the following points are elaborated upon in Benjamin I. Page, "Utilitarian Arguments for Equality," DP #547–79, Institute for Research on Poverty, University of Wisconsin, Madison, Aug. 1979. An excellent set of readings is Edmund S. Phelps, ed., *Economic Justice* (Harmondsworth, Middlesex, England: Penguin, 1973). See also Brian Barry, *The Liberal Theory of Justice* (Oxford: Clarendon Press, 1973); and Brian Barry, "Social Science and Distributive Justice," in *Value Judgment*

and Income Distribution, ed. Robert A. Solo and Charles W. Anderson (New York: Praeger, 1981), pp. 107-37.

7. Christopher Jencks points out that even if utility functions for money are not identical but are all marginally declining, the utility maximizing conditions ($dU_i/dY_i = dU_j/dY_j$ for all individuals i and j)—while probably not yielding exactly equal incomes or utilities—could lead to relatively egalitarian ones. Sybarites certainly wouldn't get all the income.

8. J. A. Mirrlees, "An Exploration in the Theory of Optimal Income Taxation," *Review of Economic Studies* 38 (1971): 175–208; Efraim Sadka, "On Progressive Taxation," *American Economic Review* 66 (Dec. 1976): 931–35; Robert Cootner, "Optimal Tax Schedules and Rates: Mirrlees and Ramsey," *American Economic Review* 68 (Dec. 1978): 756–68; John Rawls, *A Theory of Justice* (Cambridge, Mass.: Harvard University Press, 1971).

9. Evidence on these points is discussed in Chs. 2, 3, 5.

10. See Charles E. Lindblom, *Politics and Markets* (New York: Basic Books, 1977).

11. U.S. Bureau of the Census, *Current Population Reports*, Series P-60, #127, Aug. 1981, p. 15.

12. Edward C. Budd, "Postwar Changes in the Size Distribution of Income in the U.S.," *American Economic Review* 60 (1970): 247–60; *Current Population Reports*, Series P-60, various years.

13. The Gini coefficient, like any single number used to characterize a distribution, conveys only limited information. In addition, its theoretical properties are not ideal; for many purposes alternative (but less familiar) measures may be superior. See A. B. Atkinson, "On the Measurement of Inequality," *Journal of Economic Theory* 2 (1970): 244–63; Eytan Sheshinski, "Relation Between a Social Welfare Function and the Gini Index of Income Inequality," *Journal of Economic Theory* 4 (1972): 98–100; and Nanak C. Kakwani, *Income Inequality and Poverty* (New York: Oxford University Press, 1980).

14. See Morgan Reynolds and Eugene Smolensky, *Public Expenditures, Taxes and the Distribution of Income: The United States, 1950, 1961, 1970* (New York: Academic Press, 1977), Ch. 2.

15. Joseph A. Pechman and Benjamin A. Okner, *Who Bears the Tax Burden?* (Washington, D.C.: Brookings Institution, 1974), p. 46.

16. See Sheldon Danziger and Michael K. Taussig, "The Income Unit and the Anatomy of Income Distribution," *Review of Income and Wealth* (1980); Edward P. Lazear and Robert T. Michael, "Family Size and the Distribution of Real Per Capita Income," *American Economic Review* 70 (March 1980): 91–107; Harold F. Lydall, "Some Problems in Making International Comparisons of Inequality," in *Income Inequality: Trends and International Comparisons*, ed. John R. Moroney (Lexington, Mass.: Lexington, 1979), pp. 21–37.

17. Morton Paglin, "The Measurement and Trend of Inequality: A Basic Revision," *American Economic Review* 65 (Sept. 1975): 598-609; Lee Lillard, "Inequality: Earnings vs. Human Wealth," *American Economic*

Review 67 (March 1977): 42–53; Sheldon Danziger, Robert Haveman, and Eugene Smolensky, "Comment," *American Economic Review* 67 (June 1977): 505–12.

18. Dorothy S. Projector and Gertrude S. Weiss, *Survey of Financial Characteristics of Consumers* (Washington, D.C.: Federal Reserve System, Aug. 1966); Edward E. Budd, ed. *Inequality and Poverty* (New York: Norton, 1967), pp. xxi–xxiv.

19. Robert J. Lampman, *The Share of Top Wealth-Holders in National Wealth* (Ann Arbor, Mich.: University Microfilms, 1967; originally published National Bureau of Economic Research, 1962).

20. James D. Smith and Stephen D. Franklin, "The Concentration of Personal Wealth, 1922-1969," *American Economic Review* 64 (May 1974): 162–67. It is very difficult to make comparisons of the United States with other countries, but Britain may be even more unequal. See Alan Harrison, *The Distribution of Wealth in Ten Countries* (London: Royal Commission on the Distribution of Income and Wealth, 1979).

21. Rudolph G. Penner, "Drawing Back the Veil on the Very Rich," *New York Times*, July 19, 1981, sec. 3, p. 3.

22. Lester Thurow, *Generating Inequality* (New York: Basic Books, 1975); Paul L. Menchik, "Intergenerational Transmission of Inequality: An Empirical Study of Wealth Mobility," *Economica* 46 (Nov. 1979).

23. *Current Population Reports*, Series P–60, #127 (Aug. 1981), esp. pp. 27, 29, 30. See Michael Harrington, *The Other America* (New York: Macmillan, 1962); Mollie Orshansky, "Counting the Poor: Another Look at the Poverty Profile," *Social Security Bulletin* 28 (Jan. 1965): 3–29.

24. Norman Bradburn, *The Structure of Psychological Well-Being* (Chicago: Aldine, 1969); David Caplovitz, *The Poor Pay More* (New York: Free Press, 1962); Kenneth B. Clark, *Dark Ghetto* (New York: Harper, 1965); Douglas C. Glascow, *The Black Underclass* (New York: Random House, 1981); Janet M. Fitchen, *Poverty in Rural America* (Boulder, Colo.: Westview, 1981); Oscar Lewis, *La Vida* (New York: Random House, 1966).

25. See Studs Terkel, *Working* (New York: Random House, 1972). Employment problems are discussed further in Chs. 3, 5.

26. Lee Rainwater, *What Money Buys: Inequality and the Social Meaning of Income* (New York: Basic Books, 1974); Richard Sennett and Jonathan Cobb, *The Hidden Injuries of Class* (New York: Knopf, 1972).

27. Richard A. Musgrave and Peggy B. Musgrave, *Public Finance in Theory and Practice* (New York: McGraw-Hill, 1976).

28. To be sure, such a simple notion of redistribution by self-interested voters under majority rule may run afoul of Arrow's paradox. For any redistributive coalition there may exist a different majority that could defeat it so that there is no equilibrium outcome, no majority winner. Alternative game theoretic solutions seem neither determinative nor convincing. But the failure of formal theory to be conclusive on this point need not negate the common sense intuition that in a perfect democracy of selfish voters the poor would tend to soak the rich. See Kenneth J. Arrow, *Social Choice and Individual Values*, 2nd ed. (New

York: Wiley, 1963; originally published 1951); Amartya K. Sen, *Collective Choice and Social Welfare* (San Francisco, Ca.: Holden-Day, 1970); Koichi Hamada, "A Simple Majority Rule on the Distribution of Income," *Journal of Economic Theory* 6 (1973): 243–64.

Chapter 2

1. Richard A. Musgrave and Peggy B. Musgrave, *Public Finance in Theory and Practice* (New York: McGraw-Hill, 1976). For contrary arguments, see Walter J. Blum and Harry Kalven, Jr., *The Uneasy Case for Progressive Taxation* (Chicago: University of Chicago Press, 1953).

2. Roy G. Blakey and Gladys C. Blakey, *The Federal Income Tax* (New York: Longmans, Green, 1940); Sidney Ratner, *American Taxation: Its History as a Social Force in Democracy* (New York: Norton, 1942).

3. Joseph A. Pechman, *Federal Tax Policy*, 3rd ed. (Washington, D.C.: Brookings Institution, 1977), pp. 298, 301.

4. Ibid., pp. 349–50.

5. Richard Goode, *The Individual Income Tax*, rev. ed. (Washington, D.C.: Brookings Institution, 1976), pp. 248–51. See also Joseph A. Pechman and Benjamin A. Okner, *Who Bears the Tax Burden?* (Washington, D.C.: Brookings Institution, 1974), pp. 57–59.

6. Benjamin A. Okner, "Distributional Aspects of Tax Reform During the Past Fifteen Years," *National Tax Journal* 32 (March 1979): 11–27; U.S. Congress, Joint Economic Committee, "Summary of H.R. 4242: The Economic Recovery Tax Act of 1981," reprinted in *Tax Notes*, Aug. 10, 1981, pp. 273–92.

7. Pechman, *Federal Tax Policy*, p. 350.

8. Ibid., pp. 92–97, 350.

9. Ibid., pp. 83–92, 350.

10. Boris J. Bittker, "Equity, Efficiency, and Income Tax Theory: Do Misallocations Drive Out Inequities?" in *The Economics of Taxation*, ed. Henry J. Aaron and Michael J. Boskin (Washington, D.C.: Brookings Institution, 1980), pp. 19–31. See also Roger A. Freeman, *Tax Loopholes: The Legend and the Reality* (Washington, D.C.: American Enterprise Institute, 1973).

11. Martin Feldstein, "A Contribution to the Theory of Tax Expenditures: The Case of Charitable Giving," in *Economics of Taxation*, pp. 99–122; Charles T. Clotfelter and C. Eugene Steuerle, "Charitable Contributions" (and comments thereon), in *How Taxes Affect Economic Behavior*, ed. Henry J. Aaron and Joseph A. Pechman (Washington, D.C.: Brookings Institution, 1981), pp. 403–46; Susan Ackerman and David Ott, "An Analysis of the Revenue Effect of Proposed Substitutes for Tax Exemption of State and Local Bonds," *National Tax Journal* 23

(Dec. 1970): 397–406.

12. Pechman, *Federal Tax Policy*, pp. 119–22; Philip M. Stern, *The Rape of the Taxpayer* (New York: Vintage, 1974).

13. Pechman, *Federal Tax Policy*, pp. 340–41.

14. Ibid., pp. 201–19. See also John A. Brittain, *The Payroll Tax for Social Security* (Washington, D.C.: Brookings Institution, 1972).

15. U.S. Office of Management and Budget, *The Budget of the United States Government, Fiscal Year 1980* (Washington, D.C.: U.S. Government Printing Office, 1979), pp. 75–77 (hereafter cited as U.S. *Budget 1980*); and U.S. *Budget 1982*, p. 85.

16. See Karen W. Arenson, "The Quiet Repeal of the Corporate Income Tax," *New York Times*, Aug. 2, 1981, sec. 3, pp. 1, 20.

17. Arnold C. Harberger, "The Incidence of the Corporation Income Tax," *Journal of Political Economy* 70 (June 1962): 215–40.

18. Marian Krzyzaniak and Richard A. Musgrave, *The Shifting of the Corporation Income Tax* (Baltimore: Johns Hopkins University Press, 1963). On the other hand, see John G. Cragg, Arnold C. Harberger, and Peter Mieszkowski, "Empirical Evidence on the Incidence of the Corporation Income Tax," *Journal of Political Economy* 75 (Dec. 1967): 811–21.

19. Pechman, *Federal Tax Policy*, pp. 129–36.

20. Ibid., pp. 220–44, 341; U.S. *Budget 1982*, p. 562; George Cooper, *A Voluntary Tax? New Perspectives on Sophisticated Estate Tax Avoidance* (Washington, D.C.: Brookings Institution, 1979).

21. U.S. Congress, Joint Economic Committee, "Summary," p. 276.

22. Pechman, *Federal Tax Policy*, pp. 181–89; U.S. *Budget 1982*, p. 562.

23. Benjamin A. Okner, "Total U.S. Taxes and Their Effect on the Distribution of Family Income in 1966 and 1970," in *Economics of Taxation*, p. 77. See also Pechman and Okner, *Who Bears the Tax Burden?* pp. 38, 62.

24. Advisory Commission on Intergovernmental Relations, *Significant Features of Fiscal Federalism*, 1979-1980 ed. (Washington, D.C.: U.S. Government Printing Office, Oct. 1980), pp. 56, 98–107; Pechman, *Federal Tax Policy*, pp. 246–49, 369–71. Edgar Browning has come up with an ingenious argument that sales taxes are actually *progressive* (with respect to *post*-transfer income) because the poor get much of their income in untaxed in-kind benefits and inflation-indexed amounts of cash. But he relies on the dubious assumptions that in-kind benefits maintain a constant value regardless of price levels and that the poor spend no higher a proportion of their incomes on taxed goods than the rich do. See Edgar K. Browning, "The Burden of Taxation," *Journal of Political Economy* 86 (Aug. 1978): 649–71.

25. Pechman and Okner, *Who Bears the Tax Burden?* p. 59.

26. Dick Netzer, *Economics of the Property Tax* (Washington, D.C.: Brookings Institution, 1966); Henry J. Aaron, *Who Pays the Property Tax?* (Washington, D.C.: Brookings Institution, 1975), pp. 20–27.

27. Aaron, *Who Pays the Property Tax?* pp. 27–38.

28. Peter Mieszkowski, "Tax Incidence Theory: The Effects of Taxes

on the Distribution of Income," *Journal of Economic Literature* 7 (Dec. 1969): 1103–24; Peter Mieszkowski, "The Property Tax: An Excise Tax or a Profits Tax?" *Journal of Public Economics* 1 (1972): 73–96; Aaron, *Who Pays the Property Tax?* pp. 38–45.

29. Pechman and Okner, *Who Bears the Tax Burden?* p. 59; Aaron, *Who Pays the Property Tax?* pp. 45–49.

30. Jere Chapman, Elliott Sclar, and Raymond Torto, *The Rich Get Richer and the Rest Pay Taxes: A Massachusetts Tax Primer* (Lynn, Mass.: Massachusetts Public Finance Project, 1974), pp. 5–36; Robert M. Brandon et al., *Tax Politics* (New York: Random House, 1976), pp. 175–208; David E. Black, "Property Tax Incidence: The Excise-Tax Effect and Assessment Practices," *National Tax Journal* 30 (Dec. 1977): 429–33; Aaron, *Who Pays the Property Tax?* pp. 56–70.

31. Pechman, *Federal Tax Policy*, pp. 249, 269, 372–73; U.S. Advisory Commission on Intergovernmental Relations, *Significant Features of Federalism* (Washington, D.C.: U.S. Government Printing Office, 1980), pp. 110–33, esp. p. 125.

32. Okner, "Total U.S. Taxes," p. 77; see also Pechman and Okner, *Who Bears the Tax Burden?* pp. 62, 64.

33. Okner, "Total U.S. Taxes," p. 74; see also Pechman and Okner, *Who Bears the Tax Burden?* pp. 49, 51.

34. Okner, "Total U.S. Taxes," p. 82; Pechman and Okner, *Who Bears the Tax Burden?* p. 56.

35. See Walter Shapiro, "Wilbur Mills: Ways and Means of Conning the Press," *Washington Monthly*, Dec. 1974, pp. 4–13.

36. John F. Manley, *The Politics of Finance: The House Committee on Ways and Means* (Boston: Little, Brown, 1970); Benjamin I. Page, "Federal Tax Policy and Inequality," paper delivered at the 1977 annual meeting of the Midwest Political Science Association, Chicago, Ill., April 21–23.

37. Stern, *Rape of the Taxpayer*; Brandon et al., *Tax Politics*; Ralph Nader Congress Project, *The Revenue Committees: A Study of the House Ways and Means and Senate Finance Committees and the House and Senate Appropriation Committees* (New York: Grossman, 1975).

38. Manley, *Politics of Finance*; Page, "Federal Tax Policy."

39. Donald E. Stokes and Warren E. Miller, "Party Government and the Saliency of Congress," *Public Opinion Quarterly* 26 (Winter 1962). See Anthony Downs, *An Economic Theory of Democracy* (New York: Harper, 1957).

40. Sidney Verba and Norman H. Nie, *Participation in America* (New York: Harper, 1972).

41. Warren E. Miller and Donald E. Stokes, "Constituency Influence in Congress," in *Elections and the Political Order*, ed. Angus Campbell, Philip E. Converse, Warren E. Miller, and Donald E. Stokes (New York: Wiley, 1966), pp. 351–72; Benjamin I. Page, Robert Y. Shapiro, Paul M. Gronke, and Robert Rosenberg, "Constituency, Party, and Representation in Congress," unpublished, University of Chicago, Nov. 1981.

42. Manley, *Politics of Finance*; Page, "Federal Tax Policy." But see

Susan B. Hansen, "Partisan Realignment and Tax Policy, 1789-1970," paper delivered at the 1977 annual meeting of the American Political Science Association, Washington, D.C., Sept. 1–4.

43. Grant McConnell, *Private Power and American Democracy* (New York: Knopf, 1966); Theodore J. Lowi, *The End of Liberalism* (New York: Norton, 1969).

44. Mancur Olson, Jr., *The Logic of Collective Action* (Cambridge, Mass.: Harvard University Press, 1965); E. E. Schattschneider, *The Semi-Sovereign People* (New York: Holt, 1960).

45. Don A. Mele, "Organizations Seeking to Influence Tax Policy," *Tax Notes*, Sept. 21, 1981, pp. 627–36. See also Brandon et al., *Tax Politics*; Stern, *Rape of the Taxpayer*; Manley, *Politics of Finance*.

46. Stanley S. Surrey, "The Congress and the Tax Lobbyist—How Special Tax Provisions Get Enacted," *Harvard Law Review* 70 (1957): 1145–81.

47. *Wall Street Journal*, Nov. 7, 1975, p. 1.

48. Richard E. Cohen, "The Business Lobby Discovers That in Unity There Is Strength," *National Journal*, June 28, 1980, pp. 1050–55.

49. Raymond A. Bauer, Ithiel de Sola Pool, and Lewis Anthony Dexter, *American Business and Public Policy* (New York: Atherton, 1963); Lester Milbrath, *The Washington Lobbyists* (Chicago: Rand-McNally, 1963).

50. Schattschneider, *Semi-Sovereign People*; Murray Edelman, *The Symbolic Uses of Politics* (Urbana: University of Illinois Press, 1964); Murray Edelman, *Political Language: Words That Succeed and Policies That Fail* (New York: Academic Press, 1977). See also Downs, *Economic Theory of Democracy*.

51. McConnell, *Private Power*, Ch. 6.

52. "Poll Shows Public Prefers Lower U.S. Income Taxes to Simplifying Procedures," *New York Times*, July 27, 1977, p. A13.

53. *New York Times*, May 6, 1976, p. 23.

54. George H. Gallup, *The Gallup Poll: Public Opinion, 1935-1971*, 3 vols. (New York: Random House, 1972), esp. pp. 633, 686, 1152, 1549; Advisory Committee on Intergovernmental Relations, *Changing Public Attitudes on Governments and Taxes: 1976* (Washington, D.C.: U.S. Government Printing Office, 1976), pp. 6, 21; Louis Harris, press release, April 14, 1977. See also Benjamin I. Page, "Taxes and Inequality: Do the Voters Get What They Want?" discussion paper 423-77, Institute for Research on Poverty, University of Wisconsin, Madison, 1977.

55. Gallup, *Gallup Poll*, III, 1800.

56. Page, "Taxes and Inequality."

57. "Public Seen Resisting Tax Plan If Carter Tries to Change Widely Used Allowances," *Wall Street Journal*, July 27, 1977, p. 3.

58. Benjamin I. Page and Robert Y. Shapiro, "The Effects of Public Opinion on Policy," *American Political Science Review*, March 1983.

59. Ralph Miliband, *The State in Capitalist Society* (New York: Basic Books, 1969), Chs. 7, 8.

60. Robert E. Lane, "The Fear of Equality," in his *Political Ideology* (New York: Free Press, 1962), Ch. 4; Jennifer Hochschild, *What's Fair?*

American Beliefs About Distributive Justice (Cambridge, Mass.: Harvard University Press, 1981).

61. See Kevin Lancaster, "The Dynamic Inefficiency of Capitalism," *Journal of Political Economy* 81 (1973): 1092–1109.

62. E.g., Milton Friedman, *Capitalism and Freedom* (Chicago: University of Chicago Press, 1962); Robert Cooter, "Optimal Tax Schedules and Rates: Mirrlees and Ramsey," *American Economic Review* 68 (Dec. 1978): 756–68.

63. Adam Przeworski, "Material Bases of Consent: Economics and Politics in a Hegemonic System," *Political Power and Social Theory* 1 (1979); Antonio Gramsci, *Prison Notebooks*, ed. and tr. Quintin Hoare and Geoffrey Nowell Smith (New York: International, 1971).

64. Andrew Mellon, *Taxation: The People's Business* (New York: Macmillan, 1924), pp. 12–13, 20.

65. Ronald Frederick King, "The Politics of Regressive Taxation Changes: The Investment Tax Credit of 1962 as a Hegemonic Public Policy," paper delivered at the 1977 annual meeting of the Midwest Political Science Association, Chicago, Ill., April 21–23.

66. See Louis Eisenstein, *The Ideologies of Taxation* (New York: Ronald Press, 1961).

67. Robin Barlow, Harvey E. Brazer, and James N. Morgan, *Economic Behavior of the Affluent* (Washington, D.C.: Brookings Institution, 1966); Thomas Sanders, *Effects of Taxation on Executives* (Cambridge, Mass.: Harvard University Press, 1951); George F. Break, "Income Taxes and Incentives to Work: An Empirical Study," *American Economic Review* 47 (Sept. 1957): 529–49.

68. Jerry A. Hausman, "Labor Supply," in *How Taxes Affect Economic Behavior*, pp. 27–83. See also C. V. Brown, *Taxation and the Incentive to Work* (London: Oxford University Press, 1980).

69. Dale W. Jorgenson, "Econometric Studies of Investment Behavior: A Survey," *Journal of Economic Literature* 9 (Dec. 1971): 1111–47.

70. Patric H. Hendershott and Sheng-Cheng Hu, "Investment in Producers' Equipment," and George M. von Furstenberg, "Saving," both in *How Taxes Affect Economic Behavior*, pp. 85–129, 327–402. See also Gary Fromm, ed., *Tax Incentives and Capital Spending* (Washington, D.C.: Brookings Institution, 1971), esp. the skeptical comments by Franklin Fisher.

71. See Otto Eckstein and Roger Brinner, "The Complicated Question of Capital Gains Tax Reform," testimony to the Senate Finance Subcommittee on Taxation and Debt Management, June 29, 1978; Charles R. Hulten and Frank C. Wycoff, "Economic Depreciation and Accelerated Depreciation: An Evaluation of the Conable-Jones 10–5–3 Proposal," *National Tax Journal* 34 (March 1981): 45–60.

Chapter 3

1. Roger Freeman, *The Wayward Welfare State* (Stanford, Ca.: Hoover Institution, 1981); Martin Anderson, ed., *Welfare* (Stanford, Ca.: Hoover Institution, 1978); Edgar K. Browning, "How Much More Equality Can We Afford?" *Public Interest* 43 (Spring 1976): 90–110.

2. These and subsequent figures on spending, except where otherwise noted, are drawn from U.S. Office of Management and Budget, *The Budget of the United States Government, Fiscal Year 1982* (Washington, D.C.: U.S. Government Printing Office, 1981), p. 613 (hereafter cited as U.S. *Budget 1982*). See also George F. Break, "The Role of Government: Taxes, Transfers, and Spending," in *The American Economy in Transition*, ed. Martin Feldstein (Chicago: University of Chicago Press, 1980), pp. 617–56.

3. OECD study reported in "Taxes and the GDP," *New York Times*, Feb. 14, 1982, sec. F, p. 16. See also David R. Cameron, "The Expansion of the Public Economy: A Comparative Analysis," *American Political Science Review* 72 (Dec. 1978).

4. Ann Kallman Bixby, "Social Welfare Expenditures, Fiscal Year 1979," *Social Security Bulletin* 44 (Nov. 1981): 9, 10. See also Sheldon Danziger, Robert Haveman, and Robert Plotnick, "Income Transfer Programs in the United States: An Analysis of Their Structure and Impacts," prepared for the Joint Economic Committee of the United States, Special Study on Economic Change, University of Wisconsin, Madison, May 1979, pp. 7–19. For a comprehensive overview of U.S. social welfare policy, see Robert J. Myers, *Social Security*, 2nd ed. (Homewood, Ill.: Irwin, 1981). A brief account is Harrell R. Rodgers, *Poverty amid Plenty* (Reading, Mass.: Addison-Wesley, 1979).

5. Danziger, Haveman, and Plotnick, "Income Transfer Programs," p. 20. Subsequent statements about the proportion of various benefits received by the pre-transfer poor are based on this source and on Robert D. Plotnick and Felicity Skidmore, *Progress Against Poverty: A Review of the 1964-1974 Decade* (New York: Academic Press, 1976).

6. Bruce D. Schobel, "Administrative Expenses Under OASDI," *Social Security Bulletin* 44 (March 1981): 23, 24.

7. "Program Operations," *Social Security Bulletin* 45 (Jan. 1982): 2; Alicia Munnell, *The Future of Social Security* (Washington, D.C.: Brookings Institution, 1977), pp. 26, 28, 39, 59.

8. Martin Feldstein, "Social Security, Induced Retirement, and Aggregate Capital Formation," *Journal of Political Economy* 82 (Oct. 1974): 905–26; but see also Robert Barro, *The Impact of Social Security on Private Savings: Evidence from the U.S. Time Series* (Washington, D.C.: American Enterprise Institute, 1978).

9. See Peter A. Diamond, "A Framework for Social Security Analysis," *Journal of Public Economics* 8 (Dec. 1977): 275–98.

10. Munnell, *Future of Social Security*, p. 26.

11. Richard V. Burkhauser and Jennifer L. Warlick, "Disentangling the Annuity from the Redistributive Aspects of Social Security," *Journal*

of Income and Wealth (forthcoming).

12. *Social Security Bulletin* 45 (Jan. 1982): 58.

13. Martin Feldstein, "Temporary Layoffs in the Theory of Unemployment," *Journal of Political Economy* 84 (Oct. 1976): 937–57; Martin Feldstein, "The Effect of Unemployment Insurance on Temporary Layoff Unemployment," *American Economic Review* 68 (Dec. 1978): 834–46.

14. See Tom Bethell, "Real Welfare Reform," *Journal of the Institute for Socioeconomic Studies* 5 (Autumn 1980): 29–37; Susan Sheehan, *A Welfare Mother* (New York: New American Library, 1977).

15. *Social Security Bulletin* 45 (Jan. 1982): 51.

16. Richard V. Burkhauser and Timothy M. Smeeding, "The Net Impact of the Social Security System on the Poor," *Public Policy* 29 (Spring 1981): 159–78.

17. Charles L. Schultze, *The Distribution of Farm Subsidies: Who Gets the Benefits?* (Washington, D.C.: Brookings Institution, 1971).

18. For various proposals to simplify and improve the odd patchwork of programs, see Theodore R. Marmor, ed., *Poverty Policy: A Compendium of Cash Transfer Proposals* (Chicago: Aldine, 1971).

19. Maurice MacDonald, *Food, Stamps, and Income Maintenance* (New York: Academic Press, 1977).

20. See Kenneth J. Arrow, "Uncertainty and the Welfare Economics of Medical Care," *American Economic Review* 53 (Dec. 1963): 941–73; Marjorie Smith Mueller, "Private Health Insurance in 1973: A Review of Coverage, Enrollment, and Financial Experience," *Social Security Bulletin* 38 (Feb. 1975). In 1973, coverage was limited, participation was low, and administrative and sales costs were so high that only about 53 percent of premiums was paid back in health expenditure benefits.

21. Karen Davis, "A Decade of Policy Developments in Providing Health Care for Low-Income Families," in *A Decade of Federal Antipoverty Programs: Achievements, Failures, and Lessons*, ed. Robert H. Haveman (New York: Academic Press, 1977), pp. 197–231. For a general discussion of Medicare, see Karen Davis and Cathy Schoen, *Health and the War on Poverty: A Ten-Year Appraisal* (Washington, D.C.: Brookings Institution, 1978), pp. 92–119.

22. Max Baucus, "The Federal Response to Medicare Supplementary Insurance," *Journal of the Institute for Socioeconomic Studies* 5 (Autumn 1980): 65–73. Much money (perhaps $1 billion per year) was wasted on poorly integrated private supplemental insurance.

23. Joseph G. Simanis and John R. Coleman, "Health Care Expenditures in Nine Industrialized Countries, 1960–1976," *Social Security Bulletin* 43 (Jan. 1980): 3–8, actually indicate *slower* growth of medical expenses in the United States than in any of the other countries studied. But this has not been true of Canada where rigorous cost-control measures were applied. See Theodore R. Marmor, "The North American Welfare State: Social Science and Evaluation," in *Value Judgment and Income Distribution*, ed. Robert A. Solo and Charles W. Anderson (New York: Praeger, 1981), pp. 320–39.

24. Davis and Schoen, *Health and the War on Poverty*, pp. 49–91, 204.

But see also Robert Stevens and Rosemary Stevens, *Welfare Medicine in America: A Case Study of Medicaid* (New York: Free Press, 1974); H. Jack Geiger, "The Poor Still Suffer the Most," *Chicago Tribune*, March 20, 1981, sec. 3, p. 4.

25. Timothy Smeeding, "The Antipoverty Effectiveness of In-Kind Transfers," *Journal of Human Resources* 12 (Summer 1977): 360–78.

26. See Markus G. Raskin et al., eds., *The Federal Budget and Social Reconstruction: The People and the State* (New Brunswick, N.J.: Transaction, 1978), chapters by Louise Lander, Marilyn Elrod, James Gordon, and Janet Sledge and Sander Kelman, pp. 287–335; Georgia Ireland, "Home Health Care: An Alternative," *Journal of the Institute for Socioeconomic Studies* 5 (Autumn 1980): 74–81.

27. Davis and Schoen, *Health and the War on Poverty*, pp. 120–60, 161–202; Roger A. Reynolds, "Improving Access to Health Care Among the Poor—the Neighborhood Health Center Experience," *Milbank Memorial Fund Quarterly: Health and Society* 54 (Winter 1976). On Public Health Service hospitals that are gradually being closed down, see Daniel Cohen, "Social Medicine: Amputating the Wrong Leg," *Working Papers* 8 (Nov.-Dec. 1981): 17–20.

28. Chester W. Hartman, *Housing and Social Policy* (Englewood Cliffs, N.J.: Prentice-Hall, 1975); Studs Terkel, "Inequality: Barbara Hayes," in *The Capitalist System*, ed. Richard C. Edwards, Michael Reich, and Thomas Weisskopf (Englewood Cliffs, N.J.: Prentice-Hall, 1972), pp. 11–14; Lee Rainwater, *Behind Ghetto Walls: Black Family Life in a Federal Slum* (Chicago: Aldine, 1970).

29. Raymond J. Struyk, *A New System for Public Housing: Salvaging a National Resource* (Washington, D.C.: Urban Institute, 1980); "An Interview with Harry Spence," *Working Papers* 8 (Nov.-Dec. 1981): 42–49.

30. Smeeding, "Antipoverty Effectiveness."

31. Katherine L. Bradbury and Anthony Downs, eds., *Do Housing Allowances Work?* (Washington, D.C.: Brookings Institution, 1981); Raymond J. Struyk and Marc Bendick, Jr., eds., *Housing Vouchers for the Poor: Lessons from a National Experiment* (Washington, D.C.: Urban Institute, 1981).

32. Henry J. Aaron, *Shelter and Subsidies: Who Benefits from Federal Housing Policies?* (Washington, D.C.: Brookings Institution, 1972).

33. Brian D. Boyer, *Cities Destroyed for Cash: The FHA Scandal at HUD* (Chicago: Follett, 1973); Hartman, *Housing and Social Policy*, Ch. 5; U.S. Congressional Budget Office, *Federal Housing Policy: Current Programs and Recurring Issues* (Washington, D.C.: U.S. Government Printing Office, 1978).

34. Mitchell C. Lynch, "In the Protracted Cold, Free-Fuel Plan Eludes Many of Those Eligible," *Wall Street Journal*, Feb. 11, 1982, pp. 1, 23.

35. Aaron, *Shelter and Subsidies*; U.S. *Budget 1983*, Special Analysis G, "Tax Expenditures," p. 34.

36. Paul E. Peterson and J. David Greenstone, "Racial Change and Citizen Participation: The Mobilization of Low-Income Communities

Through Community Action," in *Decade of Federal Antipoverty Programs*, pp. 241–78; Daniel P. Moynihan, *Maximum Feasible Misunderstanding* (New York: Free Press, 1969).

37. U.S. Congressional Budget Office, *Public Employment and Training Assistance: Alternative Federal Approaches* (Washington, D.C.: U.S. Government Printing Office, 1977). See also Eli Ginzberg, ed., *Employing the Unemployed* (New York: Basic Books, 1980).

38. Ken Auletta, "The Underclass," *New Yorker*, Nov. 16, 1981, pp. 63–181; Nov. 22, pp. 72–175; Nov. 30, pp. 101–69.

39. John Bishop and Robert Lerman, "Wage Subsidies for Income Maintenance and Job Creation," in *Job Creation: What Works?* ed. Robert Taggart (Salt Lake City: Olympus, 1977), pp. 39–70; Emil M. Sunley, "A Tax Preference Is Born: A Legislative History of the New Jobs Tax Credit," in *The Economics of Taxation*, ed. Henry J. Aaron and Michael J. Boskin (Washington, D.C.: Brookings Institution, 1980), pp. 391–408.

40. Bixby, "Social Welfare Expenditures," p. 6.

41. John D. Owen, *School Inequality and the Welfare State* (Baltimore: Johns Hopkins University Press, 1974); Murray Milner, Jr., *The Illusion of Equality: The Effects of Education on Opportunity, Inequality, and Social Conflict* (San Francisco, Ca.: Jossey-Bass, 1972).

42. Christopher Jencks et al., *Inequality: A Reassessment of the Effect of Family and Schooling in America* (New York: Harper, 1972); and, less pessimistically, Christopher Jencks et al., *Who Gets Ahead? The Determinants of Economic Success in America* (New York: Basic Books, 1979); Raymond Boudon, *Education, Opportunity, and Social Inequality* (New York: Wiley, 1974); Ivar Berg, *Education and Jobs: The Great Training Robbery* (New York: Praeger, 1970).

43. Samuel Bowles and Herbert Gintis, *Schooling in Capitalist America* (New York: Basic Books, 1976); Ralph Miliband, *The State in Capitalist Society* (New York: Basic Books, 1969).

44. Burt S. Barnow and Glen G. Cain, "A Reanalysis of the Effect of Head Start on Cognitive Development: Methodology and Empirical Findings," *Journal of Human Resources* 12 (1977): 177–97; Victor G. Cicirelli et al., *The Impact of Head Start: An Evaluation of the Effects of Head Start on Children's Cognitive and Affective Development*, report to the Office of Economic Opportunity by the Westinghouse Learning Corporation and Ohio State University, June 1969. More broadly, see Henry M. Levin, "A Decade of Policy Developments in Improving Education and Training for Low-Income Populations," in *Decade of Federal Antipoverty Programs*, pp. 123–88; Henry J. Aaron, *Politics and the Professors: The Great Society in Perspective* (Washington, D.C.: Brookings Institution, 1978).

45. W. Lee Hansen and Burton A. Weisbrod, *Benefits, Cost, and Finance of Public Higher Education* (Chicago: Markham, 1969); Joseph A. Pechman, "The Distributional Effects of Public Higher Education in California," *Journal of Human Resources* 5 (Summer 1970): 361–70; John Conlisk, "A Further Look at the Hansen-Weisbrod-Pechman Debate," *Journal of Human Resources* 12 (1977): 147–63.

46. Edgar K. Browning, "The Trend Toward Equality in the Distribution of Net Income," *Southern Economic Journal* 43 (July 1976): 912–23; and Edgar K. Browning, "How Much More Equality Can We Afford?" *Public Interest* 43 (Spring 1976): 90–110. See also Edgar K. Browning, *Redistribution and the Welfare System* (Washington, D.C.: American Enterprise Institute, 1975); Morton Paglin and Gerald Wood, *Poverty and Transfers In-Kind* (Stanford, Ca.: Hoover Institution, 1980).

47. Timothy M. Smeeding, "On the Distribution of Net Income: Comment," *Southern Economic Journal*, Jan. 1979, pp. 932–43.

48. W. Irwin Gillespie, "Effect of Public Expenditures on the Distribution of Income," in *Essays in Fiscal Federalism*, ed. Richard A. Musgrave (Washington, D.C.: Brookings Institution, 1965), pp. 122–86; Richard A. Musgrave, Karl E. Case, and Herman Leonard, "The Distribution of Fiscal Burdens and Benefits," *Public Finance Quarterly* 2 (July 1974): 259–311; Morgan Reynolds and Eugene Smolensky, *Public Expenditures, Taxes, and the Distribution of Income: The United States, 1950, 1961, 1970* (New York: Academic Press, 1977).

49. Plotnick and Skidmore, *Progress Against Poverty*, pp. 82, 85, 112.

50. Sheldon Danziger and Robert Plotnick, "The War on Income Poverty: Achievements and Failures," in *Welfare Reform in America: Perspectives and Prospects*, ed. Paul Sommers (The Hague: Martinus Nijhoff, 1981); Sheldon Danziger and Robert Plotnick, *Has the War on Income Poverty Been Won?* (forthcoming); Danziger, Haveman, and Plotnick, "Income Transfer Programs," pp. 31, 46; and esp. Sheldon Danziger, Robert Haveman, and Robert Plotnick, "How Income Transfer Programs Affect Work, Savings, and the Income Distribution: A Critical Review," *Journal of Economic Literature* 19 (Sept. 1981): 1006–15 (section on income redistributive effects).

51. Danziger and Plotnick, "War on Income Poverty."

52. William E. Leuchtenburg, *Franklin D. Roosevelt and the New Deal, 1932–1940* (New York: Harper, 1963).

53. James L. Sundquist, *Politics and Policy: The Eisenhower, Kennedy, and Johnson Years* (Washington, D.C.: Brookings Institution, 1968); Gary Orfield, *Congressional Power: Congress and Social Change* (New York: Harcourt, 1975).

54. V. O. Key, Jr., "A Theory of Critical Elections," *Journal of Politics* 17 (Feb. 1955): 3–18; Angus Campbell, Philip E. Converse, Warren E. Miller, and Donald E. Stokes, *The American Voter* (New York: Wiley, 1960); Kristi Andersen, *The Creation of a Democratic Majority, 1928–1936* (Chicago: University of Chicago Press, 1979).

55. Benjamin I. Page, *Choices and Echoes in Presidential Elections: Rational Man and Electoral Democracy* (Chicago: University of Chicago Press, 1978), Ch. 4; Julius Turner, *Party and Constituency*, rev. ed. Edward V. Schneier, Jr. (Baltimore: Johns Hopkins University Press, 1970).

56. Walter Dean Burnham, *Critical Elections and the Mainsprings of American Politics* (New York: Norton, 1970); James L. Sundquist, *Dynamics of the Party System: Alignment and Realignment of Political Parties in*

the United States (Washington, D.C.: Brookings Institution, 1973).

57. J. David Greenstone, *Labor in American Politics* (New York: Knopf, 1968).

58. Theodore R. Marmor, *The Politics of Medicare* (Chicago: Aldine, 1970); Richard Harris, *A Sacred Trust* (New York: New American Library, 1966); Judith M. Feder, *Medicare: The Politics of Federal Hospital Insurance* (Lexington, Mass.: Heath, 1977); Robert Alford, "The Political Economy of Health Care: Dynamics Without Change," in *The Politics and Society Reader*, ed. Ira Katznelson (New York: McKay, 1974).

59. Nick Kotz, *Let Them Eat Promises: The Politics of Hunger in America* (Garden City, N.Y.: Doubleday, 1971).

60. E. E. Schattschneider, *The Semi-Sovereign People: A Realist's View of Democracy in America* (New York: Holt, 1960).

61. E. E. Schattschneider, *Party Government* (New York: Farrar, 1942); Austin Ranney, *The Doctrine of Responsible Party Government* (Urbana: University of Illinois Press, 1954).

62. Anthony Downs, *An Economic Theory of Democracy* (New York: Harper, 1957); Otto A. Davis, Melvin J. Hinich, and Peter C. Ordeshook, "An Expository Development of a Mathematical Model of the Electoral Process," *American Political Science Review* 64 (June 1970): 426–48.

63. Robert Lane, "The Fear of Equality," in his *Political Ideology* (New York: Free Press, 1962); Jennifer Hochschild, *What's Fair?* (Cambridge, Mass.: Harvard University Press, 1981); Wayne M. Alves and Peter H. Rossi, "Who Should Get What? Fairness Judgments of the Distribution of Earnings," *American Journal of Sociology* 84 (1978): 541–64.

64. Michael E. Schiltz, *Public Attitudes Toward Social Security* (Washington, D.C.: U.S. Government Printing Office, 1970); Robert S. Erikson, Norman R. Luttbeg, and Kent L. Tedin, *American Public Opinion*, 2nd ed. (New York: Wiley, 1980).

65. See Fay Lomax Cook, *Who Should Be Helped?* (Beverly Hills, Ca.: Sage, 1979).

66. Benjamin I. Page and Robert Y. Shapiro, "The Effects of Public Opinion on Policy," *American Political Science Review*, March 1983; Warren E. Miller and Donald E. Stokes, "Constituency Influence in Congress," in Angus Campbell, Philip E. Converse, Warren E. Miller, and Donald E. Stokes, eds., *Elections and the Political Order* (New York: Wiley, 1966), pp. 351–72.

67. Leonard Goodwin, *Do the Poor Want to Work? A Social-Psychological Study of Work Orientations* (Washington, D.C.: Brookings Institution, 1972).

68. Michael C. Keeley, Philip K. Robins, Robert G. Spiegelman, and Richard W. West, "The Estimation of Labor Supply Models Using Experimental Data," *American Economic Review* 68 (Dec. 1978): 873–87; Michael C. Keeley et al., "The Labor Supply Effects and Costs of Alternative Negative Income Tax Programs," *Journal of Human Resources* (Winter 1978): 3–36; Harold W. Watts and Albert Rees, *The New Jersey Income-Maintenance Experiment. Volume II: Labor Supply Responses* (New

York: Academic Press, 1977); Stanley Masters and Irwin Garfinkel, *Estimating the Labor-Supply Effects of Income-Maintenance Alternatives* (New York: Academic Press, 1977).

69. Danziger, Haveman, and Plotnick, "How Income Transfer Programs Affect Work," pp. 983–99.

70. Ibid., pp. 1015–21; David Betson, David Greenberg, and Richard Kasten, "A Simulation Analysis of the Economic Efficiency and Distributional Effects of Alternative Program Structures," in *Income-Tested Transfer Programs: The Case For and Against*, ed. Irwin Garfinkel (New York: Academic Press, 1982).

71. Joseph H. Carens, *Equality, Moral Incentives, and the Market* (Chicago: University of Chicago Press, 1981).

72. Arthur M. Okun, *Equality and Efficiency: The Big Tradeoff* (Washington, D.C.: Brookings Institution, 1975).

73. See Louis Hartz, *The Liberal Tradition in America* (New York: Harcourt, 1955).

Chapter 4

1. P. A. Samuelson, "The Pure Theory of Public Expenditure," *Review of Economics and Statistics* 36 (1954): 387–89; P. A. Samuelson, "Diagrammatic Exposition of a Theory of Public Expenditure," *Review of Economics and Statistics* 37 (1955): 350–56; Richard A. Musgrave and Peggy B. Musgrave, *Public Finance in Theory and Practice*, 2nd ed. (New York: McGraw-Hill, 1976), Chs. 1, 3.

2. Musgrave and Musgrave, *Public Finance*; Robert H. Haveman and Julius Margolis, eds., *Public Expenditures and Policy Analysis* (Chicago: Markham, 1970). Contrast Milton Friedman, *Capitalism and Freedom* (Chicago: University of Chicago Press, 1962).

3. Arthur Cecil Pigou, *The Economics of Welfare*, 4th ed. (London: Macmillan, 1932).

4. Henry Aaron and Martin McGuire, "Public Goods and Income Distribution," *Econometrica* 38 (1970): 907–20; Geoffrey Brennan, "The Distributional Implications of Public Goods," *Econometrica* 44 (March 1976): 391–99.

5. U.S. Office of Management and Budget, *The Budget of the United States Government, Fiscal Year 1982* (Washington, D.C.: U.S. Government Printing Office, 1981) (hereafter cited as U.S. *Budget 1982*). Except where otherwise noted, all spending figures in this chapter are drawn from the 1982 and 1983 fiscal year budgets.

6. U.S. Office of Management and Budget, "Federal Government Finances," unpublished, Jan. 1979, p. 36.

7. U.S. *Budget 1983*, pp. 5–9 to 5–20; Jeffrey Smith, "Reagan Proposes Huge Nuclear Buildup," *Science* 214 (Oct. 16, 1981): 309–12.

8. Kevin N. Lewis, "The Prompt and Delayed Effects of Nuclear War," *Scientific American* 241 (July 1979): 35–47.

9. For a concise description of U.S. strategic forces as of the end of the 1970s, see Charles A. Sorrels et al., "Defense Policy," in *Setting National Priorities: The 1979 Budget*, ed. Joseph A. Pechman (Washington, D.C.: Brookings Institution, 1978), pp. 233–73. Up-to-date information is available in later editions of the annual Brookings volume: e.g., William K. Kaufman, "Defense Policy," in *Setting National Priorities: Agenda for the 1980s*, ed. Joseph A. Pechman (Washington, D.C.: Brookings Institution, 1980), pp. 283–315; and, comprehensively, in Tom Gervasi, *Arsenal of Democracy II* (New York: Grove, 1981).

10. Jonathan Schell, *The Fate of the Earth* (New York: Knopf, 1982); Russell Hoban, *Riddley Walker* (New York: Summit, 1980); Committee for the Compilation of Materials on Damage Caused by the Atomic Bombs in Hiroshima and Nagasaki, *Hiroshima and Nagasaki: The Physical, Medical, and Social Effects of the Atomic Bombings* (New York: Basic Books, 1981).

11. T. B. Millar, *The East-West Strategic Balance* (London: Allen & Unwin, 1981); International Institute for Strategic Studies, *The Military Balance, 1980-1981* (London: IISS, 1980). See also Arthur Macy Cox, "The CIA's Tragic Error," *New York Review of Books*, Nov. 6, 1980, pp. 21–24.

12. Richard J. Barnet, *Intervention and Revolution* (New York: World, 1968); David Wise and Thomas B. Ross, *The Invisible Government* (New York: Random House, 1964); U.S. Congress, Senate Select Committee to Study Governmental Operations with Respect to Intelligence Activities, *Final Report* (Washington, D.C.: U.S. Government Printing Office, 1976); U.S. Congress, House Committee on Foreign Affairs, *Background Information on the Use of United States Armed Forces in Foreign Countries* (Washington, D.C.: U.S. Government Printing Office, 1970); "The CIA Report the President Doesn't Want You to Read: The Pike Papers," *Village Voice*, Feb. 16, 1976, pp. 69–92; and Feb. 23, pp. 59–69.

13. Frances FitzGerald, *Fire in the Lake: The Vietnamese and the Americans in Vietnam* (Boston: Little, Brown, 1972); David Halberstam, *The Best and the Brightest* (New York: Random House, 1972).

14. Musgrave and Musgrave, *Public Finance*, pp. 730–31. See also John Whalley, "The Worldwide Income Distributions: Some Speculative Calculations," *Review of Income and Wealth* 25 (Sept. 1979): 261–76; A. B. Atkinson, *The Economics of Inequality* (Oxford: Oxford University Press, 1975), Ch. 12.

15. See Mihajlo D. Mesarovic and Edward Pestel, *Mankind at the Turning Point* (New York: Dutton, 1974); Amartya Sen, "Just Deserts," *New York Review of Books*, March 4, 1982, pp. 3–6; L. DeWulf, "Fiscal Incidence Studies in Developing Countries: Survey and Critique," *International Monetary Fund Staff Papers* 23 (March 1975): 61–131.

16. Neil D. Fligstein, "Who Served in the Military, 1940-1973,"

Armed Forces and Society 6 (Winter 1980): 197–312; R. Berney and D. Leigh, "The Socioeconomic Distribution of American Casualties in the Indochina War: Implications for Tax Equity," *Public Finance Quarterly* 2 (April 1974): 223–35; Maurice Zeitlin, Kenneth Lutterman, and James Russell, "Death in Vietnam: Class, Poverty, and the Risks of War," in *The Politics and Society Reader*, ed. Ira Katznelson, Gordon Adams, Philip Brenner, and Alan Wolfe (New York: McKay, 1974), pp. 53–68.

17. Jeffrey G. Williamson, "The Sources of American Inequality, 1896–1948," *Review of Economics and Statistics* 58 (Nov. 1976): 387–97.

18. Wassily Leontief and Marvin Hoffenberg, "The Economic Effect of Disarmament," *Scientific American*, April 1961; Wassily Leontief, Alison Morgan, Karen Polenske, David Simpson, and Edward Tower, "The Economic Effect—Industrial and Regional—of an Arms Cut," *Review of Economics and Statistics* 47 (Aug. 1965): 217–41; Bruce M. Russett, *What Price Vigilance?* (New Haven: Yale University Press, 1970), Ch. 5.

19. Murray Weidenbaum, "Arms and the American Economy," *American Economic Association Papers and Proceedings* 58 (May 1968): 428–45; Richard F. Kaufman, *The War Profiteers* (Indianapolis: Bobbs-Merrill, 1970); W. Baldwin, *The Structure of the Defense Market, 1955–1964* (Durham, N.C.: Duke University Press, 1967); Seymour Melman, *Pentagon Capitalism* (New York: McGraw-Hill, 1970).

20. James Fellows, *National Defense* (New York: Random House, 1981).

21. Russett, *What Price Vigilance?* Ch. 5.

22. "Developing Nations Hope for a Role in Economy," *San Francisco Chronicle*, Oct. 21, 1981, p. 20.

23. Andrew J. Pierre, *The Global Politics of Arms Sales* (Princeton: Princeton University Press, 1982).

24. J. G. Tewksbury, M. S. Crandall, and W. E. Crane, "Measuring the Societal Benefits of Innovation," *Science* 209 (Aug. 8, 1980): 658-62.

25. Patricia Burke Horvath and John R. Burke, "Federal Research and Development Funding: The Grants Component and Its Distribution," in *Redistribution to the Rich and the Poor*, ed. Kenneth E. Boulding and Martin Paff (Belmont, Ca.: Wadsworth, 1972), pp. 131–48.

26. See Thomas E. Cronin, Tania Z. Cronin, and Michael E. Milakovich, *U.S. v. Crime in the Streets* (Bloomington: Indiana University Press, 1982).

27. Robert L. Lineberry, *Equality and Urban Policy: The Distribution of Municipal Public Services* (Beverly Hills, Ca.: Sage, 1977), pp. 117–19, 138–42; David L. Cingranelli, "Race, Politics, and Elites: Testing Alternative Models of Municipal Service Distribution," *American Journal of Political Science* 25 (Nov. 1981): 664–92.

28. James Q. Wilson, *Thinking About Crime* (New York: Basic Books, 1975); Malcolm Feeley, *The Process Is the Punishment* (New York: Sage, 1979).

29. Athan Theoharis, *Spying on Americans: Political Surveillance from Hoover to the Huston Plan* (Philadelphia: Temple University Press, 1978); David Wise, *The American Police State* (New York: Random House,

1977); Alan Wolfe, *The Seamy Side of Democracy: Repression in America* (New York: McKay, 1973).

30. David J. Rose, "Energy Policy in the U.S.," *Scientific American* 230 (Jan. 1974): 20–29.

31. John F. Clarke, "The Next Step in Fusion: What It Is and How It Is Being Taken," *Science* 210 (Nov. 28, 1980): 967–72.

32. Lester Thurow, *The Zero-Sum Society* (New York: Basic Books, 1980), Ch. 2.

33. Robert Dorfman, "Incidence of the Benefits and Costs of Environmental Programs," *American Economic Review* 67 (Feb. 1977): 333–40. But on the complexity of these issues, see William J. Baumol and Wallace E. Oates, *Economics, Environmental Policy, and the Quality of Life* (Englewood Cliffs, N.J.: Prentice-Hall, 1979), esp. Ch. 12.

34. John A. Ferejohn, *Pork Barrel Politics: Rivers and Harbors Legislation, 1947-1968* (Stanford, Ca.: Stanford University Press, 1974).

35. Lineberry, *Equality and Urban Policy*, pp. 108–17. Similarly, on libraries, see ibid.; also Frank Levy, Arnold J. Meltsner, and Aaron Wildavsky, *Urban Outcomes: Schools, Streets, and Libraries* (Berkeley: University of California Press, 1974).

36. Mark Frankena, "Income Distributional Effects of Urban Transit Subsidies," *Journal of Transport Economics and Policy* 7 (Sept. 1973): 215–30.

37. Levy, Meltsner, and Wildavsky, *Urban Outcomes*.

38. Charles L. Schultze, *The Distribution of Farm Subsidies: Who Gets the Benefits?* (Washington, D.C.: Brookings Institution, 1971).

39. U.S. Congress, House Committee on Banking, Finance, and Urban Affairs, Subcommittee on the City, 95th Congress, 2nd Session, "City Need and the Responsiveness of Federal Grants Programs" (Washington, D.C.: U.S. Government Printing Office, Aug. 1978); U.S. Congressional Budget Office, "Troubled Local Economies and the Distribution of Federal Dollars" (Washington, D.C.: U.S. Government Printing Office, Aug. 1977).

40. W. Irwin Gillespie, "Effect of Public Expenditures on the Distribution of Income," in *Essays in Fiscal Federalism*, ed. Richard A. Musgrave (Washington, D.C.: Brookings Institution, 1965), pp. 122–86.

41. Richard A. Musgrave, Karl E. Case, and Herman Leonard, "The Distribution of Fiscal Burdens and Benefits," *Public Finance Quarterly* 2 (July 1974): 259–311.

42. See Larry Sawyers and Howard M. Wachtel, "Theory of the State, Government Tax and Purchasing Policy, and Income Distribution," *Review of Income and Wealth*, March 1975, pp. 111–24.

43. Morgan Reynolds and Eugene Smolensky, *Public Expenditures, Taxes, and the Distribution of Income: The United States, 1950, 1961, 1970* (New York: Academic Press, 1977).

44. Ibid., Ch. 2, esp. p. 24.

45. Irwin Garfinkel points out a possible flaw in this conclusion. The social programs of the 1960s enabled some old people and others who had been dependent on their families to live alone for the first time.

Their welfare presumably improved, but they constituted a large new group of relatively low-income "families" that may have artificially inflated the apparent inequality of income. See Sheldon Danziger and Robert Plotnick, "Demographic Change, Government Transfers, and Income Distribution," *Monthly Labor Review* 100 (1977): 7–11. More recent data show that some of the effect of Great Society income transfer programs appeared only after 1970; see Sheldon Danziger, Robert Haveman, and Robert Plotnick, "How Income Transfer Programs Affect Work, Savings and the Income Distribution: A Critical Review," *Journal of Economic Literature* 19 (Sept. 1981): 975–1028. An update of the Reynolds and Smolensky analysis would probably indicate a somewhat greater degree of equality but not change the basic conclusions.

46. Harold F. Lydall, "Some Problems in Making International Comparisons of Inequality," in *Income Inequality: Trends and International Comparisons*, ed. John R. Moroney (Lexington, Mass.: Heath, 1979), pp. 21–37; DeWulf, "Fiscal Incidence Studies."

47. Mervyn A. King, "How Effective Have Fiscal Policies Been in Changing the Distribution of Income and Wealth?" *American Economic Review* 70 (May 1980): 72–76; T. Stark, "The Distribution of Income in Eight Countries," Background Paper #4 to Report #5, Royal Commission on the Distribution of Income and Wealth, London, 1977; Thomas Franzen, Kerstin Lovgren, and Irma Rosenberg, "Redistributional Effects of Taxes and Public Expenditures in Sweden," *Swedish Journal of Economics* 77 (1975): 31–47; Eugene Smolensky, Werner W. Pommerehne, and Robert E. Dalrymple, "Postfisc Income Inequality: A Comparison of the United States and West Germany," in *Income Inequality*, pp. 69–81; W. I. Gillespie, "On the Redistribution of Income in Canada," *Candian Tax Journal* 24 (July-Aug. 1976): 419–50.

48. Lydall and also Chapman in *Income Inequality*; Charles E. Lindblom, *Politics and Markets* (New York: Basic Books, 1977); William Parish, "Egalitarianism in Chinese Society," *Problems of Communism*, Jan.-Feb. 1981, pp. 37–53.

49. Benjamin I. Page, *Choices and Echoes in Presidential Elections: Rational Man and Electoral Democracy* (Chicago: University of Chicago Press, 1978), Chs. 3, 4.

50. E. E. Schattschneider, *The Semi-Sovereign People: A Realist's View of Democracy in America* (New York: Holt, 1960).

51. Theodore J. Lowi, "American Business, Public Policy, Case-Studies, and Political Theory," *World Politics* 16 (July 1964); David R. Mayhew, *Congress: The Electoral Connection* (New Haven: Yale University Press, 1974); Morris P. Fiorina, *Congress: Keystone of the Washington Establishment* (New Haven: Yale University Press, 1977); R. Douglas Arnold, *Congress and the Bureaucracy* (New Haven: Yale University Press, 1979); Barry S. Rundquist, ed., *Political Benefits* (Lexington, Mass.: Heath, 1980).

52. Lewis Anthony Dexter, "Congressmen and the Making of Military Policy," in *New Perspectives on the House of Representatives*, ed. Robert L. Peabody and Nelson W. Polsby (Chicago: Rand-McNally, 1963), pp. 305–24; Seymour Melman, *The Permanent War Economy* (New York:

Simon & Schuster, 1974); Melman, *Pentagon Capitalism*; Ralph E. Lapp, *Arms Beyond Doubt* (New York: Cowles, 1970); Congressional Quarterly, "The Military Lobby," in Peter Woll, ed., *American Politics*; Michael R. Gordon, "Are Military Contractors Part of the Problem or Part of the Solution?" *National Journal* 13 (July 11, 1981): 1232–36.

53. U.S. Department of Defense, *Soviet Military Power* (Washington, D.C.: U.S. Government Printing Office, 1981); James Fallows, "The Trap of Rearmament," *New York Review of Books*, Dec. 17, 1981, pp. 26–31; Karen Elliott House, "Reagan Says Soviets Have a Nuclear Edge That Could 'Absorb' Blows, 'Hit Us Again,' " *Wall Street Journal*, April 1, 1982, p. 3.

54. Stephen D. Krasner, *Defending the National Interest: Raw Materials Investments and U.S. Foreign Policy* (Princeton: Princeton University Press, 1978); Charles Lipson, *Standing Guard* (forthcoming).

55. Lewis F. Richardson, *Arms and Insecurity* (Pittsburgh, Pa.: Boxwood Press, 1960).

56. Arthur Hoppe, "Expensive Lives," *San Francisco Chronicle*, March 24, 1982, p. 51.

57. Bruce I. Oppenheimer, *Oil and the Congressional Process* (Lexington, Mass.: Lexington, 1974); Robert Engler, *The Politics of Oil*, 2nd ed. (Chicago: University of Chicago Press, 1961).

58. Richard Corrigan, "Relief for the Oil Interests: How the Battle Was Fought and Won," *National Journal* 13 (Aug. 15, 1981): 1454–60; William Greider, "The Education of David Stockman," *Atlantic*, Dec. 1981, pp. 27–54, at p. 51.

59. Arthur Maass, *Muddy Waters* (Cambridge, Mass.: Harvard University Press, 1951); Ferejohn, *Pork Barrel Politics*; Harry Caudill, *Night Comes to the Cumberlands* (Boston: Little, Brown, 1963); Grant McConnell, *Private Power and American Democracy* (New York: Random House, 1966), Ch. 7.

60. Jeffrey M. Berry, *Lobbying for the People* (Princeton: Princeton University Press, 1977); Andrew MacFarland, *Public Interest Lobbies: Decision-Making on Energy* (Washington, D.C.: American Enterprise Institute, 1976).

61. David Hapgood, "The Highwaymen," in Charles Peters and John Rothchild, eds., *Inside the System*, 2nd ed. (New York: Praeger, 1973), pp. 214–29.

62. Grant McConnell, *The Decline of Agrarian Democracy* (Berkeley: University of California Press, 1953); McConnell, *Private Power*, Ch. 7; Theodore J. Lowi, "How Farmers Get What They Want," *Reporter*, Sept. 14, 1964, pp. 34–37.

63. Mancur Olson, Jr., *The Logic of Collective Action* (Cambridge, Mass.: Harvard University Press, 1965); Russell Hardin, *Collective Action* (forthcoming). See also Lindblom, *Politics and Markets*, on the "privileged position" of business.

64. Paul Peterson, *City Limits* (Chicago: University of Chicago Press, 1981). See also Charles Tiebout, "The Pure Theory of Local Expenditures," *Journal of Political Economy* 64 (Oct. 1956): 416–24.

Chapter 5

1. Thomas G. Moore, "The Purpose of Licensing," *Journal of Law and Economics* 4 (Oct. 1961): 93–117; George J. Stigler, "The Theory of Economic Regulation," *Bell Journal of Economics* 2 (Spring 1971): 3–21.

2. Reuben Kessel, "The A.M.A. and the Supply of Physicians," *Law and Contemporary Problems* 35 (Spring 1970): 267–83.

3. George J. Stigler and Claire Friedland, "What Can Regulators Regulate? The Case of Electricity," *Journal of Law and Economics* 5 (Oct. 1962): 1–16.

4. Marver H. Bernstein, *Regulating Business by Independent Commission* (Princeton: Princeton University Press, 1955); Gabriel Kolko, *Railroads and Regulation, 1877–1916* (Princeton: Princeton University Press, 1965).

5. Paul W. MacAvoy, *The Economic Effects of Regulation: The Trunk Line Railroad Cartels and the Interstate Commerce Commission Before 1900* (Cambridge, Mass.: MIT Press, 1965); Robert M. Spann and Edward W. Erickson, "The Economics of Railroading: The Beginning of Cartelization and Regulation," *Bell Journal of Economics* 1 (Autumn 1970): 227–44; Richard O. Zerbe, Jr., "The Costs and Benefits of Early Regulation of the Railroads," *Bell Journal of Economics* 11 (Spring 1980): 343–50.

6. Robert C. Fellmeth, *The Interstate Commerce Commission* (New York: Grossman, 1970); Ann F. Friedlaender, *The Dilemma of Freight Transport Regulation* (Washington, D.C.: Brookings Institution, 1969); Ann F. Friedlaender and Richard H. Spady, *Freight Transport Regulation: Equity, Efficiency, and Competition in the Rail and Trucking Industries* (Cambridge, Mass.: MIT Press, 1981).

7. Richard Caves, *Air Transport and Its Regulators: An Industry Study* (Cambridge, Mass.: Harvard University Press, 1962); George Douglas and James Miller III, *Economic Regulation of Domestic Air Transport* (Washington, D.C.: Brookings Institution, 1974).

8. Ronald H. Coase, "The Federal Communications Commission," *Journal of Law and Economics* 2 (Oct. 1959): 1–40; Roger G. Noll, Merton J. Peck, and John J. McGowan, *Economic Aspects of Television Regulation* (Washington, D.C.: Brookings Institution, 1973).

9. Sam Peltzman, "Entry in Commercial Banking," *Journal of Law and Economics* 8 (Oct. 1965): 11–50.

10. Roger G. Noll, *Reforming Regulation* (Washington, D.C.: Brookings Institution, 1971), pp. 64, 74; Charles L. Schultze, *The Distribution of Farm Subsidies: Who Gets the Benefits?* (Washington, D.C.: Brookings Institution, 1971); Paul W. MacAvoy, ed., *Federal Milk Marketing Orders and Price Supports* (Washington, D.C.: American Enterprise Institute, 1977).

11. Paul W. MacAvoy, "The Regulation-Induced Shortage of Natural Gas," *Journal of Law and Economics* 14 (April 1971): 167–99; Paul W.

MacAvoy, "The Formal Work Product of the Federal Power Commissioners," *Bell Journal of Economics* 2 (Spring 1971): 379–95; Irvin C. Bupp and Jean-Claude Derian, *Light Water* (New York: Basic Books, 1978).

12. Noll, *Reforming Regulation*, p. 48; G. William Schwert, "Public Regulation of National Securities Exchanges: A Test of the Capture Hypothesis," *Bell Journal of Economics* 8 (Spring 1977): 128. For a critical assessment, see Susan M. Phillips and J. Richard Zecher, *The SEC and the Public Interest* (Cambridge, Mass.: MIT Press, 1981).

13. Noll, *Reforming Regulation*, pp. 52, 55; Sam Peltzman, "An Evaluation of Consumer Protection Legislation: The 1962 Drug Amendments," *Journal of Political Economy* 81 (Sept.-Oct. 1973): 1049–91.

14. William S. Comanor and Robert H. Smiley, "Monopoly and the Distribution of Wealth," *Quarterly Journal of Economics* 84 (May 1975): 177–94, argue that monopoly profits produce much of the inequality of wealth in the United States.

15. Ronald H. Coase, "The Problem of Social Cost," *Journal of Law and Economics* 3 (1960): 1–44.

16. Kevin Hollenbeck, "The Employment and Earnings Impacts of the Regulation of Stationary Source Air Pollution," *Journal of Environmental Economics and Management* 6 (1979): 208–21; A. Myrick Freeman, "The Incidence of the Costs of Controlling Automotive Air Pollution," in *The Distribution of Economic Well-Being*, ed. F. Thomas Juster (Cambridge, Mass.: Ballinger-NBER, 1977), pp. 163–99; Robert Dorfman, "Incidence of the Benefits and Costs of Environmental Programs," *American Economic Review, Papers and Proceedings* 67 (Feb. 1977): 337.

17. Robert Stewart Smith, *The Occupational Safety and Health Act: Its Goals and Achievements* (Washington, D.C.: American Enterprise Institute, 1976).

18. Ibid., esp. pp. 46, 51; Nina W. Cornell, Roger G. Noll, and Barry Weingast, "Safety Regulation," in *Setting National Priorities: The Next Ten Years*, ed. Henry Owen and Charles L. Schultze (Washington, D.C.: Brookings Institution, 1976), pp. 457–504; Lester B. Lave, "Health, Safety, and Environmental Regulations," in *Setting National Priorities: Agenda for the 1980s*, ed. Joseph A. Pechman (Washington, D.C.: Brookings Institution, 1980), pp. 131–68; *Wall Street Journal*, June 23, 1981, p. 12; Steven Kelman, *Regulating America, Regulating Sweden: A Comparative Study of Occupational Safety and Health Policy* (Cambridge, Mass.: MIT Press, 1981).

19. Edward Gramlich, "Impact of Minimum Wages on Other Wages, Employment, and Family Incomes," *Brookings Papers on Economic Activity* 2 (1976); John M. Peterson, *Minimum Wages: Measures and Industry Effects* (Washington, D.C.: American Enterprise Institute, 1982); Christopher Jencks, "The Minimum Wage Controversy," *Working Papers*, March-April 1978, pp. 12–14.

20. Michael E. Levine, "Revisionism Revised? Airline Deregulation and the Public Interest," *Law and Contemporary Problems*, Jan. 1981;

Aharon R. Ofer and Arie Melnick, "Price Deregulation in the Brokerage Industry: An Empirical Analysis," *Bell Journal of Economics* 9 (Autumn 1978): 633; James Worsham, "TV Industry on Threshold of Revolution," "FCC Cuts Back Sharply on Radio Station Regulation," and "ICC, at Age 94, to Take Life at a Slower Pace," *Chicago Tribune*, Jan. 16, 1981, pp. 1, 4; Jan. 19, 1981, sec. 5, pp. 9–10; Friedlaender and Spady, *Freight Transport Regulation*; Lave, "Health, Safety, and Environmental Regulations."

21. Overviews of regulatory effects (without any estimate of total distributional impact) can be found in Paul L. Joskow and Roger G. Noll, "Regulation in Theory and Practice: An Overview," in *Research in Regulation*, ed. Gary Fromm (Lexington, Mass.: Lexington, 1981); Richard A. Posner, "Theories of Economic Regulation," *Bell Journal of Economics* 5 (1974): 335–58; and Noll, *Reforming Regulation*.

22. Douglas and Miller, *Economic Regulation of Domestic Air Transport*, esp. Ch. 4 and p. 172.

23. Anthony Downs, *An Economic Theory of Democracy* (New York: Harper, 1957); Murray Edelman, *The Symbolic Uses of Politics* (Urbana: University of Illinois Press, 1964); Mancur Olson, Jr., *The Logic of Collective Action* (Cambridge, Mass.: Harvard University Press, 1965); Russell Hardin, *Collective Action* (forthcoming).

24. E. E. Schattschneider, *The Semi-Sovereign People* (New York: Holt, 1960); Theodore J. Lowi, *The End of Liberalism* (New York: Norton, 1969); Grant McConnell, *Private Power and American Democracy* (New York: Random House, 1966); William R. Cary, *Politics and the Regulatory Agencies* (New York: McGraw-Hill, 1967).

25. E. E. Schattschneider, *Politics, Pressures, and the Tariff* (New York: Prentice-Hall, 1935); Raymond A. Bauer, Ithiel de Sola Pool, and Lewis Anthony Dexter, *American Business and Public Policy* (New York: Atherton, 1963).

26. Samuel Huntington, "The Marasmus of the ICC: The Commission, the Railroads, and the Public Interest," *Yale Law Journal* 61 (1952): 467; Kolko, *Railroads and Regulation*; Fellmeth, *Interstate Commerce Commission*.

27. Bernstein, *Regulating Business by Independent Commission*; see also McConnell, *Private Power*.

28. Philip Selznick, *TVA and the Grass Roots* (Berkeley: University of California Press, 1949); Grant McConnell, *The Decline of Agrarian Democracy* (Berkeley: University of California Press, 1953); McConnell, *Private Power*; Thomas B. Edsall, "Racetracks, Banks, and Liquor Stores," *Washington Monthly*, Dec. 1974, pp. 49–55; Edmund W. Kitch, Marc Isaacson, and Daniel Kasper, "The Regulation of Taxicabs in Chicago," *Journal of Law and Economics* 14 (Oct. 1971): 285–350.

29. Stigler, "Theory of Economic Regulation"; Posner, "Theories of Economic Regulation"; Sam Peltzman, "Toward a More General Theory of Regulation," *Journal of Law and Economics* 19 (Aug. 1976): 211–40; Gary S. Becker, "Comment" (on Peltzman), *Journal of Law and Economics* 19 (Aug. 1976): 245–48.

30. Andrew S. MacFarland, *Public Interest Lobbies* (Washington, D.C.: American Enterprise Institute, 1976); Jeffery Berry, *Lobbying for the People* (Princeton: Princeton University Press, 1977); Bruce Ackerman and William T. Hassler, *Clean Air/Dirty Coal* (New Haven: Yale University Press, 1981).

31. Harrison Wellford, "How Ralph Nader, Tricia Nixon, the ABA, and Jamie Whitten Helped Turn the FTC Around," *Washington Monthly* 4 (Oct. 1972): 5–13; Robert A. Katzmann, *Regulatory Bureaucracy: The Federal Trade Commission and Antitrust Policy* (Cambridge, Mass.: MIT Press, 1980); Hardin, *Collective Action*. See also Norman Frohlich, Joe A. Oppenheimer, and Oran R. Young, *Political Leadership and Collective Goods* (Princeton: Princeton University Press, 1971). James Q. Wilson, ed., *The Politics of Regulation* (New York: Basic Books, 1980), emphasizes the complexity of regulatory politics.

32. Alan Altschuler and Roger Teal, "The Political Economy of Airline Deregulation," in *Current Issues in Transportation Policy*, ed. Alan Altschuler (Lexington, Mass.: Lexington, 1979); Levine, "Revisionism Revised?"; Stephen Breyer, "Analyzing Regulatory Failure: Mismatches, Less Restrictive Alternatives, and Reform," *Harvard Law Review* 92 (Jan. 1979): 549–609, presents a cogent neoliberal view of regulation.

33. See Douglas A. Hibbs, "Political Parties and Macroeconomic Policy," *American Political Science Review* 71 (Dec. 1977): 1467–87.

34. Helmut Frisch, "Inflation Theory 1963–1975: A 'Second Generation' Survey," *Journal of Economic Literature* 15 (Dec. 1977): 1289–1317; Douglas A. Hibbs, Jr., "Economic Interest and the Politics of Macroeconomic Policy," paper #C/75–14, Center for International Studies, MIT, revised Jan. 1976; Paul W. MacAvoy, "Good Riddance to Price Controls," *New York Times*, Feb. 15, 1981, sec. 3, p. 2.

35. David R. Cameron, "On the Limits of the Public Economy," paper delivered at the 1981 annual meeting of the American Political Science Association, New York; Karen W. Arenson, "A Closer Look at the $1 Trillion Debt," *San Francisco Chronicle*, Oct. 1, 1981, pp. 10, 11; Thomas J. More, "U.S. Balance Sheet: We're Sitting Pretty," *San Francisco Examiner*, Jan. 31, 1982, p. A15.

36. John A. Garraty, *Unemployment in History* (New York: Harper, 1978); Studs Terkel, *Hard Times: An Oral History of the Great Depression* (New York: Random House, 1970).

37. Milton Friedman, "The Role of Monetary Policy," *American Economic Review* 58 (March 1968): 1–17.

38. Emil M. Sunley, Jr., and Joseph A. Pechman, "Inflation Adjustment for the Individual Income Tax," in *Inflation and the Income Tax*, ed. Henry J. Aaron (Washington, D.C.: Brookings Institution, 1976), pp. 153–71; Edward M. Gramlich, "The Economic and Budgetary Effects of Indexing the Tax System," in *Inflation and the Income Tax*, pp. 271–90.

39. Harold T. Shapiro, "Inflation in the United States," in *Worldwide Inflation*, ed. Lawrence B. Krause and Walter S. Salant (Washington, D.C.: Brookings Institution, 1977), pp. 267–94; Barry P. Bosworth,

"Economic Policy," in *Setting National Priorities: Agenda for the 1980s*, ed. Joseph A. Pechman (Washington, D.C.: Brookings Institution, 1980), pp. 35–70; Gar Alperovitz and Jeff Faux, "Inflation Rate Is Higher for Necessities," *Chicago Tribune*, Feb. 5, 1979, p. 1.

40. G. L. Bach and James B. Stephenson, "Inflation and the Redistribution of Wealth," *Review of Economics and Statistics* 56 (Feb. 1974): 1–13; Joseph J. Minarik, "The Size Distribution of Income During Inflation," *Review of Income and Wealth* 4 (Dec. 1979): 377–92.

41. David Piachaud, "Inflation and Income Distribution," in *The Political Economy of Inflation*, ed. Fred Hirsch and John D. Goldthorpe (Cambridge, Mass.: Harvard University Press, 1978), pp. 88–116; Alan S. Blinder and Howard Y. Esaki, "Macroeconomic Activity and Income Distribution in the Postwar United States," *Review of Economics and Statistics*, 1978, pp. 604–09; Shapiro, "Inflation"; Minarik, "Size Distribution of Income During Inflation"; Christopher Jencks, "Why Worry About Inflation?" *Working Papers*, Sept.-Oct. 1978, pp. 8–11, 75–78.

42. M. Harvey Brenner, *Mental Illness and the Economy* (Cambridge, Mass.: Harvard University Press, 1973); Richard M. Cohn, "The Effect of Employment Status Change on Self-Attitudes," *Social Psychology* 41 (1978): 81–93; Harry Mauer, *Not Working: An Oral History of the Unemployed* (New York: Holt, 1979); Douglas G. Glasgow, *The Black Underclass* (New York: Random House, 1981).

43. John L. Palmer and Michael C. Barth, "The Distributional Effects of Inflation and Higher Unemployment," in *Improving Economic Measures of Well-Being*, ed. Marilyn Moon and Eugene Smolensky (New York: Academic Press, 1977), pp. 201–39; Edward M. Gramlich, "The Distributional Effects of Higher Unemployment," *Brookings Papers on Economic Activity* 2 (1974); Kim Clark and Lawrence H. Summers, "Labor Market Dynamics and Unemployment: A Reconsideration," *Brookings Papers on Economic Activity* 1 (1979): 13–60.

44. Kay Lehman Schlozman and Sidney Verba, "The New Unemployment: Does It Hurt?" *Public Policy* 26 (Summer 1978): 333–58.

45. B. Jovanovic, "Job Matching and the Theory of Turnover," *Journal of Political Economy* 87 (Oct. 1979): 972–90.

46. U.S. Office of Management and Budget, *Economic Report of the President, 1981* (Washington, D.C.: U.S. Government Printing Office, 1981), p. 269.

47. Hibbs, "Political Parties and Macroeconomic Policy"; Nathaniel Beck, "Parties, Administrations, and American Macroeconomic Outcomes," *American Political Science Review* 76 (March 1982): 83–93. See also Edward R. Tufte, *Political Control of the Economy* (Princeton: Princeton University Press, 1978), Ch. 4.

48. Hibbs, "Political Parties and Macroeconomic Policy"; Douglas A. Hibbs, Jr., "Communication," *American Political Science Review* 73 (1979): 185; David R. Cameron, "On the Limits of the Public Economy," paper delivered at the 1981 annual meeting of the American Political Science Association, New York; Louis Hartz, *The Liberal Tradition in America* (New York: Harcourt, 1955).

49. See Leon Lindberg and Charles Maier, *The Politics and Sociology of Global Inflation* (Washington, D.C.: Brookings Institution) (forthcoming).

50. Carter Goodrich, ed., *The Government and the Economy: 1783–1861* (Indianapolis: Bobbs-Merrill, 1967); Henry W. Broude, "The Role of the State in American Economic Development, 1820–1890," in *United States Economic History: Selected Readings*, ed. Harry N. Scheiber (New York: Knopf, 1964), pp. 114–35.

51. Susan B. Hansen, "Partisan Realignment and Tax Policy, 1789–1970," in *Realignment in American Politics*, ed. Bruce A. Campbell and Richard J. Trilling (Austin: University of Texas Press, 1980), documents historical party differences.

52. Ronald F. King, "The Transformation of United States Taxation Policy, 1893–1960," Ph.D. dissertation, University of Chicago, 1981, Ch. 2; Benjamin A. Okner, "Distributional Aspects of Tax Reform During the Past Fifteen Years," *National Tax Journal* 32 (March 1979): 11–27.

53. Adam Przeworski, "Material Bases of Consent: Economics and Politics in a Hegemonic System," *Political Power and Social Theory* 1 (1979); Adam Przeworski and Michael Wallerstein, "The Structure of Class Conflict in Advanced Capitalist Societies," paper presented at the 1980 annual meeting of the American Political Science Association, Washington, D.C. Of course, most neoclassical economists agree but dispute the implication that a socialist system would be superior.

54. Ralph Miliband, *The State in Capitalist Society* (New York: Basic Books, 1969), emphasizes the power of capitalists over schools and the mass media. Robert Lane, "The Fear of Equality," in his *Political Ideology* (New York: Free Press, 1962), notes some possible psychological reasons for accepting inequality and points out that people may tolerate poverty in hope (often unfounded) that their children will enjoy social mobility and success.

55. Przeworski and Wallerstein, "Structure of Class Conflict." This is akin to the general argument that information and transaction costs lead to satisficing or local optimizing rather than globally optimal behavior.

56. Malcolm Sawyer, "Income Distribution in OECD Countries," *OECD Economic Outlook: Occasional Studies*, July 1976, pp. 3–36; Bob Kuttner, "Growth with Equity," *Working Papers* 8 (Sept.-Oct. 1981): 32–43; Paul A. Samuelson, "The Public Role in the Modern American Economy," in *The American Economy in Transition*, ed. Martin Feldstein (Chicago: University of Chicago Press, 1980), pp. 656–71; Cameron, "On the Limits of the Public Economy"; Eugene Smolensky, Werner W. Pommerehne, and Robert E. Dalrymple, "Postfisc Income Inequality: A Comparison of the United States and West Germany," in *Income Inequality: Trends and International Comparisons*, ed. John R. Moroney (Lexington, Mass.: Heath, Lexington, 1979), pp. 69–81; see also sources cited in Ch. 4.

57. Harold F. Lydall, "Some Problems in Making International Comparisons of Inequality," in *Income Inequality*, pp. 21–37; Marc

Blecher, "Income Distribution in Small Rural Chinese Communities," *China Quarterly*, Dec. 1976, pp. 797–816; William Parish, "Egalitarianism in Chinese Society," *Problems of Communism*, Jan.-Feb. 1981, pp. 37–53. See also Peter Wiles, *Distribution of Income, East and West* (Amsterdam: North Holland, 1974).

58. Amartya Sen, ed., *Growth Economics* (Harmondsworth, Middlesex, England: Penguin, 1970); Dale W. Jorgenson, "Econometric Studies of Investment Behavior: A Survey," *Journal of Economic Literature* 9 (Dec. 1971): 1111–47; George M. Von Furstenberg and Burten G. Malkiel, "The Government and Capital Formation: A Survey of Recent Issues," *Journal of Economic Literature* 15 (1977): 835–78; Peter K. Clark, "Investment in the 1970s: Theory, Performance, and Prediction," *Brookings Papers on Economic Activity* 1 (1979): 173–224.

59. An eloquent statement of productivity and capital formation themes and a general hymn to capitalism (short, however, on concrete evidence) is George Gilder, *Wealth and Poverty* (New York: Basic Books, 1981). See also Jude Wanniski, *The Way the World Works* (New York: Basic Books, 1978); Michael Walzer, "Life with Father," *New York Review of Books*, April 2, 1981, pp. 3–4.

60. See, e.g., the scathing critiques of Laffer and Evans by conservative economists in Laurence H. Meyer, ed., *The Supply-Side Effects of Economic Policy* (St. Louis, Mo.: Center for the Study of American Business, May 1981), esp. Alan S. Blinder, "Thoughts on the Laffer Curve," pp. 81–92. See also Martin Gardner, "Mathematical Games: The Laffer Curve and Other Laughs in Current Economics," *Scientific American*, Dec. 1981, pp. 18–31c.

61. Gardner, "Mathematical Games."

62. Paul Blustein, "Supply-Side Theories Became Federal Policy with Unusual Speed: Politicians and Journalists, Rather Than Academics, Played a Crucial Role," *Wall Street Journal*, Oct. 8, 1981, pp. 1, 20; Chris Welles, "The Supply Side 'Cabal,' " *This World* (*San Francisco Examiner*), Sept. 20, 1981, pp. 8–12.

63. *Constitution of the United States*, Art. 1, Sec. 8; see Robert A. Goldwin and William A. Schambra, eds., *How Capitalistic Is the Constitution?* (Washington, D.C.: American Enterprise Institute, 1982).

64. Robert G. McCloskey, *The American Supreme Court* (Chicago: University of Chicago Press, 1960); Bruce A. Ackerman, *Private Property and the Constitution* (New Haven: Yale University Press, 1977).

65. McCloskey, *American Supreme Court*, p. 160.

66. Henry J. Abraham, *Freedom and the Court* (New York: Oxford University Press, 1977). One might also argue that rights of free speech encourage dissemination of egalitarian ideas and hence contribute to equality. Still, the marketplace of ideas, like the economic and political marketplaces, probably responds to the power of money.

67. Gary Orfield, *Must We Bus?* (Washington, D.C.: Brookings Institution, 1978).

68. The account of common law development presented here closely follows Morton J. Horwitz, *The Transformation of American Law,*

1780–1860 (Cambridge, Mass.: Harvard University Press, 1977). My interpretation of the distributive impact differs from Horwitz's, however.

69. A. B. Johnson, "A Defense of the Policy of Free Incorporation," in *Government and the Economy: 1783–1861*, pp. 396–405 (originally published in *Hunt's Merchants Magazine*, Dec. 1850).

70. Charles A. Beard, *An Economic Interpretation of the Constitution* (New York: Macmillan, 1913).

71. Robert E. Brown, *Charles Beard and the American Constitution* (Princeton: Princeton University Press, 1956); Forrest McDonald, *We the People: The Economic Origins of the Constitution* (Chicago: University of Chicago Press, 1958).

72. Robert A. Dahl, "The Supreme Court as a National Policy-Maker," *Journal of Public Law* 6 (1958): 279–95, accounts for Supreme Court actions chiefly in terms of political responsiveness to the "law-making majority"; Jonathan D. Casper, "The Supreme Court and National Policy Making," *American Political Science Review* 70 (1976): 50–63, attributes more autonomy to the court.

73. Contrast Joseph C. Goulden, *The Super Lawyers* (New York: Dell, 1972), with Richard A. Posner, *Economic Analysis of the Law* (Boston: Little, Brown, 1972).

Chapter 6

1. Richard A. Musgrave and Peggy B. Musgrave, *Public Finance in Theory and Practice*, 2nd ed. (New York: McGraw-Hill, 1976), p. 379.

2. Morgan Reynolds and Eugene Smolensky, *Public Expenditures, Taxes, and the Distribution of Income* (New York: Academic Press, 1977), Ch. 2, gives a sophisticated and skeptical discussion of counterfactuals.

3. Ibid., p. 67.

4. This is similar to the distinction between instrumentalist and structuralist Marxist theories, as outlined in David A. Gold, Clarence Y. H. Lo, and Erik Olin Wright, "Recent Developments in Marxist Theories of the Capitalist State," *Monthly Review*, Oct. 1975, pp. 29–43, and Nov. 1975, pp. 36–51. See also Fred Block, "The Ruling Class Does Not Rule: Notes on the Marxist Theory of the State," *Socialist Review* 7 (May–June 1977); Ira Katznelson, "Lenin or Weber? Choices in Marxist Theories of Politics," unpublished, University of Chicago, 1980.

5. Arthur M. Okun, *Equality and Efficiency: The Big Tradeoff* (Washington, D.C.: Brookings Institution, 1975); John Rawls, *A Theory of Justice* (Cambridge, Mass.: Harvard University Press, 1971).

6. Malcolm Sawyer, "Income Distribution in OECD Countries,"

OECD Economic Outlook: Occasional Studies, July 1976, pp. 3–36.

7. E. E. Schattschneider, *The Semi-Sovereign People* (New York: Holt, 1960), p. 35.

8. Mancur Olson, Jr., *The Logic of Collective Action* (Cambridge, Mass.: Harvard University Press, 1965); Russell Hardin, *Collective Action* (forthcoming).

9. Grant McConnell, *Private Power and American Democracy* (New York: Knopf, 1966).

10. See Ralf Dahrendorf, "On the Origin of Inequality Among Men," in *The Logic of Social Hierarchies*, ed. Edward O. Laumann, Paul M. Siegel, and Robert W. Hodge (Chicago: Markham, 1970), pp. 3–30; William J. Goode, *The Celebration of Heroes: Prestige as a Social Control System* (Berkeley: University of California Press, 1978).

11. See Ding Chen, "The Economic Development of China," *Scientific American* 243 (Sept. 1980): 152–65. But William Parish, "Egalitarianism in China," *Problems of Communism*, Jan.-Feb. 1981, pp. 37–53, argues that inequalities may simply have been rearranged more rationally to reward work, rather than being increased overall. Contrast the egalitarianism of Barry Reckford, *Does Fidel Eat More Than Your Father?* (New York: New American Library, 1972), with the increased salary differentials announced in *Granma* (Havana, Cuba) 16 (37) (March 25, 1980): 1, 4–5. Cuba, of course, faces the special problems of small size, few resources, and a hostile capitalist neighbor.

12. Charles E. Lindblom, *Politics and Markets* (New York: Basic Books, 1977), presents a thoughtful discussion of the relative strengths and weaknesses of markets and planning. Joseph H. Carens, *Equality, Moral Incentives and the Market: An Essay in Utopian Polito-Economic Theory* (Chicago: University of Chicago Press, 1981), offers an ingenious scheme in which social duty is the chief motivation, but efficiency is preserved by using market prices and symbolic "pre-tax incomes" to allocate resources and signal success.

13. Rudolf Meidner, *Employee Investment Funds: An Approach to Collective Capital Formation* (London: Allen & Unwin, 1978).

14. Some creative egalitarian thinking can be found in Herbert J. Gans, *More Equality* (New York: Random House, 1973); Martin Carnoy and Derek Shearer, *Economic Democracy: The Challenge of the 1980s* (White Plains, N.Y.: M. E. Sharpe, 1980); and various issues of *Working Papers*. Concrete policy ideas might be adapted from Japan and Germany, Scandinavia, the Low Countries, and elsewhere.

15. See Irwin Garfinkel, ed., *Income-Tested Transfer Programs: The Case For and Against* (New York: Academic Press, 1982).

INDEX

Designer:	Barbara Llewellyn
Compositor:	Wilsted & Taylor
Printer:	Vail-Ballou
Binder:	Vail-Ballou
Text:	10/12 Palatino
Display:	Palatino